criticism, on the ... and is one of Britain's foremost thinkers. Her published work includes *Woman's Estate* and *Women: The Longest Revolution* and, with Jacqueline Rose, *Feminine Sexuality: Jacques Lacan and the école freudienne*.

Juliet Mitchell is now a psychoanalyst practising in London, where she lives with her husband and daughter.

THE SELECTED
MELANIE KLEIN

Edited by Juliet Mitchell

Penguin Books

PENGUIN BOOKS

Published by the Penguin Group
Penguin Books Ltd, 27 Wrights Lane, London W8 5TZ, England
Penguin Books USA Inc., 375 Hudson Street, New York, New York 10014, USA
Penguin Books Australia Ltd, Ringwood, Victoria, Australia
Penguin Books Canada Ltd, 10 Alcorn Avenue, Toronto, Ontario, Canada M4V 3B2
Penguin Books (NZ) Ltd, 182–190 Wairau Road, Auckland 10, New Zealand

Penguin Books Ltd, Registered Offices: Harmondsworth, Middlesex, England

This selection first published in Peregrine Books 1986
Reprinted in Penguin Books 1991
10 9 8 7 6 5 4

Printed in England by Clays Ltd, St Ives plc
Typeset in VIP Plantin

CONTENTS

EDITOR'S NOTE

The main writings of Melanie Klein have been published in four volumes of collected works by the Hogarth Press and The Institute of Psychoanalysis under the general editorship of Roger Money-Kyrle. I have used the first full English publication for this selection, but references in the Introduction other than to essays printed here are to the Collected Works as these are more easily available. The final essay, 'A Study of Envy and Gratitude', is the second lecture version on which the book of that title was based. It has not been published previously.

The notes on pp. 230–41 are Melanie Klein's own footnotes, with minor revisions to bring the bibliographical details up to date.

The following abbreviations are used:

CW	*Collected Works of Melanie Klein*, Vols. I–IV, 1975, London, Hogarth Press and The Institute of Psychoanalysis.
SE	*Standard Edition of the Complete Psychological Works of Sigmund Freud*, Vols. I–XXIV, 1953–74, London, Hogarth Press and The Institute of Pyschoanalysis.
Int. J. Psycho-Anal.	*International Journal of Psycho-Analysis*, London.

ACKNOWLEDGEMENTS

I would like to thank the Melanie Klein Trust for giving permission to produce this selection of the works of Melanie Klein, and in particular Mrs Elizabeth Spillius, Secretary of the Trust, for her generous advice and assistance, and Dr Hanna Segal, the Trust's Chairwoman, for recalling the original lecture of one of Klein's major books, *Envy and Gratitude*, and for allowing me to reprint it here for the first time.

I am grateful to the *International Journal of Psycho-Analysis* (London) for permission to reprint the first English versions of Chapters 2–7 and Chapter 9.

I also wish to thank Enid Balint-Edmonds, Jill Duncan, Harry Karnac, Martin Rossdale and Margaret Walters.

INTRODUCTION

MELANIE KLEIN:
HER PSYCHOANALYTIC HERITAGE

Psychoanalysis starts but does not end with Freud. Yet his work remains the reference point, the still explosively creative point of departure or of return both for clinicians and for theorists. Melanie Klein started work as a psychoanalyst at the time of the First World War and died, still working, practising and developing her ideas, in 1960. In her first ten years as a psychoanalyst she was anxious to stress that her work was a direct and loyal extension of Freud's thinking. Gradually she acknowledged an occasional, important disagreement. By the second half of the thirties, her contribution to psychoanalysis, though at least to her and her followers' minds remaining within a Freudian framework, was developing into an autonomous unit, a growing independent body.

To recount the many arguments as to where the ideas of Klein and Freud conform and where they differ would be tedious here. More important, in a brief introduction it would be misleading. It is for the new territories she explored and started to chart, not for the failures or successes of orthodoxy, that Melanie Klein should be acclaimed. What she did was new. She was an outstanding clinician and her ideas, despite problems with their presentation, represent an important new departure in the theory of mental processes. Yet, this having been said, her ideas, like all ideas, were not self-created; their context and their relationship to Freud's innovation are important.

In 1910 Melanie Klein, with her husband and two children, went to live in Budapest. There she discovered psychoanalysis. Probably in 1912, she started her analytic training with Sándor Ferenczi and became a member of the Hungarian Psychoanalytic Society. In 1921, she moved to Berlin and continued her psychoanalytic work there. From the beginning of 1924 until the summer of 1925, Karl Abraham was her analyst. Abraham's importance for Klein's work is always emphasized – both by herself and by her commentators. The period in Budapest with Ferenczi is mentioned only briefly. As far as conscious influence is concerned, this bias is undoubtedly correct – as regards unconscious influence, I am less sure. The Budapest Psychoanalytic Society, in the crucial years when Klein was there, was vibrant and inventive, a small, dynamic group of creative thinkers with Ferenczi at their centre. Sándor Ferenczi was a maverick. By contrast with Budapest, Berlin, though the world's most active psychoanalytic city, was more rivalrous and conscious of its intellectual proximity to Freud's Vienna. Karl Abraham's work is important, and interesting particularly on the period of earliest infantile development, but it never quite escapes from his reverence for Freud. Where Ferenczi loves, quarrels and bursts with ideas, Karl Abraham respects, smooths things over and binds his new insights in a strait-jacket of dubious loyalty. Intellectually, consciously, there is no doubt that Melanie Klein owed most to Karl Abraham's encouragement and to his ideas. Spiritually, something of the freedom of Ferenczi and the excitement of Budapest seems to have found its unconscious echo in her. But ultimately more important than either Budapest or Berlin was Klein's move to England where she was most warmly welcomed. Once in England, her work became freer and more coherent.

In July 1925 Klein's good friend Alix Strachey, with the help of her husband, James, arranged for Klein to lecture at the Institute of Psychoanalysis in London. At Christmas, after an illness that had fluctuated for months, Abraham died. Early in 1926 Klein settled permanently in Britain.

In England analysts thought in ways similar to Klein's; she was not struggling with an ill-fitting coat. British empirical traditions, which privileged direct and careful observations and, at their best, an open-mindedness that resulted from the lack of a habit of reference to and reverence for an over-arching philosophical mode of thought, were not only congenial to a new investigator but in Klein's case coincided with her own propensities. In addition, although interest in child analysis was becoming strong on the Continent, perhaps in London it was given added impetus by that aspect of English culture which had for three hundred years, and more emphatically since the Romantic poets and nineteenth-century novelists, put the determinative effect of childhood at the centre of its world-view. It was

Wordsworth, not Freud, who first said that 'the child is father to the man'. Also, there was at the turn of the century in England an efflorescence of interest in the mother–child relationship. It was this relationship that was to dominate psychoanalysis in Britain until the present day. When she started work, Klein was a mother with young children.

THE CHANGING PSYCHOANALYTIC BACKGROUND

1 · Theory and Therapy – Free Association and Reconstruction. Sexuality, the Unconscious and Psychic Reality

By the beginning of the twenties, psychoanalysis, though in no sense 'accepted', was an established body of thought. The theory concerned the formative importance of early childhood. Therapeutically Freud and his adherents treated patients whose free associations led to their unconscious life and whose imagined histories were interpreted and reconstructed within a clinical session.

Over time, Freud developed 'free association' as the fundamental rule of psychoanalysis. The patient says everything, however trivial or unpleasant, that comes to mind – this gives access to unconscious chains of associations, to the unconscious determinants of communication. In this way one's actions or the language of the body is squeezed into words. Instead, for instance, of getting locked out of one's home repeatedly or having a cramp in one's neck for which there is no physical explanation, one hears the chain of associations that leads to one having lost the key idea or to finding out what or who is a pain in the neck. In interpreting a dream, although symbolism may be important, access to its meanings is through the patient's free associations. A patient dreams of two cars crashing: in recounting the dream his first association is of the supermarket he had visited the day before; he had come out, seen a car like his own but in better condition, and, envious, hoped it would crash. Another patient with a similar dream-story thinks first how she hates travelling by car, she gets car-sick, she's suffering from morning sickness, she's frightened of giving birth . . . it's so violent . . . Between different individuals, a similar dream-image may have some symbolic aspects in common – but the particular history of the individual patient, discovered through his or her free associations, gives access to the particular meaning of the symbol and the wish. This is why interpretations of dreams can only take place in an analytic setting. The dream of crashing cars immediately suggests a 'primal scene' (phantasies of parents in intercourse) – but it is useless to say this, for the many-layered meaning depends on the person's hitherto undiscovered history, past and present, which is reconstructed through associations to something that is latent in the unconscious.

Roughly speaking, during the first twenty years of this century the very diverse preoccupations of Freud's work can be subjugated to two central tenets: the formative importance of infantile sexuality and the existence of an unconscious mind that works on principles quite distinct from those of the conscious mind. These two discoveries come together in Freud's theory of the Oedipus complex and its destruction by the castration complex. Together these organize, and offer normative possibilities for the psychological expression of sexuality in human life. The structuring role of these complexes makes them for Freud the nuclei of the neurosis and the key tenets of psychoanalytic understanding.

Until the 1920s the term 'unconscious' had been used either loosely, as still it is today in non-psychoanalytic discussions, to describe everything which is not present to consciousness, or more strictly, and as the object of psychoanalytic inquiry, as a mental process, a system in its own right containing all that has been repressed from consciousness. Crudely speaking, within the Freudian unconscious there is a hypothetical area that is always unfathomable and which is produced by what is known as 'primal repression'. Then there is an area (whose testing-ground is the psychoanalytical clinical setting) produced by the restriction of the wishes of infancy and early childhood: by repression 'proper'. Repression proper acts on illicit or unacceptable wishes so that they disappear from consciousness to form an unconscious domain with its own laws, the so-called 'primary process'. The wishes are forgotten and the result is an amnesia that covers our earliest years.

In Freud's theory the same sexual energy that originally belonged to the wishes tries to push the ideas back into consciousness. If they manage to re-emerge from the unconscious, they do so in a form that is distorted by the marks of the prohibition on them. They come back not as direct wishes, but as hidden, disguised, displaced wishes represented in the symptoms of neuroses, in 'normal' slips of the pen or tongue, in dreams – these can be 'interpreted' and the history of the original wish reconstructed so that it is made more acceptable to consciousness. For the patient, at its centre, this is a painful and a brave endeavour.

The concepts of the Oedipus and castration complexes include the observation that the human infant is born with sexual drives which will only eventually – and then never in a final or absolute way – become dominated by genital urges. A primary relationship to the mother becomes culturally problematic at the stage or level when the child wants to occupy the place already filled by the father, when, in a phallic and hence competitive way, it wants to be everything for the mother, to have everything she needs to satisfy her and thus to have exclusive rights to her.

The forbidden wishes and all the phantasies connected with them constitute the core of what is called 'psychic reality'. This concept replaced Freud's first idea that some actual occurrence such as seduction in childhood caused the later production of neurotic symptoms. Unconscious processes completely replace external reality (with which they have no truck) by psychical reality. Psychical reality is not commensurate with an inner world in general or with all psychological productions; it is a hard core, a nugget, felt to be as real as the grass and the trees, as real as (and not unconnected with) the fact that one is born to two parents and is either a boy or a girl. Like other realities, with time and effort it can, if it is so wished, be modified to a degree. Historical reality both is and is not changed by new ways of seeing and experiencing – so too is psychical reality.

2 · The Ego, the Object, Life, Death and Anxiety

Freud developed psychoanalysis through an attempt to understand some inexplicable occurrence, a symptom, a dream, or an hysterical (not an organic) illness. In the years after the First World War other aspects of his work were being taken up, developed, and diverged from. Instead of the symptoms that indicated the primary process of a system of the unconscious, aspects of human relationships that determined the psychological dimension of character development started to come to the fore. In Vienna, interest increased in the agency that implemented the repression along with other defences. Eventually this led to the emergence of 'ego psychology', which was vastly extended when it was transported by refugee analysts to North America. In Berlin, Abraham emphasized the significance of the earliest oral and anal experiences of the nursing baby and the toilet-trained infant. In Budapest, Ferenczi, back from work with war neurosis, was interested, among other things, in the present analyst–patient relationship and in working out a therapy that utilized it more actively. In London, an interest in children and their human environment and in the vicissitudes of 'normal' development led to a tendency known as 'object relations analysis'. The period prior to (or, speaking structurally, 'underneath') the Oedipus complex gained in theoretical and clinical importance.

Under the impact of clinical experience, speculative necessity and confrontation with colleagues' differing psychoanalytic theories, Freud's work itself was changing. Here, I shall select the new theories that are of relevance to Klein's thinking. In *Beyond the Pleasure Principle* (1919) Freud subsumed the previous dominance of the sexual drive under a 'life drive' that, while still sexual (and hence not to be confused with Jungian notions), also included the urge for self-preservation. He introduced, in opposition to the life drive, the highly controversial speculation of a death drive, a force that strove to return the human being back into a state of inertia, of the inorganic. Clinically it is seen in masochism, in an unconscious sense of guilt, in the quality of driven-ness within the compulsion to repeat certain experiences and in the wish not to recover.

In 1923, in *The Ego and the Id* (*SE*, XIX), Freud introduced a new metapsychology. Though the division between unconscious, preconscious and conscious continues to be used by Freud after the twenties, it is superseded by a new topographical division of the mind: the id, the ego, the super-ego. All have unconscious parts and origins – the id is completely unconscious and inherits the characteristics of the previous system of the unconscious. Finally, in 1926, prompted explicitly by Otto Rank's argument that the nature and degree of the trauma of birth is causative of all future development, but also by a more general tendency of psychoanalytic work of which Klein's was an important part, Freud revised his understanding of the affectual state of anxiety. Earlier he had thought that when a sexual idea is repressed the idea becomes unconscious but the feelings are converted into anxiety. Now he argues that, although this does happen to a degree (particularly in what were known as the 'actual neuroses'), in most other cases the feeling of anxiety comes first and warns of the danger inherent in certain sexual desires and ideas.

Freud's many revisions did not cancel out his earlier ideas: they are more like new layers on old rock – affecting it and changing its composition, but not annihilating it.

FREUD'S NEW IDEAS: DIVISION AND THE WEARISOME CONDITION OF HUMANITY

In the 1920s Freud argued that the neonate is born with what is to become the id, the ego and the super-ego undifferentiated. The ego and the super-ego (in that order) are carved – never totally, never for ever – out of the id. The id (like the previous system of the 'unconscious') is the repository of ideational representatives of human drives and desires. The ego is the organized part of the mental structure. The super-ego is the protector and critic of this ego. While originating in the id, the super-ego takes its form from an internalization of particular external injunctions and prohibitions and of particular 'inherited' ones – of the world's *thou shalts* and *thou shalt nots*. Freud wrote:

thus a child's super-ego is in fact constructed on the model not of its parents but of its parents' super-ego; the contents which fill it are the same and it becomes the vehicle of tradition and of all the time-resisting judgements of value which have propagated themselves in this manner from generation to generation. (*SE*, XXII, p. 67)

The concepts of id, ego and super-ego are metapsychological descriptions – phenomenologically the distinctions may well not be perceived. (We shall see this lack of differentiation again later in Klein's observation of the proximity of conscious, preconscious and unconscious in the very young child.) Freud thought that the division into ego and id characterized humankind and was one of three factors that might well be causative of our unique (or exceptional) proclivity to neurosis.

Freud mentions certain preconditions which he saw as crucial for the unique development of the human psyche.

The human baby is born prematurely. Its instincts are weak – it seems to have only a slight instinctual notion of how to avoid danger or to get satisfaction for its own needs from the outside. It is thus much more helpless and dependent on others for the satisfaction of its vital needs than even those mammals most closely related to human beings. When its caretaker (usually – but, more important, prototypically – its mother) satisfies the baby, she is 'at one' with it and hence not felt as separate. When, however, she is felt to fail to satisfy the baby's need, she (or her breast) is experienced as separate from the baby and hence as the first distinct psychological object. When she is thus perceived to be missing, two things happen. One is that the loss or the removal of the means whereby its needs are met make the baby feel anxious. Anxiety is an affectual state that warns the baby of a danger. The danger is not experienced directly but is apprehended as a danger on the model of a preceding danger that was actually experienced (a 'trauma' – such as birth). The second is that the baby re-creates the mother for itself, making the satisfaction she has represented seem now to be inside itself (for instance, by hallucinating a 'good feed'); it thus forms a separate area within itself – which in part becomes its ego (the ego is 'the precipitate of abandoned object cathexes').

For the prematurely born infant there is a perception of the danger of helplessness and a signal of anxiety. The ego is formed on this bed of helplessness and anxiety. But the infant's helplessness relates to its inside as well as to its outside world. The internal needs and wishes, which are the instigators of the problem, themselves come to feel dangerous. Thus the ego which is being constructed has to cope with dangers from two directions: it develops means of avoiding external dangers and of rejecting internal ones that emanate from the id – these means are termed the ego's defences.

The biphasic nature of human sexuality is a further condition that Freud always felt was responsible for the predisposition of human-kind to neuroses. In other mammals there seems to be a straightfor-ward uninterrupted progression to sexual maturity; in humans amnesia overtakes infancy. The first phase is the efflorescent gener-alized sexuality of the infant (called 'polymorphously perverse'), then for a period sexuality is 'forgotten' and only latent, then it re-emerges in a second phase of ebullient sexuality in puberty and adolescence. This biphasic situation of infantile and then pubertal sexuality with a gap between them indicates the repression of infantile sexuality, the mark of the unconscious. Once again it suggests a division within the subject which seems to be the hallmark of the human being and which can be seen in an exaggerated version in the neurotic. It is through the exaggerations of the neuroses that normality can be seen.

Freud's work emphasizes the divisions that condition the human subject. He is concerned with the construction of different areas of mental life. There is one mind, but something divides it. For him, the wearisome condition of humanity (in the words of the renaissance poet Fulke Greville), which produces both creativity and neurosis, is that we are born under one law yet to another bound. Human beings bring something with them, but the mind's divisions are set up by the encounter with the world, with the commands, phantasies and wishes of others – with humankind's culture, laws and prohibitions.

MELANIE KLEIN: CHILD ANALYSIS
AND THE PLAY TECHNIQUE

When Melanie Klein started to work with children she was not the first analyst to do so, but the field was a completely new one. When Freud had been working with adults in the first decades of the century, others joined him, coming together, submitting to the dominance of his ideas or parting in hostility. The different analysts who started to work with children after the First World War repeated this experience – but with a difference. For them there was a body of psychoanalytic theory already dominated by Freud's writings – their own theories had all to be contained within a reference to this work.

Klein started her psychoanalytic work with observations of a normal child – her first papers all show her applying basic psychoanalytic ideas to child development. Soon, Abraham was to encourage her to extend her observations into proper, full analyses of very young children. Klein always argued that, though there were differences in the mental apparatus of children and adults, the same psychoanalytic treatment could be applied to both.

It is Freud's early theories of sexuality and the unconscious that Klein uses in her first published paper. The first part she read originally in 1919 to the Hungarian Psychoanalytic Society and the second part to the Berlin Society in 1921. She discusses a later revised version of it in her retrospective essay on play technique (Chapter 1 in this volume). Klein describes the prophylactic treatment she carried out on a five-year-old boy, Fritz (see p. 230, n. 2). Where, in the case of 'Little Hans', his famous analysis of a childhood phobia, Freud talked to the father, Klein talks directly and listens to Fritz. But this was not a psychoanalysis – nor intended as such – but rather a re-education of mother and child using Freudian theories. Klein also watches what Fritz does. He was a late speaker and soon Klein was working with two-year-olds or with autistic children – if language is not available, something else must replace it. From this work Melanie Klein developed her 'play technique' – the central method of her analysis. In the consulting room, the child has access to general play materials – water, pencils, paper, etc. – and its own set of 'neutral' toys – small basic human figures, a train, a car and so on. How it deals with these toys and the whole analytic space is observed and interpreted. Although she did not, of course, use the technique with older children and adults, its use with very young and verbally disturbed child patients led to her insights into the earliest preverbal ways of communication and to her account of the phantasies and psychic contents of the neonatal and infantile mind.

Klein's own interests always centred on the very young child or the infant in the older child and in the adult, but her ideas led other analysts into working with psychotic conditions in which the patient may have no access to language or may not be able to use the normal structures of language.

Melanie Klein claimed that the play technique, as a technique for gaining access to the unconscious, was the complete equivalent of free association. She writes:

. . . the brick, the little figure, the car, not only represent things which interest the child in themselves, but in his play with them they always have a variety of symbolical meanings as well which are bound up with his phantasies, wishes, and experiences. This archaic mode of expression is also the language with which we are familiar in dreams, and it was by approaching the play of the child in a way similar to Freud's interpretation of dreams, that I found I could get access to the child's unconscious. But we have to consider each child's use of symbols in connection with his particular emotions and anxieties and in relation to the whole situation which is presented in the analysis; mere generalized translations of symbols are meaningless. (p. 51)

Play, like dream-thoughts, can be a manifest expression with a latent unconscious content. In using it, we have to consider each child's game in connection with its particular emotions and anxieties. When a child crashes a toy car into another, it may do so enthusiastically, nervously, lethargically, sadistically . . . We also have to note what it does before and after each action. In this way the interpretation of play and the understanding of the symbols, displacements and affects in their context are very similar to the interpretation of dreams or symptoms through the patient's free associations.

MELANIE KLEIN: THE BABY AND ITS WORLD

1 · The Ego's Defences, the Paranoid-schizoid and the Depressive Positions, Normality and the Psychoses

Observing and working in an intensive and extensive psychoanalytic practice with children and adults, Klein developed a model of mental development which she amended and amplified throughout her life. Simplifying somewhat, I would suggest that Klein's basic model is that the neonate brings into the world two main conflicting impulses: love and hate. In Klein's later formulations, love is the manifestation of the life drive; hate, destructiveness and envy are emanations of the death drive. The life drive and death drive are two innate instincts in conflict with each other. From the very beginning the neonate tries to deal with the conflict between these two drives, either by bringing them together in order to modify the death drive with the life drive or by expelling the death drive into the outside world. The baby brings with it the effects of these two instincts, its various impulses and a body with sensations and a primitive residual ego which is endangered by the baby's own impulses and which develops different, ever more mature mechanisms for dealing with them. Furthermore, the baby encounters a world which is both satisfying and frustrating. It exists from the start in a relationship to another person or part of that person (prototypically its mother and her breast). Gradually, its world becomes more complex and includes a father. The relationship between the ego and the impulses, drives and body-feelings on the one hand, and between these and the outside world on the other (represented by mother-and-father at first combined together), are the two poles whose interaction Klein describes.

Freud made the act of repression critical for the formation of that aspect of psychic life which psychoanalysis could decipher; it was the particular defence which constructed the unconscious whose manifestations could be understood in the distortions of neurosis. But Klein, along with a growing number of analysts, paid attention to the ego's earlier mechanisms of defence. There are many things the threatened infantile ego can do by way of protecting itself. It can, for instance, deny or repudiate unwelcome reality; but there are other mechanisms which, in the clinical setting of the relationship between the patient and the analyst, can be seen as communicating an experience that cannot be verbalized.

In this connection I would single out four mechanisms which are central to an understanding of Klein's work. *Splitting* – the ego can stop the bad part of the object contaminating the good part, by dividing it, or it can split off and disown a part of itself. In fact, each kind of splitting always entails the other. In *projection*, the ego fills the object with some of its own split feelings and experience; in *introjection*, it takes into itself what it perceives or experiences of the object. *Projective identification* was first described by Klein but has been developed much more fully by Kleinians subsequently. In this the ego projects its feelings into the object which it then identifies with, becoming like the object which it has already imaginatively filled with itself. The ego makes use of these defences to cope with the inner world and the constant interaction between inner and outer. Its own destructive feelings – emanations of the death drive – make the baby very anxious. It fears that the object on which it vents its rage (e.g. the breast that goes away and frustrates it) will retaliate. In self-protection it splits itself and the object into a good part and a bad part and projects all its badness into the outside world so that the hated breast becomes the hateful and hating breast. Klein describes this as the paranoid-schizoid position (see particularly Chapter 8). As developmentally the ego becomes able to take in the whole person, to see that good and bad can exist together in the same person, it continues to rage against the mother for the frustrations she causes, but now, instead of fearing retaliation, it feels guilt and anxiety for the damage it itself has done in phantasy. This Klein calls the depressive position. In overcoming this position the baby wishes to undo or repair the earlier phantasized destruction of the actual and the internalized mother. As it does so it also takes in the damaged and then restored mother, adding these new internalizations as part of the self's inner world. These two positions, the paranoid-schizoid and the depressive, develop in the first months of life, but they always remain as part of our personality, of our normal and our psychotic development.

We all use these mechanisms unconsciously as part of our daily lives; in psychoses, one or other of them takes over and dominates over any other form of communication. Perception of inner and outer reality can become so distorted that normal communication is impossible.

Every infant introjects, projects, splits its objects and hence its ego – excessive use of these defences is psychotic. In the normal course of events, every child does its best to repudiate undesirable parts of reality; severe repudiation is at the heart of psychosis. A difference of degree can become a difference of kind.

In a clinical setting all these defences and positions that Klein describes are discoverable in the present relationship between patient and analyst; they are primitive, preverbal or extra-verbal ways of communicating an experience, and they can be understood and put into words in an interpretation which can bring clarity and relief. A clear description of the practice is given in Klein's account of four-year-old Dick (see Chapter 5).

2 · Anxiety, Symbolism, Phantasy and the Toy

Three concepts cover the area of Klein's observations: anxiety, symbolism and phantasy. All three work together – each is a condition or product of the others.

From the very beginning, Melanie Klein stressed the importance of anxiety as a diagnostic tool. An increase in anxiety, and its diminution, seemed to her to indicate that the analyst was getting near to the trouble. Even to a lay person, it is noticeable how a child becomes acutely anxious and then relieved if one touches on a secret, shameful problem. Klein, in conformity with Freud's first theories, thought anxiety was a transformation of frustrated or prohibited desire; later she saw it as the manifestation of the death drive. As her work developed, she specified types of anxiety. Each position has its appropriate anxiety – persecutory in the paranoid-schizoid position, depressive in the depressive position. The type of anxiety is thus the key to the level of the condition.

Klein's work with child patients, her use of the play technique in particular, privileged symbolism. At first her understanding was that similar pleasures derived from different objects made the baby equate the objects symbolically. Soon she realized that this was a static model and she proposed that anxiety produced the movement within the development of symbol formation. Anxious lest its negativity destroy an object, the infant moves to another which thus relates symbolically to the one left behind. If, as in some psychotic conditions, no anxiety is expressed, then there is stasis and no, or severely reduced, symbol formation including language.

How the baby relates to the conjunction of its inner and outer worlds psychically is expressed in Klein's notion of phantasy. (The 'ph' spelling is used to indicate that the process is unconscious.)

By later Kleinians and critics alike, phantasy is often seen as identical to Freud's concept of psychic reality. Klein herself was right to think it is not the same.

To see the distinction between them it is perhaps easiest to start with the observation that Freud's concept of a human drive is never as something that is equivalent to an animal instinct. A human drive initially has no object. As humans, probably because of our premature birth, we are weak in instincts. For Freud our drives take shape in relation to this weakness of our instincts and to the greatness of our dependence. But as humans we are, of course, also animals. An animal instinct knows and goes for its object – as a calf finds a nipple, or a chick follows a hen. Presumably we too have some residual animal instinct expressed in human terms. I would argue that the Kleinian concept of phantasy describes the human being's vast elaboration through perceptions and experience of this animal, biological instinct. Klein herself writes:

My hypothesis is that the infant has an innate unconscious awareness of the existence of the mother. We know that young animals at once turn to the mother and find their food from her. The human animal is not different in that respect, and this instinctual knowledge is the basis for the infant's primal relation to his mother . . . (*CW*, III, 248.)

Kleinian 'phantasy' cannot be reduced to this, but this is its origin and in this it differs from Freud's concept of psychical reality, which is something not innate but produced by the peculiar conditions of the human being. In Klein's concept, phantasy emanates from within and imagines what is without, it offers an unconscious commentary on instinctual life and links feelings to objects and creates a new amalgam: the world of imagination. Through its ability to phantasize, the baby tests out, primitively 'thinks' about, its experiences of inside and outside. External reality can gradually affect and modify the crude hypotheses phantasy sets up. Phantasy is both the activity and its products.

It is in the light of the concept of phantasy that we must view Klein's major technical innovation in child analysis: the use of toys. A toy on the one hand is archetypal, but it can be used in various ways according to the individual's phantasy: a train can be cuddled like a baby as well as more obviously driven furiously into a tunnel/womb. A typical or archetypal toy such as Klein used is something that bridges the gap between an external object and the inner world. Toys represent the object of phantasy and of object relations. As Hanna Segal says, for Freud, the psychological object is the object of the drive and for Klein it is the object of the child, most importantly of the child's phantasy. A toy stands for this object. Klein moves the symbol into the consulting room and offers it to the child, senses its anxiety and discovers its phantasies.

I would suggest that the centrepoint of Klein's therapy is her understanding of anxiety; the key concept of her theory is not the system of the unconscious (the key concept of Freud's psychoanalysis) but 'phantasy'.

FREUD AND KLEIN: THE UNCONSCIOUS AND PHANTASY

When Klein started writing, Anton von Freund in Budapest said that she was only dealing with preconscious material: the sexual questions and answers were available to the child, but were just put out of mind – descriptively 'unconscious', technically only 'preconscious'. In response, Klein gave interpretations to the child that went deeper. In particular, she talked of what could be assumed to be unknown: the father's role in coitus and procreation.

It is sometimes argued that Klein's concept of the unconscious conforms to Freud's notion of 'primal repression', but it does not do so exactly. Primal repression in Freud's sense is something that happens in the individual's prehistory or in its taking in of human prehistory. For Klein, what is unconscious is the biological and affectual condition of the human being. In essence, by the time of her later writings, the unconscious is equivalent to the instincts: to the life drive and death drive and their affects. The unconscious exists as a condition and from it emerge preconsciousness and consciousness. The Kleinian unconscious is a container full of contents; it is not another system of thought; it does not have its own laws which would bear the mark of its construction. There are unconscious mechanisms, the unconscious ego's many defences, but not mechanisms of the unconscious as a system. Freud's system of the unconscious knows neither time nor contradiction, but works primarily through displacing, condensing or symbolizing different elements. In Klein's theory there is no clear distinction between what Freud called the primary process (the unconscious) and the secondary processes (the conscious and the preconscious). There is unconscious symbolism but not symbolism as a basic manifestation of the unconscious. The ego displaces and condenses but, though done unconsciously, these are not defining characteristics of 'an unconscious'. Klein's theory reflects her observation of children – the distinction between conscious, unconscious and preconscious is not sharp. Despite her response to Anton von Freund, Klein's concept of the unconscious is of something not dynamic but descriptive. It is not surprising that some eminent analysts who started work in Klein's footsteps, such as Wilfred Bion, rarely use the concept. In a way it has become uninteresting; after all, in what way can we say a baby phantasizing a breast is unconscious of it?

Klein's unconscious phantasy and Freud's unconscious as a mental area utterly distinct in its laws of operation from consciousness are different concepts. All Klein's interest, therapeutically and theoretically, is directed to finding the unconscious content of the phantasies and the work of the unconscious ego. As Klein's friend and colleague Susan Isaacs wrote: 'The primary *content* of all mental processes are unconscious phantasies. Such phantasies are the basis of all unconscious and conscious thought processes' (my italics). Klein is not concerned with how the unconscious as a mode of thought works. The content not the dream-work is central to her interpretation of dreams. This orientation towards phantasy contents and the ego's defences suggests there must be some differences between free association and the play technique.

FREUD AND KLEIN: TIME PAST AND FUTURE.
TIME PRESENT

In the 1880s Freud became increasingly struck by the psychological nature of physiological symptoms. The picture of the neuroses was confused, and, in conformity with scientific practice, his aim was to sort it out – while always realizing that the phenomena themselves and their clinical presentation would remain for ever confused.

The differentiating pattern that Freud first espoused divided the neuroses into two conditions: the 'actual' neuroses and the psychoneuroses. Throughout his life, Freud continued to be interested in the distinction, but he never fully developed it. Its use declined to the extent that it is hardly heard today. I am resurrecting it here to help me clarify an important difference that I find in the theories of Klein and Freud. The actual neuroses – anxiety attacks, neurasthenia, hypochondria and possibly the war neuroses – were psychological conditions provoked by contemporary, that is to say 'actual', situations such as prolonged sexual abstinence, violence or persistent frustration.

In the 1890s Freud had advanced a crucial argument: the psychoneuroses, hysteria and the actual anxiety neurosis had much in common and were often found together, but, despite this, hysteria was a distinct structure with a determinant from the past. At first, perhaps as a reflection of the mixed presentation of the neuroses, Freud thought that an actual event (childhood seduction) had taken place in the past and had caused the trouble in the present. Freud's hysterical patients 'suffered from reminiscences'. The psychoneurosis of hysteria became more differentiated from the actual neuroses when he realized that it was an infantile sexual phantasy (a version of what he later called the Oedipus complex) that was its main determinant. The determining instance is no longer historically real; yet it is a case of the past, in a complex way, producing the present. As the existence or the significance of an actual past trauma was abandoned by Freud, the notion of a key phantasy formed in the past but operating by deferred action in the present replaced the notion of reminiscences. There is, however, never an absolute distinction – the important point is the 'pastness': 'Up to the present we have not succeeded in pointing to any difference in the consequences, whether phantasy or reality has had a greater share in these events of childhood' (*SE*, XVI, p. 370).

In brief, I would suggest that, through all its vicissitudes, Freud's theory revolves around the question of a past. Psychically speaking, there is no past until after the repression of Oedipal wishes by the castration complex. The castration complex destroys the phantasy of an eternally satisfying relationship with the mother, it introduces the command that the Oedipus complex be over and done with: if you accept it as past you will be able to have a new version (be a father in your turn with a woman of your own) in the future. (The theory's phallocentrism is outside the scope of this introduction.) The castration complex, bearing the injunction of human history, inaugurates history within the individual.

The clearly observed phenomenon of an amnesia that covers our infancy indicates the construction of memory. The paradox here is only apparent.

Infancy is a perpetual present. This could be linked with the small child's extraordinary memory – which is not memory, but a continuous actuality. So too, because of the Oedipus and castration complexes, only humans have yesterdays. As far as we can tell neither animals nor pre-Oedipal human infants divide time into future, past and present. Time for them would seem to be nearer to spatial relationships: here, there; come, gone; horizontal, punctuated duration rather than an historical, vertical temporal perspective.

By contrast with the psychoneuroses, the expressions of the actual neuroses are not over-determined by the complexity and multifacetedness of a person's history. They may use a physical weakness or an affective condition which may well exist in a person's past as well as in their present, or the trauma may be cumulative – but this past condition does not determine or give the pattern to the present situation. Repeated exposure to warfare may stir an individual's anxiety about their own aggression; persistent sexual frustration or seduction may provoke tabooed fantasies. What is produced in the actual neurosis is a hidden, probably hitherto unused, but nevertheless continuing possibility of the personality. 'Pastness' is unimportant.

Freud argued that the actual neuroses were the grain of sand around which the oyster produced the pearl of the psychoneuroses; Klein's work leads in another direction. From her observations of normal children she is led to an analysis of infantile development that finds the points of psychosis which at the present time, or repeated in the future because they are always current, will be echoed in a psychotic illness. At first, it looks as though we have here a parallel with Freud's work. It is often claimed that, where Freud found the child was father to the man, Klein found the infant gave birth to the child and adult. The resemblance between the two notions is illusory. Freud's historical imagination examines the present (the adult illness) and from it reconstructs a hypothetical past determinant. For Klein the past and the present are one.

Today the concept of actual neurosis has been replaced by the idea of psychosomatic illness. The shift preserves the bodily and affectual traits but loses the dimension of present time. Defining the actual neurosis in their *Language of Psycho-Analysis* (see the Selected Bibliography, p. 242), Laplanche and Pontalis end with this comment:

It is worth noting that it is only the lack of satisfaction of the sexual instincts which is taken into consideration by Freud's theory. In attempting to understand the genesis of actual and psychosomatic symptoms we should be well advised to pay some attention too to the suppression of aggressiveness.

Klein is not interested in psychosomatic illness, and when she started work actual neurosis was a current but soon to recede diagnosis. It is not one she makes use of. However, I suggest that her work finds the links between the psychology of the actual neurosis and the psychosis. From a particular perspective, in doing this she has already taken into account Laplanche and Pontalis's proposals – she has found an important place for the effects (one of which is aggressiveness) of the death drive.

The very nature of Klein's first observations makes the obsolete category of actual neurosis useful.

Klein's first work was with inhibited children. Their difficulties resemble those of neurasthenics:

The following characteristics proved in a number of cases and in a typical way to be inhibitions: awkwardness in games and athletics and distaste for them, little or no pleasure in lessons, lack of interest in any particular subject or in general, the varying degrees of so-called laziness. (*CW*, I, p. 77)

In placing anxiety at the centre of the theoretical elaboration of the clinical picture Klein is once more dealing with present-day or persistent, potential actuality. The unanswered questions, the practice of masturbation once it is no longer acceptable, produce anxiety. The child of three or four is dealing with sexual or aggressive problems or hypochondriacal worries in the present. Where in Freud repression is a defence that creates a past and a symptom is a return of that past, Klein is appropriately more interested in the defences which have no such dimension of time past and with atemporal inhibitions of the ego, not with symptoms.

Although Klein worked often with latency children and later with adults, her innovation in theory and practice is with Freud's 'pre-Oedipal' child. By definition, the pre-Oedipal child, but also the psychotic, whether child or adult, has not negotiated the Oedipus complex, has not acquired a history. Klein's contribution is to chart an area where present and past are one and time is spatial, not historical. This area has all the characteristics of a descriptive unconsciousness, an unconscious that has not been constructed by repression.

This absence of historical time is evident both in Klein's innovations and in her omissions. Thus the concept of regression plays no role in Klein's theory. She has no explanation of infantile amnesia and she and her followers show an ever-decreasing interest in the castration complex. Her discovery of an early Oedipus complex is not of something overcome by an internalization of a prohibition but rather of an internal unconscious sociology of immediate object relations that are come to terms with through the activities and phantasies of the depressive position. Even experientially, what is depressing about depression (among other things) is that, though it may come and go, the sufferer from it has no sense of a past or hence of a future freedom. Klein's crucial concept of a 'position' speaks to this different, earlier, prehistorical sense of time – a position is a mental space in which one is sometimes lodged.

In the psychotherapeutic setting, the anxiety, the nature and contents of the phantasies, the mechanisms of their operation, all come into the present situation with the analyst. Because psychotic elements are present all the time in everyone and psychoses themselves are not regressed to, these states are potentially present all the time; they are not activated by the analytic situation – the analytic situation provides the space and the skills for their comprehension and their mitigation. The instances of our ego's earliest defences can be worked through in a particular type of transference that deals not with the past but with the 'here and now' – the total present of the relationship between analyst and analysand (see Chapter 9).

Whatever the shifts in Freud's theory, the central creation remains the same. Freud's psychoanalytic theory of the psychoneuroses is about the production of a psychic domain which is not reducible to either or both of two poles. If we imagine two overlapping triangles, the Freudian unconscious is at the apex of one whose two sides are the inner drives and the laws and history of the outer world; the psychoneuroses are at the apex of another whose base points are the bipolar opposition between sexuality and its prohibition.

Freud thought the ego could regress to early protopsychotic mechanisms, tunnel back to its beginnings – use the grain of sand; Klein, looking at the flat earth of infancy, the direct relationship between normality and psychosis, sees that past and present are one. Not surprisingly, in the clinical picture Klein finds what Freud finds – for instance, an Oedipus complex and a super-ego, both of which she places much earlier. In fact, though what Klein describes may be, as she asserts, the kernel of the later developments, they are not, I would suggest, even residually the same conceptions at the level of a theoretical understanding of them. In Klein these situations are all products of the ego's phantasized relations with its external world, they are not in any dynamic sense triangular structures; neither the 'combined parents' nor the 'father-inside-the-mother' that she proposes, constitute a different third term. Hence these key concepts do not describe another psychic domain.

Klein's model is a two-way process from inner to outer and back again. For Klein the construction of a third independent psychic structure does not arise. It does not arise because what she is observing, describing and theorizing is the very absence of history and of historical time.

Klein is not a scientific theorist in the nineteenth-century tradition. The great theorists of the nineteenth century – Darwin, Marx and Freud – explain the present by the past. The dominant sociological phenomenologies of the twentieth century in which Klein participated study lateral, horizontal, not vertical, relationships. But Klein is also observing something different from the neuroses: she is working with the prototypes of psychotic behaviours whose mechanisms, like those of the actual neuroses, may well be only bipolar oppositions.

KLEIN AND FREUD: MOTHERS AND FATHERS

Freud was always intent on differentiation. This was and is the scientific tradition: separation, categorization – Wordsworth's 'we murder to dissect'. (Recently it has been identified as 'masculine'. Certainly psychoanalysis itself could provide an explanation of why this might be so.) The clinical picture is always mixed but to Freud the theory must not echo this state of affairs. Early in his work, he wrote to his friend Fliess: 'In my opinion it is possible to deal with hysteria, freed from any admixture, as something independent; and to do so in every respect *except in that of therapeutics.*' (*SE*, II, p. 261, my italics) The situation is muddled, the task of science is to sort it out – recognizing that such sorting is an imposition:

We cannot do justice to the characteristics of the mind by linear outlines like those in a drawing or in a primitive painting, but rather by areas of colour melting into one another as they are represented by modern artists. After making the separation we must allow what we have separated to merge together once more. (*SE*, XII, p. 79)

It is always recognized that Klein's theory itself can be somewhat confused. It is held that the confusion arises because her theory is really more a descriptive phenomenology that sticks close to the complexity of her clinical material. Without doubt such an explanation is correct. Freud always thought of himself as a poor therapist, Klein was a superb clinician. But this distinction and this explanation raise more questions than they solve. To be a good clinician or even a good experimental scientist demands the ability to identify and to be intuitive on the basis of endlessly accumulated experience. The geneticist Barbara McClintock describes her work thus: 'I found that the more I worked with [the chromosomes] the bigger and bigger they got, and when I was really working with them, I wasn't outside, I was down there. I was part of the system. I was right down there with them, and everything got big . . . it surprised me because I actually felt as if I were right down there and these were my friends' (see Selected Bibliography). Identification and intuition on the basis of accumulated experience are maternal characteristics – they are the mechanisms by which a mother comes to know the meaning of her baby's cry. (Masculine dissections are no more limited to men than maternal abilities for identification are limited to women.) Being a good clinician is not the same as being a good theoretician, but being good at identifying with what one observes in order to follow what is going on in something other than oneself and then describing it constitutes an intermediary level of conceptualization. This is Klein's achievement – but it is more than that. Just as Freud theorizes the construction of what scientific theory itself is about, so too, Klein identifies and describes what intuitive identification and clinical observation are about: areas of confusion, fusion, lack of boundaries, of communicating without the differential structures of speech.

MELANIE KLEIN: THE PSYCHOSES, THE DEATH DRIVE AND THE EGO

Klein effected a major shift within an important branch of psychoanalysis. She explored the borderland between the physiological and the psychological, seeing the one emanating from the other under the provocation of the external world. In doing so she effected a shift in interest from the neuroses to the psychoses. Concomitant with this is a change in the orientation from the effects of sexuality to the effects of the death drive.

In her early writings Klein is concerned with Freudian sexual explanations but there is an ever-increasing reference to the death drive as a given cause of mental development. Klein's concept of a death drive differs from Freud's, though once again, as both are psychoanalysts, the clinical material they are elucidating mostly looks the same. The question of a death drive in Freud's writing is highly complicated, but it is clear, and of relevance to Klein, that its manifestations (though for Freud always mixed with sexuality) relate to the ego, to the ego's struggle to preserve itself. From the very beginning it is the ego that interests Klein. She extends the concept to cover what would nowadays probably be called 'the self'.

Everything in her early orientation, long before she accepted the notion of a death drive and when she was working within a Freudian framework of the Oedipus and castration complexes, can be seen to harbinger her later development. In starting work with the problems of the normal child she rediscovered an ego psychology that existed before Freud started psychoanalysis with his attempt to understand the neurotic symptom. Klein brought to her rediscovery the insights and techniques of Freud's psychoanalysis and thereby profoundly changed it. Psychoses or narcissistic neuroses are illnesses of the ego. Where Freud had proposed that, to produce the psychoses, the neuroses must be closed off or regressed from, Klein sees a spider's web of direct lines between normal ego development and psychosis. In Klein's theory the ego works with both the death and the life drive, fending off annihilation, moving towards integration; expressing envy, feeling gratitude. While in all senses using Freud's development of psychoanalysis, Klein changes the terrain and thereby changes the task.

RETROSPECTIVE

CHAPTER ONE

'The Psycho-Analytic Play Technique' was written as the introductory contribution to the volume *New Directions in Psycho-Analysis*, published in 1955. An earlier version had been read to the Royal Medico-Psychological Association on 12 February, but this did not give such full child case histories. Other contributors to the volume included Paula Heimann and Susan Isaacs. The Melanie Klein Trust was established this year.

In this paper Klein surveys her work, tracing how her earliest clinical work enabled her to make the observations that became the keystones of her theory. The paper is a retrospective account in which all Klein's development and concepts are referred to briefly; their elaboration at the time of their birth will be found in the subsequent essays (all of which, except for 'A Study in Envy and Gratitude', were written earlier).

The survey is interesting for two overriding reasons: it is Klein's only published account of how she sees her own history as a psychoanalyst and it gives a full and clear description of her discovery that a child's play could be used as the equivalent of an adult's 'free association' – a means of gaining access to the unconscious modes of thought, which for Klein is always the task of psychoanalysis.

THE PSYCHO-ANALYTIC PLAY TECHNIQUE: ITS HISTORY AND SIGNIFICANCE (1955)

In offering a paper mainly concerned with play technique . . . I have been prompted by the consideration that my work with both children and adults, and my contributions to psycho-analytic theory as a whole, derive ultimately from the play technique evolved with young children. I do not mean by this that my later work was a direct application of the play technique; but the insight I gained into early development, into unconscious processes, and into the nature of the interpretations by which the unconscious can be approached, has been of far-reaching influence on the work I have done with older children and adults.

I shall, therefore, briefly outline the steps by which my work developed out of the psycho-analytic play technique, but I shall not attempt to give a complete summary of my findings. In 1919, when I started my first case, some psycho-analytic work with children had already been done, particularly by Dr Hug-Hellmuth (1921). However, she did not undertake the psycho-analysis of children under six and, although she used drawings and occasionally play as material, she did not develop this into a specific technique.

At the time I began to work it was an established principle that interpretations should be given very sparingly. With few exceptions psycho-analysts had not explored the deeper layers of the unconscious – in children such exploration being considered potentially dangerous. This cautious outlook was reflected in the fact that then, and for years to come, psycho-analysis was held to be suitable only for children from the latency period onwards.[1]

My first patient was a five-year-old boy. I referred to him under the name 'Fritz' in my earliest published papers.[2] To begin with I thought it would be sufficient to influence the mother's attitude. I suggested that she should encourage the child to discuss freely with her the many unspoken questions which were obviously at the back of his mind and were impeding his intellectual development. This had a good effect, but his neurotic difficulties were not sufficiently alleviated and it was soon decided that I should psycho-analyse him. In doing so, I deviated from some of the rules so far established, for I interpreted what I thought to be most urgent in the material the child presented to me and found my interest focusing on his anxieties and the defences against them. This new approach soon confronted me with serious problems. The anxieties I encountered when analysing this first case were very acute, and although I was strengthened in the belief that I was working on the right lines by observing the alleviation of anxiety again and again produced by my interpretations, I was at times perturbed by the intensity of the fresh anxieties which were being brought into the open. On one such occasion I sought advice from Dr Karl Abraham. He replied that since my interpretations up to then had often produced relief and the analysis was obviously progressing, he saw no ground for changing the method of approach. I felt encouraged by his support and, as it happened, in the next few days the child's anxiety, which had come to a head, greatly diminished, leading to further improvement. The conviction gained in this analysis strongly influenced the whole course of my analytic work.

The treatment was carried out in the child's home with his own toys. This analysis was the beginning of the psycho-analytic play technique, because from the start the child expressed his phantasies and anxieties mainly in play, and I consistently interpreted its meaning to him, with the result that additional material came up in his play. That is to say, I already used with this patient, in essence, the method of interpretation which became characteristic of my technique. This approach corresponds to a fundamental principle of psycho-analysis – free association. In interpreting not only the child's words but also his activities with his toys, I applied this basic principle to the mind of the child, whose play and varied activities – in fact his whole behaviour – are means of expressing what the adult expresses predominantly by words. I was also guided throughout by two other tenets of psycho-analysis established by Freud, which I have from the beginning regarded as fundamental: that the exploration of the unconscious is the main task of psycho-analytic procedure, and that the analysis of the transference is the means of achieving this aim.

Between 1920 and 1923 I gained further experience with other child cases, but a definite step in the development of play technique was the treatment of a child of two years and nine months whom I psycho-analysed in 1923. I have given some details of this child's case under the name 'Rita' in my book *The Psycho-Analysis of Children*.[3] Rita suffered from night terrors and animal phobias, was very ambivalent towards her mother, at the same time clinging to her to such an extent that she could hardly be left alone. She had a marked obsessional neurosis and was at times very depressed. Her play was inhibited and her inability to tolerate frustrations made her upbringing increasingly difficult. I was very doubtful about how to tackle this case since the analysis of so young a child was an entirely new experiment. The first session seemed to confirm my misgivings. Rita, when left alone with me in her nursery, at once showed signs of what I took to be a negative transference: she was anxious and silent and very soon asked to go out into the garden. I agreed and went with her – I may add, under the watchful eyes of her mother and aunt, who took this as a sign of failure. They were very surprised to see that Rita was quite friendly towards me when we returned to the nursery some ten to fifteen minutes later. The explanation of this change was that while we were outside I had been interpreting her negative transference (this again being against the usual practice). From a few things she said, and the fact that she was less frightened when we were in the open, I concluded that she was particularly afraid of something which I might do to her when she was alone with me in the room. I interpreted this and, referring to her night terrors, I linked her suspicion of me as a hostile stranger with her fear that a bad woman would attack her when she was by herself at night. When, a few minutes after this interpretation, I suggested that we should return to the nursery, she readily agreed. As I mentioned, Rita's inhibition in playing was marked, and to begin with she did hardly anything but obsessionally dress and undress her doll. But soon I came to understand the anxieties underlying her obsessions, and interpreted them. This case strengthened my growing conviction that a precondition for the psycho-analysis of a child is to understand and to interpret the phantasies, feelings, anxieties and experiences expressed by play or, if play activities are inhibited, the causes of the inhibition.

As with Fritz, I undertook this analysis in the child's home and with her own toys; but during this treatment, which lasted only a few months, I came to the conclusion that psycho-analysis should not be carried out in the child's home. For I found that, although she was in great need of help and her parents had decided that I should try psycho-analysis, her mother's attitude towards me was very ambivalent and the atmosphere was on the whole hostile to the treatment. More important still, I found that the transference situation – the backbone of the psycho-analytic procedure – can only be established and maintained if the patient is able to feel that the consulting-room or the play-room, indeed the whole analysis, is something separate from his ordinary home life. For only under such conditions can he overcome his resistances against experiencing and expressing thoughts, feelings and desires, which are incompatible with convention, and in the case of children, felt to be in contrast to much of what they have been taught.

I made further significant observations in the psycho-analysis of a girl of seven, also in 1923. Her neurotic difficulties were apparently not serious, but her parents had for some time been concerned about her intellectual development. Although quite intelligent she did not keep up with her age group, she disliked school, and sometimes played truant. Her relation to her mother, which had been affectionate and trusting, had changed since she had started school: she had become reserved and silent. I spent a few sessions with her without achieving much contact. It had become clear that she disliked school, and from what she diffidently said about it, as well as from other remarks, I had been able to make a few interpretations which produced some material. But my impression was that I should not get much further in that way. In a session in which I again found the child unresponsive and withdrawn I left her, saying that I would return in a moment. I went into my own children's nursery, collected a few toys, cars, little figures, a few bricks and a train, put them into a box and returned to the patient. The child, who had not taken to drawing or other activities, was interested in the small toys and at once began to play. From this play I gathered that two of the toy figures represented herself and a little boy, a school-mate about whom I had heard before. It appeared that there was something secret about the behaviour of these two figures and that other toy people were resented as interfering or watching and were put aside. The activities of the two toys led to catastrophes, such as their falling down or colliding with cars. This was repeated with signs of mounting anxiety. At this point I interpreted, with reference to the details of her play, that some sexual activity seemed to have occurred between herself and her friend, and that this had made her very frightened of being found out and therefore distrustful of other people. I pointed out that while playing she had become anxious and seemed on the point of stopping her play. I reminded her that she disliked school, and that this might be connected with the fear that the teacher would find out about her relation with her school-mate and punish her. Above all she was frightened and therefore distrustful of her mother, and now she might feel the same way about me. The effect of this interpretation on the child was striking: her anxiety and distrust first increased, but very soon gave way to obvious relief. Her facial expression changed, and although she neither admitted nor denied what I had interpreted, she subsequently showed her agreement by producing new material and by becoming much freer in her play and speech; also her attitude towards me became much more friendly and less suspicious. Of course the negative transference, alternating with the positive one, came up again and again; but, from this session onwards, the analysis progressed well. Concurrently there were favourable changes, as I was informed, in her relation to her family – in particular to her mother. Her dislike of school diminished and she became more interested in her lessons, but her inhibition in learning, which was rooted in deep anxieties, was only gradually resolved in the course of her treatment.

II

I have described how the use of the toys I kept especially for the child patient in the box in which I first brought them proved essential for her analysis. This experience, as well as others, helped me to decide which toys are most suitable for the psycho-analytic play technique.[4] I found it essential to have *small* toys because their number and variety enable the child to express a wide range of phantasies and experiences. It is important for this purpose that these toys should be non-mechanical and that the human figures, varying only in colour and size, should not indicate any particular occupation. Their very simplicity enables the child to use them in many different situations, according to the material coming up in his play. The fact that he can thus present simultaneously a variety of experiences and phantasies or actual situations also makes it possible for us to arrive at a more coherent picture of the workings of his mind.

In keeping with the simplicity of the toys, the equipment of the play-room is also simple. It does not contain anything except what is needed for the psycho-analysis.[5] Each child's playthings are kept locked in one particular drawer, and he therefore knows that his toys and his play with them, which is the equivalent of the adult's associations, are only known to the analyst and to himself. The box in which I first introduced the toys to the little girl mentioned above turned out to be the prototype of the individual drawer, which is part of the private and intimate relation between analyst and patient, characteristic of the psycho-analytic transference situation.

I do not suggest that the psycho-analytic play technique depends entirely on my particular selection of play material. In any case, children often spontaneously bring their own things and the play with them enters as a matter of course into the analytic work. But I believe that the toys provided by the analyst should on the whole be of the type I have described, that is to say, simple, small and non-mechanical.

Toys, however, are not the only requisites for a play analysis. Many of the child's activities are at times carried out round the wash-hand-basin, which is equipped with one or two small bowls, tumblers and spoons. Often he draws, writes, paints, cuts out, repairs toys, and so on. At times he plays games in which he allots roles to the analyst and himself such as playing shop, doctor and patient, school, mother and child. In such games the child frequently takes the part of the adult, thereby not only expressing his wish to reverse the roles but also demonstrating how he feels that his parents or other people in authority behave towards him – or *should* behave. Sometimes he gives vent to his aggressiveness and resentment by being, in the role of parent, sadistic towards the child, represented by the analyst. The principle of interpretation remains the same whether the phantasies are presented by toys or by dramatization. For, whatever material is used, it is essential that the analytic principles underlying the technique should be applied.[6]

Aggressiveness is expressed in various ways in the child's play, either directly or indirectly. Often a toy is broken or, when the child is more aggressive, attacks are made with knife or scissors on the table or on pieces of wood; water or paint is splashed about and the room generally becomes a battlefield. It is essential to enable the child to bring out his aggressiveness; but what counts most is to understand why at this particular moment in the transference situation destructive impulses come up and to observe their consequences in the child's mind. Feelings of guilt may very soon follow after the child has broken, for instance, a little figure. Such guilt refers not only to the actual damage done but to what the toy stands for in the child's unconscious, e.g. a little brother or sister, or a parent; the interpretation has therefore to deal with these deeper levels as well. Sometimes we can gather from the child's behaviour towards the analyst that not only guilt but also persecutory anxiety has been the sequal to his destructive impulses and that he is afraid of retaliation.

I have usually been able to convey to the child that I would not tolerate physical attacks on myself. This attitude not only protects the psycho-analyst but is of importance for the analysis as well. For such assaults, if not kept within bounds, are apt to stir up excessive guilt and persecutory anxiety in the child and therefore add to the difficulties of the treatment. I have sometimes been asked by what method I prevented physical attacks, and I think the answer is that

I was very careful not to inhibit the child's aggressive *phantasies*; in fact he was given the opportunity to act them out in other ways, including verbal attacks on myself. The more I was able to interpret in time the motives of the child's aggressiveness the more the situation could be kept under control. But with some psychotic children it has occasionally been difficult to protect myself against their aggressiveness.

III

I have found that the child's attitude towards a toy he has damaged is very revealing. He often puts aside such a toy, representing for instance a sibling or a parent, and ignores it for a time. This indicates dislike of the damaged object, due to the persecutory fear that the attacked person (represented by the toy) has become retaliatory and dangerous. The sense of persecution may be so strong that it covers up feelings of guilt and depression which are also aroused by the damage done. Or guilt and depression may be so strong that they lead to a reinforcing of persecutory feelings. However, one day the child may search in his drawer for the damaged toy. This suggests that by then we have been able to analyse some important defences, thus diminishing persecutory feelings and making it possible for the sense of guilt and the urge to make reparation to be experienced. When this happens we can also notice that a change in the child's relation to the particular sibling for whom the toy stood, or in his relations in general, has occurred. This change confirms our impression that persecutory anxiety has diminished and that, together with the sense of guilt and the wish to make reparation, feelings of love which had been impaired by excessive anxiety have come to the fore. With another child, or with the same child at a later stage of the analysis, guilt and the wish to repair may follow very soon after the act of aggression, and tenderness towards the brother or sister who may have been damaged in phantasy becomes apparent. The importance of such changes for character formation and object relations, as well as for mental stability, cannot be overrated.

It is an essential part of the interpretative work that it should keep in step with fluctuations between love and hatred; between happiness and satisfaction on the one hand and persecutory anxiety and depression on the other. This implies that the analyst should not show disapproval of the child having broken a toy; he should not, however, encourage the child to express his aggressiveness, or suggest to him that the toy could be mended. In other words, he should enable the child to experience his emotions and phantasies as they come up. It was always part of my technique not to use educative or moral influence, but to keep to the psycho-analytic procedure only, which, to put it in a nutshell, consists in understanding the patient's mind and in conveying to him what goes on in it.

The variety of emotional situations which can be expressed by play activities is unlimited: for instance, feelings of frustration and of being rejected; jealousy of both father and mother, or of brothers and sisters; aggressiveness accompanying such jealousy; pleasure in having a playmate and ally against the parents; feelings of love and hatred towards a newborn baby or one who is expected, as well as the ensuing anxiety, guilt and urge to make reparation. We also find in the child's play the repetition of actual experiences and details of everyday life, often interwoven with his phantasies. It is revealing that sometimes very important actual events in his life fail to enter either into his play or into his associations, and that the whole emphasis at times lies on apparently minor happenings. But these minor happenings are of great importance to him because they have stirred up his emotions and phantasies.

IV

There are many children who are inhibited in play. Such inhibition does not always completely prevent them from playing, but may soon interrupt their activities. For instance, a little boy was brought to me for one interview only (there was a prospect of an analysis in the future; but at the time the parents were going abroad with him). I had some toys on the table and he sat down and began to play, which soon led to accidents, collisions and toy people falling down whom he tried to stand up again. In all this he showed a good deal of anxiety, but since no treatment was yet intended, I refrained from interpreting. After a few minutes he quietly slipped out of his chair and saying: 'Enough of playing', went out. I believe from my experience that if this had been the beginning of a treatment and I had interpreted the anxiety shown in his actions with the toys and the corresponding negative transference towards me, I should have been able to resolve his anxiety sufficiently for him to continue playing.

The next instance may help me to show some of the causes of a play inhibition. The boy, aged three years nine months, whom I described under the name 'Peter' in *The Psycho-Analysis of Children*, was very neurotic.[7] To mention some of his difficulties: he was unable to play, could not tolerate any frustration, was timid, plaintive and unboyish, yet at times aggressive and overbearing, very ambivalent towards his family and strongly fixated on his mother. She told me that Peter had greatly changed for the worse after a summer holiday during which at the age of eighteen months he shared his parents' bedroom and had opportunity of observing their sexual intercourse. On that holiday he became very difficult to manage, slept badly and relapsed into soiling his bed at night, which he had not done for some months. He had been playing freely until then, but from that summer onwards he stopped playing and became very destructive towards his toys; he would do nothing with them but break them. Shortly afterwards his brother was born, and this increased all his difficulties.

In the first session Peter started to play; he soon made two horses bump into each other, and repeated the same action with different toys. He also mentioned that he had a little brother. I interpreted to him that the horses and the other things which had been bumping together represented people, an interpretation which he first rejected and then accepted. He again bumped the horses together, saying that they were going to sleep, covered them up with bricks, and added: 'Now they're quite dead; I've buried them.' He put the motor-cars front to rear in a row which, as became clear later in the analysis, symbolized his father's penis, and made them run along, then suddenly lost his temper and threw them about the room, saying: 'We always smash our Christmas presents straight away; we don't want any.' Smashing his toys thus stood in his unconscious for smashing his father's genital. During this first hour he did in fact break several toys.

In the second session Peter repeated some of the material of the first hour, in particular the bumping together of cars, horses, etc., and speaking again of his little brother, whereupon I interpreted that he was showing me how his Mummy and Daddy bumped their genitals (of course using his own word for genitals) and that he thought that their doing so caused his brother to be born. This interpretation produced more material, throwing light on his very ambivalent relation towards his little brother and towards his father. He laid a toy man on a brick which he called a 'bed', threw him down and said he was 'dead and done for'. He next re-enacted the same thing with two toy men, choosing figures he had already damaged. I interpreted that the first toy man stood for his father whom he wanted to throw out of his mother's bed and kill, and that one of the two toy men was again the father and the other represented himself to whom his father would do the same. The reason why he had chosen two damaged figures was that he felt that both his father and himself would be damaged if he attacked his father.

This material illustrates a number of points, of which I shall only mention one or two. Because Peter's experience of witnessing the sexual intercourse of his parents had made a great impact on his mind, and had aroused strong emotions such as jealousy, aggressiveness and anxiety, this was the first thing which he expressed in his play. There is no doubt that he had no longer any conscious knowledge of this experience, that it was repressed, and that only the symbolical expression of it was possible for him. I have reason to believe that if I had not interpreted that the toys bumping together were people, he might not have produced the material which came up in the second hour. Furthermore, had I not, in the second hour, been able to show him some of the reasons for his inhibition in play, by interpreting the damage done to the toys, he would very likely – as he did in ordinary life – have stopped playing after breaking the toys.

There are children who at the beginning of treatment may not even play in the same way as Peter, or the little boy who came for one interview only. But it is very rare for a child completely to ignore the toys laid out on the table. Even if he turns away from them, he often gives the analyst some insight into his motives for not wishing to play. In other ways, too, the child analyst can gather material for interpretation. Any activity, such as using paper to scribble on or to cut out, and every detail of behaviour, such as changes in posture or in facial expression, can give a clue to what is going on in the child's mind, possibly in connection with what the analyst has heard from the parents about his difficulties.

I have said much about the importance of interpretations for play technique and have given some instances to illustrate their content. This brings me to a question which I have often been asked: 'Are young children intellectually able to understand such interpretations?' My own experience and that of my colleagues has been that if the interpretations relate to the salient points in the material, they are fully understood. Of course the child analyst must give his interpretations as succinctly and as clearly as possible, and should also use the child's expressions in doing so. But if he translates into simple words the essential points of the material presented to him, he gets into touch with those emotions and anxieties which are most operative at the moment; the child's conscious and intellectual understanding is often a subsequent process. One of the many interesting and surprising experiences of the beginner in child analysis is to find in even very young children a capacity for insight which is often far greater than that of adults. To some extent this is explained by the fact that the connections between conscious and unconscious are closer in young children than in adults, and that infantile repressions are less powerful. I also believe that the infant's intellectual capacities are often underrated and that in fact he understands more than he is credited with.

I shall now illustrate what I have said by a young child's response to interpretations. Peter, of whose analysis I have given a few details, had strongly objected to my interpretation that the toy man he had thrown down from the 'bed' and who was 'dead and done for' represented his father. (The interpretation of death wishes against a loved person usually arouses great resistance in children as well as in adults.) In the third hour Peter again brought similar material, but now accepted my interpretation and said thoughtfully: 'And if I were a Daddy and someone wanted to throw me down behind the bed and make me dead and done for, what would I think of it?' This shows that he had not only worked through, understood and accepted my interpretation, but that he had also recognized a good deal more. He understood that his own aggressive feelings towards his father contributed to his fear of him, and also that he had projected his own impulses on to his father.

One of the important points in play technique has always been the analysis of the transference. As we know, in the transference on the analyst the patient repeats earlier emotions and conflicts. It is my experience that we are able to help the patient fundamentally by taking his phantasies and anxieties back in our transference interpretations to where they originated – namely, in infancy and in relation to his first objects. For by re-experiencing early emotions and phantasies and understanding them in relation to his primal objects, he can, as it were, revise these relations at their root, and thus effectively diminish his anxieties.

V

In looking back over the first few years of my work, I would single out a few facts. I mentioned at the beginning of this paper that in analysing my earliest child case I found my interest focusing on his anxieties and defences against them. My emphasis on anxiety led me deeper and deeper into the unconscious and into the phantasy life of the child. This particular emphasis ran counter to the psycho-analytical point of view that interpretations should not go very deep and should not be given frequently. I persisted in my approach, in spite of the fact that it involved a radical change in technique. This approach took me into new territory, for it opened up the understanding of the early infantile phantasies, anxieties and defences, which were at that time still largely unexplored. This became clear to me when I began the theoretical formulation of my clinical findings.

One of the various phenomena which struck me in the analysis of Rita was the harshness of her super-ego. I have described in *The Psycho-Analysis of Children* how Rita used to play the role of a severe and punishing mother who treated the child (represented by the doll or by myself) very cruelly. Furthermore, her ambivalence towards her mother, her extreme need to be punished, her feelings of guilt and her night terrors led me to recognize that in this child aged two years and nine months – and quite clearly going back to a much earlier age – a harsh and relentless super-ego operated. I found this discovery confirmed in the analyses of other young children and came to the conclusion that the super-ego arises at a much earlier stage than Freud assumed. In other words, it became clear to me that the super-ego, as conceived by him, is the end-product of a development which extends over years. As a result of further observations, I recognized that the super-ego is something which is felt by the child to operate internally in a concrete way; that it consists of a variety of figures built up from his experiences and phantasies and that it is derived from the stages in which he had internalized (introjected) his parents.

These observations in turn led, in the analyses of little girls, to discovery of the leading female anxiety situation: the mother is felt to be the primal persecutor who, as an external and internalized object, attacks the child's body and takes from it her imaginary children. These anxieties arise from the girl's phantasied attacks on the mother's body, which aim at robbing her of its contents, i.e. of faeces, of the father's penis and of children, and result in the fear of retaliation by similar attacks. Such persecutory anxieties I found combined or alternating with deep feelings of depression and guilt, and these observations then led to my discovery of the vital part which the tendency to *make reparation* plays in mental life. Reparation in this sense is a wider concept than Freud's concepts of 'undoing in the obsessional neurosis' and of 'reaction-formation'. For it includes the variety of processes by which the ego feels it undoes harm done in phantasy, restores, preserves and revives objects. The importance of this tendency, bound up as it is with feelings of guilt, also lies in the major contribution it makes to all sublimations, and in this way to mental health.

In studying the phantasied attacks on the mother's body, I soon came upon anal- and urethral-sadistic impulses. I have mentioned above that I recognized the harshness of the super-ego in Rita (1923) and that her analysis greatly helped me to understand the way in which destructive impulses towards the mother become the cause of feelings of guilt and persecution. One of the cases through which the anal- and urethral-sadistic nature of these destructive impulses became clear to me was that of 'Trude', aged three years and three months, whom I analysed in 1924.[8] When she came to me for treatment, she suffered from various symptoms, such as night terrors and incontinence of urine and faeces. Early on in her analysis she asked me to pretend that I was in bed and asleep. She would then say that she was going to attack me and look into my buttocks for faeces (which I found also represented children) and that she was going to take them out. Such attacks were followed by her crouching in a corner, playing that she was in bed, covering herself with cushions (which were to protect her body and which also stood for children); at the same time she actually wetted herself and showed clearly that she was very much afraid of being attacked by me. Her anxieties about the dangerous internalized mother confirmed the conclusions I first formed in Rita's analysis. Both these analyses had been of short duration, partly because the parents thought that enough improvement had been achieved.[9]

Soon afterwards I became convinced that such destructive impulses and phantasies could always be traced back to oral-sadistic ones. In fact Rita had already shown this quite clearly. On one occasion she blackened a piece of paper, tore it up, threw the scraps into a glass of water which she put to her mouth as if to drink from it, and said under her breath 'dead woman'.[10] This tearing up and soiling of paper I had at the time understood to express phantasies of attacking and killing her mother which gave rise to fears of retaliation. I have already mentioned that it was with Trude that I became aware of the specific anal- and urethral-sadistic nature of such attacks. But in other analyses, carried out in 1924 and 1925 (Ruth and Peter, both described in *The Psycho-Analysis of Children*), I also became aware of the fundamental part which oral-sadistic impulses play in destructive phantasies and corresponding anxieties, thus finding in the analysis of young children full confirmation of Abraham's discoveries.[11] These analyses, which gave me further scope for observation, since they lasted longer than Rita's and Trude's,[12] led me towards a fuller insight into the fundamental role of oral desires and anxieties in mental development, normal and abnormal.[13]

As I have mentioned, I had already recognized in Rita and Trude the internalization of an attacked and therefore frightening mother – the harsh super-ego. Between 1924 and 1926 I analysed a child who was very ill indeed.[14] Through her analysis I learned a good deal about the specific details of such internalization and about the phantasies and impulses underlying paranoid and manic-depressive anxieties. For I came to understand the oral and anal nature of her introjection processes and the situations of internal persecution they engendered. I also became more aware of the ways in which internal persecutions influence, by means of projection, the relation to external objects. The intensity of her envy and hatred unmistakably showed its derivation from the oral-sadistic relation to her mother's breast, and was interwoven with the beginnings of her Oedipus complex. Erna's case much helped to prepare the ground for a number of conclusions which I presented to the Tenth International Psycho-Analytical Congress in 1925,[15] in particular the view that the early super-ego, built up when oral-sadistic impulses and phantasies are at their height, underlies psychosis – a view which two years later I developed by stressing the importance of oral-sadism for schizophrenia.[16]

Concurrently with the analyses so far described I was able to make some interesting observations regarding anxiety situations in boys. The analyses of boys and men fully confirmed Freud's view that castration fear is the leading anxiety of the male, but I recognized that owing to the early identification with the mother (the feminine position which ushers in the early stages of the Oedipus complex) the anxiety about attacks on the inside of the body is of great importance in men as well as women, and in various ways influences and moulds their castration fears.

The anxieties derived from phantasied attacks on the mother's body and on the father she is supposed to contain, proved in both sexes to underlie claustrophobia (which includes the fear of being imprisoned or entombed in the mother's body). The connection of these anxieties with castration fear can be seen for instance in the phantasy of losing the penis or having it destroyed inside the mother – phantasies which may result in impotence.

I came to see that the fears connected with attacks on the mother's body and of being attacked by external and internal objects had a particular quality and intensity which suggested their psychotic nature. In exploring the child's relation to internalized objects, various situations of internal persecution and their psychotic contents became clear. Furthermore, the recognition that fear of retaliation derives from the individual's own aggressiveness led me to suggest that the initial defences of the ego are directed against the anxiety aroused by destructive impulses and phantasies. Again and again, when these psychotic anxieties were traced to their origin, they were found to stem from oral-sadism. I recognized also that the oral-sadistic relation to the mother and the internalization of a devoured, and therefore devouring, breast create the prototype of all internal persecutors; and furthermore that the internalization of an injured and therefore dreaded breast on the one hand, and of a satisfying and helpful breast on the other, is the core of the super-ego. Another conclusion was that, although oral anxieties come first, sadistic phantasies and desires from all sources are operative at a very early stage of development and overlap the oral anxieties.[17]

The importance of the infantile anxieties I have described above was also shown in the analysis of very ill adults, some of whom were border-line psychotic cases.[18]

There were other experiences which helped me to reach yet a further conclusion. The comparison between the undoubtedly paranoiac Erna and the phantasies and anxieties that I had found in less ill children, who could only be called neurotic, convinced me that psychotic (paranoid and depressive) anxieties underlie infantile neurosis. I also made similar observations in the analyses of adult neurotics. All these different lines of exploration resulted in the hypothesis that anxieties of a psychotic nature are in some measure part of normal infantile development and are expressed and worked through in the course of the infantile neurosis.[19] To uncover these infantile anxieties the analysis has, however, to be carried into deep layers of the unconscious, and this applies both to adults and to children.[20]

It has already been pointed out in the introduction to this paper that my attention from the beginning focused on the child's anxieties and that it was by means of interpreting their contents that I found myself able to diminish anxiety. In order to do this, full use had to be made of the symbolic language of play which I recognized to be an essential part of the child's mode of expression. As we have seen, the brick, the little figure, the car, not only represent things which interest the child in themselves, but in his play with them they always have a variety of symbolical meanings as well which are bound up with his phantasies, wishes, and experiences. This archaic mode of expression is also the language with which we are familiar in dreams, and it was by approaching the play of the child in a way similar to Freud's interpretation of dreams that I found I could get access to the child's unconscious. But we have to consider each child's use of symbols in connection with his particular emotions and anxieties and in relation to the whole situation which is presented in the analysis; mere generalized translations of symbols are meaningless.

The importance I attributed to symbolism led me – as time went on – to theoretical conclusions about the process of symbol formation. Play analysis had shown that symbolism enabled the child to transfer not only interests, but also phantasies, anxieties and guilt to objects other than people.[21] Thus a great deal of relief is experienced in play and this is one of the factors which make it so essential for the child. For instance, Peter to whom I have referred earlier, pointed out to me, when I interpreted his damaging a toy figure as representing attacks on his brother, that he would not do this to his *real* brother, he would only do it to the *toy* brother. My interpretation of course made it clear to him that it was really his brother whom he wished to attack; but the instance shows that only by symbolic means was he able to express his destructive tendencies in the analysis.

I have also arrived at the view that, in children, a severe inhibition of the capacity to form and use symbols, and so to develop phantasy life, is a sign of serious disturbance.[22] I suggested that such inhibitions, and the resulting disturbance in the relation to the external world and to reality, are characteristic of schizophrenia.[23]

In passing I may say that I found it of great value from the clinical and theoretical point of view that I was analysing both adults and children. I was thereby able to observe the infant's phantasies and anxieties still operative in the adult and to assess in the young child what his future development might be. It was by comparing the severely ill, the neurotic, and the normal child, and by recognizing infantile anxieties of a psychotic nature as the cause of illness in adult neurotics, that I had arrived at the conclusions I have described above.[24]

VI

In tracing, in the analyses of adults and children, the development of impulses, phantasies and anxieties back to their origin, i.e. to the feelings towards the mother's breast (even with children who have not been breast-fed), I found that object relations start almost at birth and arise with the first feeding experience; furthermore, that all aspects of mental life are bound up with object relations. It also emerged that the child's experience of the external world, which very soon includes his ambivalent relation to his father and to other members of his family, is constantly influenced by – and in turn influences – the internal world he is building up, and that external and internal situations are always interdependent, since introjection and projection operate side by side from the beginning of life.

The observations that in the infant's mind the mother primarily appears as good and bad breast split off from each other, and that within a few months, with growing ego integration the contrasting aspects are beginning to be synthesized, helped me to understand the importance of the processes of splitting and keeping apart good and bad figures,[25] as well as the effect of such processes on ego development. The conclusion to be drawn from the experience that depressive anxiety arises as a result of the ego synthesizing the good and bad (loved and hated) aspects of the object led me in turn to the concept of the depressive position which reaches its climax towards the middle of the first year. It is preceded by the paranoid position, which extends over the first three or four months of life and is characterized by persecutory anxiety and splitting processes.[26] Later on, in 1946,[27] when I reformulated my views on the first three or four months of life, I called this stage (making use of a suggestion of Fairbairn's)[28] the paranoid-schizoid position, and, in working out its significance, sought to co-ordinate my findings about splitting, projection, persecution and idealization.

My work with children and the theoretical conclusions I drew from it increasingly influence my technique with adults. It has always been a tenet of psycho-analysis that the unconscious, which originates in the infantile mind, has to be explored in the adult. My experience with children had taken me much deeper in that direction than was formerly the case, and this led to a technique which made access to those layers possible. In particular, my play technique had helped me to see which material was most in need of interpretation at the moment and the way in which it would be most easily conveyed to the patient; and some of this knowledge I could apply to the analysis of adults.[29] As has been pointed out earlier, this does not mean that the technique used with children is identical with the approach to adults. Though we find our way back to the earliest stages, it is of great importance in analysing adults to take account of the adult ego, just as with children we keep in mind the infantile ego according to the stage of its development.

The fuller understanding of the earliest stages of development, of the role of phantasies, anxieties and defences in the emotional life of the infant has also thrown light on the fixation points of adult psychosis. As a result there has opened up a new way of treating psychotic patients by psycho-analysis. This field, in particular the psycho-analysis of schizophrenic patients, needs much further exploration; but the work done in this direction by some psycho-analysts . . . seems to justify hopes for the future.

THE
'BRITISH'
PSYCHOANALYST

CHAPTER TWO

'The Psychological Principles of Infant Analysis' was Melanie Klein's first essay to be published originally in an English-language journal. Earlier essays had appeared first in German-language journals and in English journals subsequently. 'The Psychological Principles' appeared in the *International Journal of Psycho-Analysis* (Vol. VIII). (It is reprinted in *CW*, Vol. I, as 'The Psychological Principles of Early Analysis'.) This volume of the *International Journal* included an interesting discussion on lay analysis and a review by J. C. Flugel of Freud's major revision of his metapsychology, *The Ego and the Id*. It also contained Ernest Jones's crucial paper on 'The Development of Female Sexuality'. Klein was clearly working in a changed atmosphere (see Introduction). Later that year she was the leading speaker at a Symposium on Child Analysis held by the British Psychoanalytical Society (4 May and 18 May), in response to the publication of Anna Freud's book *Introduction to the Technique of the Analysis of Children* (Vienna, 1927). Support for Klein's criticism of Anna Freud was strong from the other contributors. Klein expressed the views of 'Psychological Principles' yet more trenchantly in her contribution to the Symposium.

By the time she came to lecture and then settle in London, Klein was working with both normally disturbed and more seriously disturbed children and making no distinction in their treatment. This paper is interesting because in it she explicitly states that child analysis is in principle the same as adult analysis. The technique differs: a child's play and the features that surround it take the place of dreaming and of free associations to dreams. Her theoretical framework is still Freud's: the infant is first of all narcissistic – relating only to itself, its own ego; its first relationship to other people (objects) is a result of the narcissistic pleasure it derives from them. If this pleasure is withdrawn the child either copes adequately with the state of affairs and thus adapts to reality or it does not and it becomes commensurately disturbed. Thus already *adaptation to reality* rather than the resolution of a neurotic symptom had become a central endeavour of the therapy. At this stage Klein still believes that the frustrations and deprivations of the Oedipus complex are paramount. Already, however, she is stressing that the Oedipus complex starts very early, when the baby is being fed – in the oral phase – and is a gradual process over years, only eventually culminating in what to Freud was the Oedipus complex: the period when phallic desires are dominant and are soon to be prohibited by the castration complex. Furthermore, where Freud argued that a sense of guilt was a result of internalizing the later prohibiting father of the castration complex, Klein discovers it far earlier – a result of what she calls early *introjects* of mother and father who, in the child's phantasy, punish its destructive or forbidden impulses. With typical observational acumen, she finds this exemplified in a child's practice of hurting itself, 'being in the wars' – a kind of self-inflicted punishment.

A great number of theories that Klein was to develop are already present: play observation as the technique of child analysis; an Oedipus complex and a castration complex which start early, develop and are prolonged; the early sense of guilt for the child's own impulses; symbolic phantasies in games; the use of identification in a way that foreshadows her later concept of projective identification – the putting of a part of oneself into another person with whom one then identifies; the emphasis on the relative lack of separation between the unconscious and the conscious life in a small child; the fact that what is all happening takes place in the present and does not need to be reconstructed. These new ideas are presented within an old framework whose bounds they are already bursting.

THE PSYCHOLOGICAL PRINCIPLES
OF INFANT ANALYSIS
(1926)

In the following paper I propose to discuss in detail certain differences between the mental life of young children and that of adults. These differences require us to use a technique adapted to the mind of the young child, and I shall try to show that there is a certain analytical *play technique* which fulfils this requirement. This technique is planned in accordance wtih certain points of view which I shall discuss in some detail in this paper.

As we know, children form relations with the outside world by directing to objects from which pleasure is obtained the libido that was originally attached exclusively to the child's own ego. A child's relation to these objects, whether they be living or inanimate, is in the first instance purely narcissistic. It is in this way, however, that children arrive at their relations with reality also. I should like to illustrate the relation of young children to reality by means of an example.

Trude, a child of three and a quarter, went on a journey with her mother, having previously had a single hour's analysis. Six months later the analysis was continued. It was only after some considerable time that she spoke of anything that had happened to her in the interval, the occasion of her touching on it being a dream which she related to me. She dreamt that she was with her mother again in Italy, in a familiar restaurant. The waitress did not give her any raspberry-syrup, for there was none left. The interpretation of this dream showed, amongst other things, that the child was still suffering from the deprivation of the mother's breast when she was weaned; further, it revealed her envy of her little sister. As a rule Trude told me all sorts of apparently irrelevant things, and also repeatedly mentioned details of her first hour's analysis six months previously, but it was only the connection with the deprivation she had experienced which caused her to think of her travels, otherwise they were of no interest to her.

At a very early age children become acquainted with reality through the deprivations which it imposes on them. They try to defend themselves against it by repudiating it. The fundamental thing, however, and the criterion of all later capacity for adaptation to reality, is the degree in which they are able to tolerate the deprivations that result from the Oedipus situation. Hence, even in little children, an exaggerated repudiation of reality (often disguised under an apparent 'adaptability' and 'docility') is an indication of neurosis and differs from the flight from reality of adult neurotics only in the forms in which it manifests itself. Even in the analysis of young children, therefore, one of the final results to be attained is successful adaptation to reality. One way in which this shows itself in children is in the disappearance of the difficulties encountered in their education. In other words, such children have become capable of tolerating real deprivations.

Observation of children often shows, as early as in the beginning of their second year, a marked preference for the parent of the opposite sex and other indications of incipient Oedipus tendencies. *When* the ensuing conflicts begin, that is, at what point the child actually becomes dominated by the Oedipus complex, is less clear; for we infer its existence only from certain changes which we notice in the child.

The analysis of one child of two years and nine months, another of three years and a quarter, and several children of about four years old, has led me to conclude that, in them, the Oedipus complex exercised a powerful influence as early as their second year.[1] I will illustrate this from the development of a little patient. Rita showed a preference for her mother up to the beginning of her second year; after that she showed a striking preference for her father. For instance, at the age of fifteen months she would constantly demand to stay alone in the room with him and, sitting on his knee, look at books with him. At the age of eighteen months, however, her attitude changed again, and once more she preferred her mother. Simultaneously she began to suffer from *pavor nocturnus* and a dread of animals. She developed an excessive fixation to her mother and a very pronounced father identification. At the beginning of her third year she displayed increasing ambivalence, and was more and more difficult to train, so that when she was two years and nine months she was brought for analytic treatment. At this time she had for some months shown very considerable inhibition in play, as well as an inability to tolerate deprivations, an excessive sensitivity to pain, and marked moodiness. The following experiences had contributed to this development. Up till the age of nearly two years Rita had slept in her parents' room, and the effects of the primal scene showed plainly in her analysis. The occasion of the outbreak of her neurosis, however, was the birth of her little brother. Soon after this, still greater difficulties manifested themselves and constantly increased. There can be no doubt that there is a close connection between neurosis and such profound effects of the Oedipus complex experienced at so early an age. I cannot determine whether it is neurotic children whom the early working of the Oedipus complex affects so intensely, or whether children become neurotic because this happens to them. It is, however, certain that experiences such as I have mentioned here make the conflict more severe and therefore either increase the neurosis or cause it to break out.

I will now select from this case the features which the analysis of children of different ages has taught me are typical. They are seen most directly in the analysis of *little* children. In several cases in which I analysed anxiety attacks in quite little children, these attacks proved to be the repetition of a *pavor nocturnus* which had occurred in the second half of the child's second year and at the beginning of its third year. This fear was at once an effect and a neurotic elaboration of the Oedipus complex. There are innumerable elaborations of this sort and they lead us to certain positive conclusions as to the effects of the Oedipus complex.[2]

Amongst such elaborations, in which the connection with the Oedipus situation was quite clear, are to be reckoned the way in which children constantly fall and hurt themselves, their exaggerated sensitivity, their incapacity to tolerate deprivations, their inhibitions in play, their highly ambivalent attitude towards festive occasions and presents, and finally, various difficulties in education which often make their appearance at a surprisingly early age. But I found that the cause of these very common phenomena was a particularly strong sense of guilt, the development of which I will now examine in detail.

How strongly the sense of guilt operates even in *pavor nocturnus* I will show from an example. Trude, at the age of four and a quarter, constantly played in the analytic hour that it was night. We both had to go to sleep. Then she came out of the particular corner which she called her room, stole up to me and made all sorts of threats. She would stab me in the throat, throw me into the courtyard, burn me up, or give me to the policeman. She tried to tie my hands and feet, she lifted the sofa-cover and said she was making '*po-kacki-kucki*'.[3]

It turned out that she was looking into the mother's 'popo' for the kackis, which to her represented children. Another time she wanted to hit me on the stomach and declared that she was taking out the 'a-a's' (faeces) and making me poor. She then pulled down the cushions, which she constantly called 'children', and hid herself with them in the corner of the sofa, where she crouched down with vehement signs of fear, covered herself up, sucked her thumb and wetted herself. This always directly followed her attacks on me. Her attitude was, however, similar to that which, at the age of not quite two, she had adopted in bed when she began to suffer from intense *pavor nocturnus*. At that time, too, she used constantly to run into her parents' bedroom in the night without being able to tell them what she wanted. When her sister was born she was two years old, and the analysis succeeded in revealing what was in her mind at the time and also what were the causes of her anxiety and of her wetting and dirtying her bed. Analysis also succeeded in getting rid of these symptoms. At that time she had already wished to rob her mother, who was pregnant, of her children, to kill her and to take her place in coitus with the father. These tendencies to hate and aggression were the cause of her fixation to her mother (which, at the age of two years, was becoming peculiarly strong), the cause also of her sense of anxiety and guilt. At the time when these phenomena were so prominent in Trude's analysis, she managed to hurt herself almost always just before the analytic hour. I found out that the objects against which she hurt herself (tables, cupboards, stoves, etc.), signified to her (in accordance with the primitive childish identification) her mother, or at times her father who was punishing her. In general I have found, especially in very little children, that constantly 'being in the wars' and falling and hurting themselves is closely connected with the castration complex and the sense of guilt.

Children's games enable us to form certain special conclusions about the infantile sense of guilt. As early as her second year, those with whom Rita came into contact were struck by her remorse for every naughtiness, however small, and her hypersensitiveness to any sort of blame. For instance, she burst into tears when her father playfully threatened a bear in a picture-book. Here, what determined her identification with the bear was her fear of blame from her *real* father. Again, her inhibition in play proceeded from her sense of guilt. When she was only two and a half she repeatedly declared when playing with her doll (a game which she did not much enjoy), that she was not the baby doll's mother. Analysis showed that she did not *dare* to play at being the mother because the baby doll stood to her amongst other things for the little brother whom she had wanted to take away from her mother, even during the pregnancy. But here the prohibition of the childish wish no longer emanated from the *real* mother, but from an introjected mother, whose role she enacted for me in many ways and who exercised a harsher and more cruel influence upon her than her real mother had ever done. One obsessional symptom which Rita developed at the age of two was a sleep ceremonial which wasted a great deal of time. The main point of this was that she insisted on being tightly rolled up in the bedclothes for fear that 'a mouse or a butty might come through the window and bite off her butty (genital)'.[4] Her games revealed other determinants: the doll had always to be rolled up in the same way as Rita herself, and on one occasion an elephant was put beside its bed. This elephant was supposed to prevent the baby doll from getting up; otherwise it would steal into the parents' bedroom and do them some harm or take something away from them. The elephant (a father-imago) was intended to take over the part of hinderer. This part the introjected father had played within her since the time when, between the ages of eighteen months and two years, she had wanted to usurp her mother's place with her father, to steal from her mother the child with which she was pregnant, and to injure and castrate the parents. The reactions of rage and anxiety which followed on the punishment of the 'child' during such games showed, too, that Rita was inwardly playing both parts: that of the authorities who sit in judgement and that of the child who is punished.

A fundamental and universal mechanism in the game of acting a part serves to separate those different identifications at work in the child which are tending to form a single whole. By the division of roles the child succeeds in expelling the father and mother whom, in the elaboration of the Oedipus complex, it has absorbed into itself and who are now tormenting it inwardly by their severity. The result of this expulsion is a sensation of relief, which contributes in great measure to the pleasure derived from the game. Though this game of acting often appears quite simple and seems to represent only primary identifications, this is only the surface appearance. To penetrate behind this appearance is of great importance in the analysis of children. It can, however, have its full therapeutic effect only if the investigation reveals all the underlying identifications and determinations and, above all, if we have found our way to the sense of guilt which is here at work.

In the cases which I have analysed the inhibitory effect of feelings of guilt was clear at a very early age. What we here encounter corresponds to that which we know as the super-ego in adults. The fact that we assume the Oedipus complex to reach its zenith somewhere about the fourth year of life and that we recognize the development of the super-ego as the end-result of the complex seems to me in no way to contradict these observations. Those definite, typical phenomena, the existence of which in the most clearly developed form we can establish when the Oedipus complex has reached its zenith and which precede its waning, are simply the termination of a development which occupies *years*. The analysis of little children shows that, immediately the Oedipus complex arises, they begin to work it through and thereby to develop the super-ego.

The effects of this childish super-ego upon the child are analogous to those of the super-ego upon the adult, but they weigh far more heavily upon the weaker, childish ego. As the analysis of children teaches us, we strengthen that ego when the analytic procedure curbs the excessive demands of the super-ego. There can be no doubt that the ego of little children differs from that of older children or of adults. But, when we have freed the little child's ego from neurosis, it proves perfectly equal to such demands of reality as it encounters – demands as yet less serious than those made upon adults.[5]

Just as the minds of little children differ from those of older children, so their reaction to psycho-analysis is different in early childhood from what it is later. We are often surprised at the facility with which *for the time being* our interpretations are accepted: sometimes children even express considerable pleasure in them. The reason why this process is different from that met with in the analysis of adults is that in certain strata of the child-mind there is a much easier communication between Cs and Ucs (the system conscious and unconscious), and therefore it is much simpler to retrace the steps from the one to the other. This accounts for the rapid effect of our interpretation, which of course is never given except on the basis of adequate material. Children, however, often produce such material surprisingly quickly and in amazing variety. The effect, too, is often astonishing, even when the children have not seemed at all receptive of the interpretation. The play which was interrupted owing to the setting-up of resistances is resumed; it deepens, expands and expresses deeper strata of the mind; the relation between the child and the analyst is strengthened. The pleasure in play, which visibly ensues after an interpretation has been given, is also due to the fact that the expenditure necessitated by a repression is no longer required after the interpretation. But soon we once more encounter resistances for a time, and here matters are no longer made easy by what has gone before. On the contrary, we have to wrestle with the greatest possible difficulties. This is especially the case when we encounter the sense of guilt.

In their play children represent symbolically phantasies, wishes and experiences. Here they are employing the same language, the same archaic, phylogenetically acquired mode of expression as we are familiar with from dreams. We can only fully understand it if we approach it by the method Freud has evolved for unravelling dreams. Symbolism is only a part of it; if we want rightly to comprehend children's play in connection with their whole behaviour during the analytic hour, we must take into account not only the symbolism which often appears so clearly in their games, but also all the means of representation and the mechanisms employed in dream work, and we must bear in mind the necessity of examining the whole nexus of phenomena.[6]

If we employ this technique we soon find that children produce no fewer associations to the separate features of their games than do adults to the fragments of their dreams. The details of the play point the way for an attentive observer; and, in between, the child tells all sorts of things which must be given their full weight as associations.

Besides this archaic mode of representation children employ another primitive mechanism, that is to say, they substitute actions (which were the original precursors of thoughts) for words: with children, *acting* plays a prominent part.

In *The History of an Infantile Neurosis*,[7] Freud says: 'An analysis which is conducted upon a neurotic child itself must, as a matter of course, appear to be more trustworthy, but it cannot be very rich in material; too many words and thoughts have to be lent to the child, and even so the deepest strata may turn out to be impenetrable to consciousness.'

If we approach children with the technique appropriate to the analysis of adults we shall assuredly not succeed in penetrating to the deepest layers of the child's mental life. But it is precisely these layers which are of moment for the value and success of an analysis. If, however, we take into account the psychological differences between children and adults and bear in mind the fact that in children we find *Ucs* still in operation side by side with *Cs*, the most primitive tendencies side by side with those most complicated developments known to us, such as the super-ego – if, that is to say, we rightly understand the child's mode of expression, all these doubtful points and unfavourable factors vanish. For we find that, as regards the depth and scope of the analysis, we may expect as much from children as from adults. And more still, in the analysis of children we can go back to experiences and fixations which in analysing adults we can only *reconstruct*, while in children they are *directly* represented.[8] Take for instance, the case of Ruth who, as an infant, had gone hungry for some time because her mother had little milk to give her. At the age of four years and three months, when playing with the wash-basin, she called the water-tap a milk-tap. She declared that the milk was running into mouths (the holes of the waste-pipe), but that only a very little was flowing. This unsatisfied oral demand made its appearance in countless games and dramatizations and showed itself in her whole attitude. For instance, she asserted that she was poor, that she only had one coat, and that she had very little to eat – none of these statements being in the least in accordance with reality.

Another little patient who suffered from obsessional neurosis was the six-year-old Erna, whose neurosis was based on impressions received during the period of training in cleanliness.[9] These impressions she dramatized for me in the minutest detail. Once she placed a little doll on a stone, pretended that it was defecating and stood other dolls round it which were supposed to be admiring it. After this dramatization Erna brought the same material into a game of acting. She wanted me to be a baby in long clothes which made itself dirty, while she was the mother. The baby was a spoilt child and an object of admiration. This was followed by a reaction of rage in Erna, and she played the part of a cruel teacher who knocked the child about. In this way Erna enacted before me one of the first traumata in her experience: the heavy blow her narcissism received when she imagined that the measures taken to train her meant the loss of the excessive affection bestowed on her in her infancy.

In general, in the analysis of children we cannot over-estimate the importance of translation into action and of phantasy at the bidding of the compulsion to repetition. Naturally, *little* children use the vehicle of action to a far greater extent, but even older ones constantly have recourse to this primitive mechanism, especially when analysis has removed some of their repressions. It is indispensable for carrying on the analysis that children should have the pleasure that is bound up with this mechanism, but the pleasure must always remain only a means to the end. It is just here that we see the predominance of the pleasure principle over the reality principle. We cannot appeal to the sense of reality in little patients as we can in older ones.

Just as children's means of expression differ from those of adults, so the analytic situation in the analysis of children is of a wholly different character. It is, however, in both cases *essentially* the same. Constant interpretation, the gradual solving of resistances and the constant tracing of the transference to earlier situations – these constitute in children as in adults the correct analytic situation.

I have said that in the analysis of young children I have again and again proved how rapidly the interpretations take effect. It is a striking fact that, though there are numerous unmistakable indications of this effect: the development of play, the consolidating of the transference, the lessening of anxiety, etc., nevertheless for quite a long time the child does not consciously elaborate the interpretations. I have been able, however, to prove that this elaboration does set in later. For instance, children begin to distinguish between the 'pretence' mother and the real mother and between the wooden baby doll and the live baby brother. They then firmly insist that they wanted to do this or that injury to the toy baby only – the real baby, they say, of course they love. Only when very powerful and long-standing resistances have been overcome, do children admit that their aggressive acts were directed against the *real* objects. When this admission is made, however, the result, even in quite little children, is generally a notable step forward in adaptation to reality. My impression is that the interpretation is at first only unconsciously assimilated. It is not till later that its relation to reality gradually penetrates the child's understanding. The process of enlightenment is analogous. For a long time analysis brings to light only the material for sexual theories and birth phantasies and interprets this material without any 'explanation'. Thus, enlightenment takes place bit by bit with the removal of the unconscious resistances which operate against it.

Hence, the first thing that happens as a result of psycho-analysis is that the emotional relation to the parents improves; it is only when this has taken place that understanding comes. This understanding is admitted at the bidding of the super-ego, whose demands have been modified by analysis so that it can tolerate and comply with an ego which is less oppressed and therefore stronger. Thus the child is not *suddenly* confronted with the situation of admitting a new knowledge of its relation to the parents or, in general, of being obliged to absorb knowledge which burdens it. It has always been my experience that the effect of such knowledge, gradually elaborated, is simply to *relieve* the child, to establish a fundamentally more favourable relation to the parents and thus to increase its power of social adaptation.

When this has taken place children also are quite able to replace repression to some extent by reasoned rejection. We see this from the fact that at a later stage of the analysis children have advanced so far from various anal-sadistic or cannibalistic cravings (which at an earlier stage were still so powerful) that they can now at times adopt an attitude of humorous criticism towards them. When this happens I hear even very little children making jokes to the effect, for instance, that some time ago they really wanted to eat up their mummy or cut her into bits. When this change takes place, not only is the sense of guilt inevitably lessened, but at the same time the children are enabled to *sublimate* the wishes which previously were wholly repressed. This manifests itself in practice in the disappearance of inhibitions in play and in a beginning of numerous interests and activities.

To sum up what I have said: the special primitive peculiarities of the mental life of children necessitate a separate technique adapted to them, consisting of the analysis of their play. By means of this technique we can reach the deepest repressed experiences and fixations and this enables us fundamentally to influence the children's development.

It is a question simply of a difference of *technique*, not of the *principles* of treatment. The criteria of the psycho-analytic method proposed by Freud, namely, that we should use as our starting-point the facts of transference and resistance, that we should take into account infantile impulses, repression and its effects, amnesia and the compulsion to repetition and, further, that we should discover the primal scene, as he requires in the 'History of an Infantile Neurosis' – all these criteria are maintained in their entirety in the play technique. The method of play preserves all the principles of psycho-analysis and leads to the same results as the classic technique. Only it is adapted to the minds of children in the technical means employed.

CHAPTER THREE

At the Tenth International Psychoanalytic Congress held in Innsbruck in September 1927, Melanie Klein read her paper, 'Early Stages of the Oedipus Conflict'. It was published a year later in the *International Journal of Psycho-Analysis* (Vol. IX, 1928). By this point Klein had received considerable support for her development of child analysis from her colleagues in England. In this paper she ties together her ideas on the very early appearance of the Oedipus complex with her previous interest in the child's urge for knowledge – the epistemophilic impulse. She discusses the similar and different development of boys and girls. Here she is in the company of analysts whose work challenged Freud's phallocentrism – his use of the boy as the model for the development of sexual difference.

Klein suggests that children of both sexes first identify with the mother in what she calls the 'femininity phase'. They, like her, want to produce babies and milk and contain the father's penis, but also fear that their wish to destroy the things of which they are envious in their mother will provoke her retaliation. They thus introject a beneficent maternal imago – a model of bounty – but also a rapacious, thieving, violent one who is the basis of a very primitive, very punitive super-ego. The child's curiosity about the mother's body is also a model for its curiosity in general – the vicissitudes of this (which will differ in the two sexes) will affect the child's relationship to the acquisition of knowledge.

Klein and Ernest Jones, in particular, argue that the girl's phallic stage (when in Freud's theory she is 'like a little boy') is a secondary defence against her primary femininity. This is in accordance with Klein's later notion of neurotic syndromes acting as a *defence* against earlier positions.

EARLY STAGES OF THE OEDIPUS CONFLICT (1928)

In my analyses of children, especially of children between the ages of three and six, I have come to a number of conclusions of which I shall here present a summary.

I have repeatedly alluded to the conclusion that the Oedipus complex comes into operation earlier than is usually supposed. In my last paper, 'The Psychological Principles of Infant Analysis', I discussed this subject in greater detail. The conclusion which I reached there was that the Oedipus tendencies are released in consequence of the frustration which the child experiences at weaning, and that they make their appearance at the end of the first and the beginning of the second year of life; they receive reinforcement through the anal frustrations undergone during training in cleanliness. The next determining influence upon the mental processes is that of the anatomical difference between the sexes.

The boy, when he finds himself impelled to abandon the oral and anal positions for the genital, passes on to the aim of *penetration* associated with possession of the penis. Thus he changes not only his libido position, but its *aim*, and this enables him to retain his original love-object. In the girl, on the other hand, the *receptive* aim is carried over from the oral to the genital position: she changes her libido position, but retains its aim, which has already led to disappointment in relation to her mother. In this way receptivity of the penis is induced in the girl, who then turns to the father as her love-object.

The very onset of the Oedipus wishes, however, already becomes associated with incipient dread of castration and feelings of guilt.

The analysis of adults, as well as of children, has familiarized us with the fact that the pregenital instinctual impulses carry with them a sense of guilt, and it was thought at first that the feelings of guilt were of subsequent growth, displaced back on to these tendencies, though not originally associated with them. Ferenczi assumes that, connected with the urethral and anal impulses, there is a 'kind of physiological forerunner of the super-ego', which he terms 'sphincter morality'. According to Abraham, anxiety makes its appearance on the cannibalistic level, while the sense of guilt arises in the succeeding early anal-sadistic phase.

My findings lead rather further. They show that the sense of guilt associated with pregenital fixation is already the direct effect of the Oedipus conflict. And this seems to account satisfactorily for the genesis of such feelings, for we know the sense of guilt to be simply a result of the introjection (already accomplished or, as I would add, in process of being accomplished) of the Oedipus love-objects: that is, a sense of guilt is a product of the formation of the super-ego.

The analysis of little children reveals the structure of the super-ego as built up of identifications dating from very different periods and strata in the mental life. These identifications are surprisingly contradictory in character, over-indulgence and excessive severity existing side by side. We find in them, too, an explanation of the severity of the super-ego, which comes out specially plainly in these infant analyses. It does not seem clear why a child of, say, four years old should set up in his mind an unreal, phantastic image of parents who devour, cut and bite. But it *is* clear why in a child of about *one year* old the anxiety caused by the beginning of the Oedipus conflict takes the form of a dread of being devoured and destroyed. The child himself desires to destroy the libidinal object by biting, devouring and cutting it, which leads to anxiety, since awakening of the Oedipus tendencies is followed by introjection of the object, which then becomes one from which punishment is to be expected. The child then dreads a punishment corresponding to the offence: the super-ego becomes something which bites, devours and cuts.

The connection between the formation of the super-ego and the pregenital phases of development is very important from two points of view. On the one hand, the sense of guilt attaches itself to the oral and anal-sadistic phases, which as yet predominate; and, on the other, the super-ego comes into being while these phases are in the ascendant, which accounts for its sadistic severity.

These conclusions open up a new perspective. Only by strong repression can the still very feeble ego defend itself against a super-ego so menacing. Since the Oedipus tendencies are at first chiefly expressed in the form of oral and anal impulses, the question of which fixations will predominate in the Oedipus development will be mainly determined by the degree of the repression which takes place at this early stage.

Another reason why the direct connection between the pregenital phase of development and the sense of guilt is so important is that the oral and anal frustrations, which are the prototypes of all later frustrations in life, at the same time signify *punishment* and give rise to anxiety. This circumstance makes the frustration more acutely felt, and this bitterness contributes largely to the hardship of all subsequent frustrations.

We find that important consequences ensue from the fact that the ego is still so little developed when it is assailed by the onset of the Oedipus tendencies and the incipient sexual curiosity associated with them. Still quite undeveloped intellectually, it is exposed to an onrush of problems and questions. One of the most bitter grievances which we come upon in the unconscious is that this tremendous questioning impulse, which is apparently only partly conscious and even so far as it is cannot yet be expressed in words, remains unanswered. Another reproach follows hard upon this, namely, that the child could not understand words and speech. Thus his first questions go back beyond the beginnings of his understanding of speech.

In analysis both these grievances give rise to an extraordinary amount of hate. Singly or in conjunction they are the cause of numerous inhibitions of the epistemophilic impulse: for instance, the incapacity to learn foreign languages, and, further, hatred of those who speak a different tongue. They are also responsible for direct disturbances in speech, etc. The curiosity which shows itself plainly later on, mostly in the fourth or fifth year of life, is not the beginning, but the climax and termination, of this phase of development, which I have also found to be true of the Oedipus conflict in general.

The early feeling of *not knowing* has manifold connections. It unites with the feeling of being incapable, impotent, which soon results from the Oedipus situation. The child also feels this frustration the more acutely because he *knows nothing* definite about sexual processes. In both sexes the castration complex is accentuated by this feeling of ignorance.

The early connection between the epistemophilic impulse and sadism is very important for the whole mental development. This instinct, roused by the striving of the Oedipus tendencies, at first mainly concerns itself with the mother's womb, which is assumed to be the scene of all sexual processes and developments. The child is still dominated by the anal-sadistic libido-position which impels him to wish to *appropriate* the contents of the womb. He thus begins to be curious about what it contains, what it is like, etc. So the epistemophilic instinct and the desire to take possession come quite early to be most intimately connected with one another and at the same time with the sense of guilt aroused by the incipient Oedipus conflict. This significant connection ushers in a phase of development in both sexes which is of vital importance, hitherto not sufficiently recognized. It consists of a very early identification with the mother.

The course run by this 'femininity' phase must be examined separately in boys and in girls, but, before I proceed to this, I will show its connection with the previous phase, which is common to both sexes.

In the early anal-sadistic stage the child sustains his second severe trauma, which strengthens his tendency to turn away from the mother. She has frustrated his oral desires, and now she also interferes with his anal pleasures. It seems as though at this point the anal deprivations cause the anal tendencies to amalgamate with the sadistic tendencies. The child desires to get possession of the mother's faeces, by penetrating into her body, cutting it to pieces, devouring and destroying it. Under the influence of his genital impulses, the boy is beginning to turn to his mother as love-object. But his sadistic impulses are in full activity, and the hate originating in earlier frustrations is powerfully opposed to his object love on the genital level. A still greater obstacle to his love is his dread of castration by the father, which arises with the Oedipus impulses. The degree in which he attains to the genital position will partly depend on his capacity for tolerating this anxiety. Here the intensity of the oral-sadistic and anal-sadistic fixations is an important factor. It affects the degree of hatred which the boy feels towards the mother; and this, in its turn, hinders him to a greater or lesser extent in attaining a positive relation to her. The sadistic fixations exercise also a decisive influence upon the formation of the super-ego, which is coming into being whilst these phases are in the ascendant. The more cruel the super-ego the more terrifying will be the father as castrator, and the more tenaciously in the child's flight from his genital impulses will he cling to the sadistic levels, from which his Oedipus tendencies in the first instance then also take their colour.

In these early stages all the positions in the Oedipus development are cathected in rapid succession. This, however, is not noticeable, because the picture is dominated by the pregenital impulses. More-over, no rigid line can be drawn between the active heterosexual attitude which finds expression on the anal level and the further stage of identification with the mother.

We have now reached that phase of development of which I

spoke before under the name of the 'femininity phase'. It has its basis on the anal-sadistic level and imparts to that level a new content, for faeces are now equated with the child that is longed for, and the desire to rob the mother now applies to the child as well as to faeces. Here we can discern two aims which merge with one another. The one is directed by the desire for children, the intention being to appropriate them, while the other aim is motivated by jealousy of the future brothers and sisters whose appearance is expected and by the wish to destroy them in the womb. A third object of the boy's oral-sadistic tendencies in the mother's womb is the father's penis.

As in the castration complex of girls, so in the femininity complex of the male, there is at bottom the frustrated desire for a special organ. The tendencies to steal and destroy are concerned with the organs of conception, pregnancy and parturition, which the boy assumes to exist in the womb, and further with the vagina and the breasts, the fountain of milk, which are coveted as organs of receptivity and bounty from the time when the libidinal position is purely oral.

The boy fears punishment for his destruction of his mother's body, but, besides this, his fear is of a more general nature, and here we have an analogy to the anxiety associated with the castration wishes of the girl. He fears that his body will be mutilated and dismembered, and amongst other things castrated. Here we have a direct contribution to the castration complex. In this early period of development the mother who takes away the child's faeces signifies also a mother who dismembers and castrates him. Not only by means of the anal frustrations which she inflicts does she pave the way for the castration complex: in terms of psychic reality she *is* also already the *castrator*.

This dread of the mother is so overwhelming because there is combined with it an intense dread of castration by the father. The destructive tendencies whose object is the womb are also directed with their full oral- and anal-sadistic intensity against the father's penis, which is supposed to be located there. It is upon his penis that the dread of castration by the father is focused in this phase. Thus the femininity phase is characterized by anxiety relating to the womb and the father's penis, and this anxiety subjects the boy to the tyranny of a super-ego which devours, dismembers and castrates and is formed from the image of father and mother alike.

The aims of the incipient genital libido positions are thus criss-crossed by and intermingled with the manifold pregenital tendencies. The greater the preponderance of sadistic fixations the more does the boy's identification with his mother correspond to an attitude of rivalry towards the woman, with its blending of envy and hatred; for on account of his wish for a child he feels himself at a disadvantage and inferior to the mother.

Let us now consider why the femininity complex of men seems so much more obscure than the castration complex in women, with which it is equally important.

The amalgamation of the desire for a child with the epistemophilic impulse enables a boy to effect a displacement on to the intellectual plane; his sense of being at a disadvantage is then concealed and over-compensated by the superiority he deduces from his possession of a penis, which is also acknowledged by girls. This exaggeration of the masculine position results in excessive protestations of masculinity. In her paper entitled 'Notes on Curiosity',[1] Mary Chadwick, too, has traced the man's narcissistic over-estimation of the penis and his attitude of intellectual rivalry towards women to the frustration of his wish for a child and the displacement of this desire on to the intellectual plane.

A tendency to excess in the direction of aggression, which very frequently occurs, has its source in the femininity complex. It goes with an attitude of contempt and 'knowing better', and is highly asocial and sadistic; it is partly conditioned as an attempt to mask the anxiety and ignorance which lie behind it. In part it coincides with the boy's protest (originating in his fear of castration) against the feminine role, but it is rooted also in his dread of his mother, whom he intended to rob of the father's penis, her children and her female sexual organs. This excessive aggression unites with the pleasure in attack which proceeds from the direct, genital Oedipus situation, but it represents that part of the situation which is by far the more asocial factor in character formation. This is why a man's rivalry with women will be far more asocial than his rivalry with his fellow men, which is largely prompted through the genital position. Of course the quantity of sadistic fixations will also determine the relationship of a man to other men when they are rivals. If, on the contrary, the identification with the mother is based on a more securely established genital position, on the one hand his relation to women will be positive in character, and on the other the desire for a child and the feminine component, which play so essential a part in men's work, will find more favourable opportunities for sublimation.

In both sexes one of the principal roots of inhibitions in work is the anxiety and sense of guilt associated with the femininity phase. Experience has taught me, however, that a thorough analysis of this phase is, for other reasons as well, important from a therapeutic point of view, and should be of help in some obsessional cases which seem to have reached a point where nothing more could be resolved.

In the boy's development the femininity phase is succeeded by a prolonged struggle between the pregenital and the genital positions of the libido. When at its height, in the third to the fifth year of life, this struggle is plainly recognizable as the Oedipus conflict. The anxiety associated with the femininity phase drives the boy back to identification with the father; but this stimulus in itself does not provide a firm foundation for the genital position, since it leads mainly to repression and over-compensation of the anal-sadistic instincts, and not to overcoming them. The dread of castration by the father strengthens the fixation to the anal-sadistic levels. The degree of constitutional genitality also plays an important part as regards a favourable issue, i.e. the attainment of the genital level. Often the outcome of the struggle remains undecided, and this gives rise to neurotic troubles and disturbances of potency.[2] Thus the attainment of complete potency and reaching the genital position will in part depend upon the favourable issue of the femininity phase.

I will now turn to the development of girls. As a result of the process of weaning, the girl child has turned from the mother, being impelled more strongly to do so by the anal deprivations she has undergone. The genital now begins to influence her mental development.

I entirely agree with Helene Deutsch,[3] who holds that the genital development of the woman finds its completion in the successful displacement of oral libido on to the genital. Only, my results lead me to believe that this displacement begins with the first stirrings of the genital impulses and that the oral, receptive aim of the genital exercises a determining influence in the *girl's turning to the father*. Also I am led to conclude that not only an unconscious awareness of the vagina, but also sensations in that organ and the rest of the genital apparatus, are aroused as soon as the Oedipus impulses make their appearance. In girls, however, onanism does not afford anything like so adequate an outlet for these quantities of excitation as it does in boys. Hence the accumulated lack of satisfaction provides yet another reason for more complications and disturbances of female sexual development. The difficulty of obtaining complete gratification by onanism may be another cause, besides those indicated by Freud, for the girl's repudiation of the practice, and may partly explain why, during her struggle to give it up, manual masturbation is generally replaced by pressing the legs together.

Besides the receptive quality of the genital organ, which is brought into play by the intense desire for a new source of gratification, envy and hatred of the mother who possesses the father's penis seem, at the period when these first Oedipus impulses are stirring, to be a further motive for the little girl's turning to the father. His caresses have now the effect of a seduction and are felt as 'the attraction of the opposite sex'.[4]

In the girl identification with the mother results directly from the Oedipus impulses: the whole struggle caused in the boy by his castration anxiety is absent in her. In girls as well as boys this identification coincides with the anal-sadistic tendencies to rob and destroy the mother. If identification with the mother takes place at a stage at which the oral- and anal-sadistic tendencies predominate, dread of a primitive maternal super-ego will lead to the repression and fixation of this phase and interfere with further genital development. Dread of the mother, too, impels the little girl to give up identification with her, and identification with the father begins.

The little girl's epistemophilic impulse is first roused by the Oedipus complex; the result is that she discovers her lack of a penis. She feels this lack to be a fresh cause of hatred of the mother, but at the same time her sense of guilt makes her regard it as a punishment. This embitters her frustration in this direction, and it, in its turn, exercises a profound influence on the whole castration complex.

This early grievance about the lack of a penis is greatly magnified later on, when the phallic phase and the castration complex are in full swing. Freud has stated that the discovery of the lack of a penis causes the turning from the mother to the father. My findings show, however, that this discovery operates only as a reinforcement in this direction, since it follows on a very early stage in the Oedipus conflict, and is succeeded by the wish for a child, by which it is actually replaced in later development. I regard the deprivation of the breast as the most fundamental cause of the turning to the father.

Identification with the father is less charged with anxiety than that with the mother; moreover, the sense of guilt towards her impels to over-compensation through a fresh love relation with her. Against this new love relation with her there operates the castration complex which makes a masculine attitude difficult, and also the hatred of her which sprang from the earlier situations. Hate and rivalry of the mother, however, again lead to abandoning the identification with the father and turning to him as the object to be secured and loved.

The little girl's relation with her mother causes that to her father to take both a positive and a negative direction. The frustration undergone at his hands has as its very deepest basis the disappointment already suffered in relation to the mother; a powerful motive in the desire to possess him springs from the hatred and envy against the mother. If the sadistic fixations remain predominant, this hatred and its over-compensation will also materially affect the woman's relation to men. On the other hand, if there is a more positive relation to the mother, built up on the genital position, not only will the woman be freer from a sense of guilt in her relation to her children, but her love for her husband will be strongly reinforced, since for the woman he always stands at one and the same time for the mother who gives what is desired and for the beloved child. On this very significant foundation is built up that part of the relation which is connected exclusively with the father. At first it is focused on the act of the penis in coitus. This act, which also promises gratification of the desires that are now displaced on to the genital, seems to the little girl a most consummate performance.

Her admiration is, indeed, shaken by the Oedipus frustration, but unless it is converted into hate, it constitutes one of the fundamental features of the woman's relation to the man. Later, when full satisfaction of the love impulses is obtained, there is joined with this admiration the great gratitude ensuing from the long-pent-up deprivation. This gratitude finds expression in the greater feminine capacity for complete and lasting surrender to a love-object, especially to the 'first love'.

One way in which the little girl's development is greatly handicapped is the following. Whilst the boy does in reality *possess* the penis, in respect of which he enters into rivalry with the father, the little girl has only the *unsatisfied* desire for motherhood, and of this, too, she has but a dim and uncertain, though a very intense, awareness.

It is not merely this uncertainty which disturbs her hope of future motherhood. It is weakened far more by anxiety and sense of guilt, and these may seriously and permanently damage the maternal capacity of a woman. Because of the destructive tendencies once directed by her against the mother's body (or certain organs in it) and against the children in the womb, the girl anticipates retribution in the form of destruction of her own capacity for motherhood or of the organs connected with this function and of her own children. Here we have also one root of the constant concern of women (often so excessive) for their personal beauty, for they dread that this too will be destroyed by the mother. At the bottom of the impulse to deck and beautify themselves there is always the motive of *restoring* damaged comeliness, and this has its origin in anxiety and sense of guilt.[5]

It is probable that this deep dread of the destruction of internal organs may be the psychic cause of the greater susceptibility of women, as compared with men, to conversion hysteria and organic diseases.

It is this anxiety and sense of guilt which is the chief cause of the repression of feelings of pride and joy in the feminine *role*, which are originally very strong. This repression results in depreciation of the capacity for motherhood, at the outset so highly prized. Thus the girl lacks the powerful support which the boy derives from his possession of the penis, and which she herself might find in the anticipation of motherhood.

The girl's very intense anxiety about her womanhood can be shown to be analogous to the boy's dread of castration, for it certainly contributes to the checking of her Oedipus impulses. The course run by the boy's castration anxiety concerning the penis which *visibly* exists is, however, different; it might be termed more *acute* than the more chronic anxiety of the girl concerning her internal organs, with which she is necessarily less familiar. Moreover, it is bound to make a difference that the boy's anxiety is determined by the paternal and the girl's by the maternal super-ego.

Freud has said that the girl's super-ego develops on different lines from that of the boy. We constantly find confirmation of the fact that jealousy plays a greater part in women's lives than in men's, because it is reinforced by deflected envy of the male on account of the penis. On the other hand, however, women especially possess a great capacity, which is not based merely on an over-compensation, for disregarding their own wishes and devoting themselves with self-sacrifice to ethical and social tasks. We cannot account for this capacity by the blending of masculine and feminine traits which, because of the human being's bisexual disposition, does in individual cases influence the formation of character, for this capacity is so plainly maternal in nature. I think that, in order to explain how women can run so wide a gamut from the most petty jealousy to the most self-forgetful loving kindness, we have to take into consideration the peculiar conditions of the formation of the feminine super-ego. From the early identification with the mother in which the anal-sadistic level so largely preponderates, the little girl derives jealousy and hatred and forms a cruel super-ego after the maternal imago. The super-ego which develops at this stage from a father identification can also be menacing and cause anxiety, but it seems never to reach the same proportions as that derived from the mother identification. But the more the identification with the mother becomes stabilized on the genital basis, the more will it be characterized by the devoted kindness of an indulgent mother ideal. Thus this positive affective attitude depends on the extent to which the maternal mother ideal bears the characteristics of the pregenital or of the genital age. But when it comes to the active conversion of the emotional attitude into social or other activities, it would seem that it is the paternal ego ideal which is at work. The deep admiration felt by the little girl for the father's genital activity leads to the formation of a paternal super-ego which sets before her active aims to which she can never fully attain. If, owing to certain factors in her development, the incentive to accomplish these aims is strong enough, their very impossibility of attainment may lend an impetus to her efforts which, combined with the capacity for self-sacrifice which she derives from the maternal super-ego, gives a woman, in individual instances, the capacity for very exceptional achievements on the intuitive plane and in specific fields.

The boy, too, derives from the feminine phase a maternal super-ego which causes him, like the girl, to make both cruelly primitive and kindly identifications. But he passes through this phase to resume (it is true, in varying degrees) identification with the father. However much the maternal side makes itself felt in the formation of the super-ego, it is yet the *paternal* super-ego which from the beginning is the decisive influence for the man. He too sets before himself a figure of an exalted character upon which to model himself, but, because the boy *is* 'made in the image of' his ideal, it is not unattainable. This circumstance contributes to the more sustained and objective creative work of the male.

The dread of injury to her womanhood exercises a profound influence on the castration complex of the little girl, for it causes her to over-estimate the penis which she herself lacks; this exaggeration is then much more obvious than is the underlying anxiety about her own womanhood. I would remind you here of the work of Karen Horney, who was the first to examine the sources of the castration complex in women in so far as those sources lie in the Oedipus situation.

In this connection I must speak of the importance for sexual development of certain early experiences in childhood. In the paper which I read at the Salzburg Congress in 1924, I mentioned that when observations of coitus take place at a later stage of development they assume the character of traumata, but that if such experiences occur at an early age they become fixated and form part of the sexual development. I must now add that a fixation of this sort may hold in its grip not only that particular stage of development, but also the super-ego which is then in process of formation, and may thus injure its further development. For the more completely the super-ego reaches its zenith in the genital stage the less prominent will the sadistic identifications be in its structure and the more surely will an ethically fine personality be developed and greater possibilities of mental health be secured.

There is another kind of experience in early childhood which strikes me as typical and exceedingly important. These experiences often follow closely in time upon the observations of coitus and are induced or fostered by the excitations set up thereby. I refer to the sexual relations of little children with one another, between brothers and sisters or playmates, which consist in the most varied acts: looking, touching, performing excretion in common, fellatio, cunnilingus and often direct attempts at coitus. They are deeply repressed and have a cathexis of profound feelings of guilt. These feelings are mainly due to the fact that this love-object, chosen under the pressure of the excitation due to the Oedipus conflict, is felt by the child to be a substitute for the father or mother or both. Thus these relations, which seem so insignificant and which apparently no child under the stimulus of the Oedipus development escapes, take on the character of an Oedipus relation actually realized, and exercise a determining influence upon the formation of the Oedipus complex, the subject's detachment from that complex and upon his later sexual relations. Moreover, an experience of this sort forms an important fixation point in the development of the super-ego. In consequence of the need for punishment and the repetition compulsion, these experiences often cause the child to subject himself to sexual traumata. In this connection I would refer you to Abraham,[6] who showed that experiencing sexual traumata is one part of the sexual development of children. The analytic investigation of these experiences, during the analysis of adults as well as of children, to a great extent clears up the Oedipus situation in its connection with early fixations and is therefore important from the therapeutic point of view.

To sum up my conclusions: I wish above all to point out that they do not, in my opinion, contradict the statements of Professor Freud. I think that the essential point in the additional considerations which I have advanced is that I date these processes earlier and that the different phases (especially in the initial stages) merge more freely into one another than was hitherto supposed.

The early stages of the Oedipus conflict are so largely dominated by pregenital phases of development that the genital phase, when it begins to be active, is at first heavily shrouded and only later, between the third and fifth years of life, becomes clearly recognizable. At this age the Oedipus complex and the formulation of the super-ego reach their climax. But the fact that the Oedipus tendencies begin so much earlier than we supposed, the pressure of the sense of guilt which therefore falls upon the pregenital levels, the determining influence thus exercised so early upon the Oedipus development on the one hand and that of the super-ego on the other, and accordingly upon character formation, sexuality and all the rest of the subject's development – all these things seem to me of great and hitherto unrecognized importance. I found out the therapeutic value of this knowledge in the analyses of children, but it is not confined to these. I have been able to test the resulting conclusions in the analysis of adults and have found not only that their theoretical correctness was confirmed, but that their therapeutic importance was established.

CHAPTER FOUR

On 15 May 1929 Melanie Klein read her paper 'Infantile Anxiety Situations Reflected in a Work of Art and in the Creative Impulse' to the British Psychoanalytical Society. It was published in the *International Journal* in the same year. The paper extends the theme of the previous essay in this volume into a study of literature and art: the boy and girl have the same wish to attack the envied mother's body. In the libretto of Ravel's opera *L'Enfant et les sortilèges*, the nature of the boy's fear of reprisal is discovered – he fears the retaliation of the father within his mother. The girl, as exemplified by the story of the artist Ruth Kjär, fears that the mother will return her attacks on her insides – will destroy her capacity to bear babies. In both cases the restoration of an internal mother who is not too attacking is the key to progress. In the instance of Ruth Kjär we can see foreshadowed Klein's later theories of the importance of envy and of the 'depressive position' in which the infant tries to make reparation to the mother for its phantasied attacks. Klein's work, well illustrated in this paper, has been a fruitful source of inspiration for the analysis of art and literature.

Here the question of the theory of anxiety is coming to the fore. Klein refers to Freud's new account of anxiety (see Introduction) in his short book, *Hemmung, Symptom und Angst* (only translated as *Inhibitions, Symptoms and Anxiety* ten years later). The same number of the *International Journal* published a review of Freud's book by R. Wälder from Vienna – the differences between the English and Viennese emphases that were to become explicit by the mid-1930s are already in evidence.

INFANTILE ANXIETY SITUATIONS REFLECTED IN A WORK OF ART AND IN THE CREATIVE IMPULSE (1929)

My first subject is the highly interesting psychological material underlying an opera of Ravel's, now being revived in Vienna. My account of its content is taken almost word for word from a review by Eduard Jakob in the *Berliner Tageblatt*.

A child of six years old is sitting with his homework before him, but he is not doing any work. He bites his pen-holder and displays that final stage of laziness, in which *ennui* has passed into *cafard*. 'Don't want to do the stupid lessons,' he cries in a sweet soprano. 'Want to go for a walk in the park! I'd like best of all to eat up all the cake in the world, or pull the cat's tail or pull out all the parrot's feathers! I'd like to scold every one! Most of all I'd like to put mama in the corner!' The door now opens. Everything on the stage is shown very large – in order to emphasize the smallness of the child – so all that we see of his mother is a skirt, an apron and a hand. A finger points and a voice asks affectionately whether the child has done his work. He shuffles rebelliously on his chair and puts out his tongue at his mother. She goes away. All that we hear is the rustle of her skirts and the words: 'You shall have dry bread and no sugar in your tea!' The child flies into a rage. He jumps up, drums on the door, sweeps the teapot and cup from the table, so that they are broken into a thousand pieces. He climbs on the window-seat, opens the cage and tries to stab the squirrel with his pen. The squirrel escapes through the open window. The child jumps down from the window and seizes the cat. He yells and swings the tongs, pokes the fire furiously in the open grate, and with his hands and feet hurls the kettle into the room. A cloud of ashes and steam escapes. He swings the tongs like a sword and begins to tear the wallpaper. Then he opens the case of the grandfather-clock and snatches out the copper pendulum. He pours the ink over the table. Exercise-books and other books fly through the air. Hurrah! . . .

The things he has maltreated come to life. An armchair refuses to let him sit in it or have the cushions to sleep on. Table, chair, bench and sofa suddenly lift up their arms and cry: 'Away with the dirty little creature!' The clock has a dreadful stomach-ache and begins to strike the hours like mad. The teapot leans over the cup, and they begin to talk Chinese. Everything undergoes a terrifying change. The child falls back against the wall and shudders with fear and desolation. The stove spits out a shower of sparks at him. He hides behind the furniture. The shreds of the torn wallpaper begin to sway and stand up, showing shepherdesses and sheep. The shepherd's pipe sounds a heart-breaking lament; the rent in the paper, which separates Corydon from his Amaryllis, has become a rent in the fabric of the world! But the doleful tale dies away. From under the cover of a book, as though out of a dog's kennel, there emerges a little old man. His clothes are made of numbers, and his hat is like a pi. He holds a ruler and clatters about with little dancing steps. He is the spirit of mathematics, and begins to put the child through an examination: millimetre, centimetre, barometer, trillion – eight and eight are forty. Three times nine is twice six. The child falls down in a faint!

Half suffocated he takes refuge in the park round the house. But here again the air is full of terror, insects, frogs (lamenting in muted thirds), a wounded tree-trunk, which oozes resin in long drawn-out bass notes, dragon-flies and oleander-flies all attack the newcomer. Owls, cats and squirrels come along in hosts. The dispute as to who is to bite the child becomes a hand-to-hand fight. A squirrel which has been bitten falls to the ground, screaming beside him. He instinctively takes off his scarf and binds up the little creature's paw. There is great amazement amongst the animals, who gather together hesitatingly in the background. The child has whispered: 'Mama!' He is restored to the human world of helping, 'being good'. 'That's a good child, a very well-behaved child,' sing the animals very seriously in a soft march – the finale of the piece – as they leave the stage. Some of them cannot refrain from themselves calling out 'Mama'.

I will now examine more closely the details in which the child's pleasure in destruction expresses itself. They seem to me to recall the early infantile situation which in my most recent writings I have described as being of fundamental importance both for neurosis in boys and for their whole development. I refer to the attack on the mother's body and on the father's penis in it. The squirrel in the cage and the pendulum wrenched out of the clock are plain symbols of the penis in the mother's body. The fact that it is the *father's* penis and that it is in the act of coitus with the mother is indicated by the rent in the wallpaper 'which separates Corydon from his Amaryllis', of which the author says that to the boy it has become 'a rent in the fabric of the world'. Now what weapons does the child employ in this attack on his united parents? The ink poured over the table, the emptied kettle, from which a cloud of ashes and steam escapes, represent the weapons which very little children have at their disposal: namely, the device of soiling with excrement.

Smashing things, tearing them up, using the tongs as a sword – these represent the other weapons of the child's primary sadism, which employs his teeth, nails, muscles, and so on.

In my paper at the last Congress (1927) and on other occasions in our society I have described this early phase of development, the content of which is the attack made on the mother's body with all the weapons that the child's sadism has at its disposal. Now, however, I can add to this earlier statement and say more exactly where this phase is to be inserted in the scheme of sexual development proposed by Abraham. My results lead me to conclude that the phase in which sadism is at its zenith in all the fields whence it derives precedes the earlier anal stage and acquires a special significance from the fact that it is also the stage of development at which the Oedipus tendencies first appear. That is to say, that the Oedipus conflict begins under the complete dominance of sadism. My supposition that the formation of the super-ego follows closely on the beginning of the Oedipus tendencies, and that, therefore, the ego falls under the sway of the super-ego even at this early period, explains, I think, why this sway is so tremendously powerful. For, when the objects are introjected, the attack launched upon them with all the weapons of sadism rouses the subject's dread of an analogous attack upon himself from the external and the internalized objects. I wanted to recall these notions of mine to your minds because I can make a bridge from them to a notion of Freud's: one of the most important of the new conclusions which he has put before us in his *Hemmung, Symptom und Angst*. I refer to the hypothesis of an early infantile situation of anxiety or danger. I think that this places analytic work on a yet more exactly defined and firmer basis than heretofore, and thus gives our methods an even plainer direction. But in my view it also makes a fresh demand upon analysis. Freud's hypothesis is that there is an infantile danger situation which undergoes modification in the course of development, and which is the source of the influence exercised by a series of *anxiety situations*. Now the new demand upon the analyst is this – that analysis should fully uncover these anxiety situations right back to that which lies deepest of all. This demand for a *complete* analysis is allied to that which Freud suggests as a new demand at the conclusion of his 'History of an Infantile Neurosis', where he says that a complete analysis must reveal the primal scene. This latter requirement can have its full effect only in conjunction with that which I have just put forward. If the analyst succeeds in the task of discovering the infantile danger situations, working at their resolution and elucidating in each individual case the relations between the anxiety situations and the neurosis on the one hand and the ego development on the other – then, I think, he will achieve more completely the main aim of psycho-analytic therapy: removal of the neuroses. It seems to me, therefore, that everything that can contribute to the elucidation and exact description of the infantile danger situations is of great value, not only from the theoretical, but also from the therapeutic point of view.

Freud assumes that the infantile danger situation can be reduced ultimately to the loss of the beloved (longed-for) person. In girls, he thinks, the loss of the object is the danger situation which operates most powerfully; in boys it is castration. My work has proved to me that both these danger situations are a modification of yet earlier ones. I have found that in boys the dread of castration by the father is connected with a very special situation, which, I think, proves to be the earliest anxiety situation of all. As I pointed out, the attack on the mother's body, which is timed psychologically at the zenith of the sadistic phase, implies also the struggle with the father's penis in the mother. A special intensity is imparted in this danger situation by the fact that a union of the two parents is in question. According to the early sadistic super-ego, which has already been set up, these united parents are extremely cruel and much dreaded assailants. Thus the anxiety situation relating to castration by the father is a modification, in the course of development, of the earliest anxiety situation as I have described it.

Now I think that the anxiety engendered in this situation is plainly represented in the libretto of the opera which was the starting-point of my paper. In discussing the libretto, I have already dealt in some detail with the *one* phase – that of the sadistic attack. Let us now consider what happens after the child has given rein to his lust for destruction.

At the beginning of his review the writer mentions that all the things on the stage are made very large, in order to emphasize the smallness of the child. But the child's anxiety makes things and people seem gigantic to him – far beyond the actual difference in size. Moreover, we see what we discover in the analysis of every child: that things represent human beings, and therefore are things of anxiety. The writer of the review writes as follows: 'The mal-treated things begin to live.' The armchair, the cushion, table, chair, etc., attack the child, refuse to serve him, banish him outside. We find that things to sit and lie upon, as well as beds, occur regularly in children's analyses as symbols for the protecting and loving mother. The strips of the torn wallpaper represent the injured interior of the mother's body, while the little old number-man who comes out of the book-cover is the father (represented by his penis), now in the character of judge, and about to call the child, who faints with anxiety, to his reckoning for the damage he has done and the theft he has committed in the mother's body. When the boy flees into the world of nature, we see how it takes on the role of the mother whom he has assaulted. The hostile animals represent a multiplication of the father, whom he has also attacked, together with the children assumed to be in the mother. We see the incidents which took place inside the room now reproduced on a bigger scale in a wider space and in larger numbers. The world, transformed into the mother's body, is in hostile array against the child and persecutes him.

In ontogenetic development sadism is overcome when the subject advances to the genital level. The more powerfully this phase sets in, the more capable does the child become of object love, and the more able is he to conquer his sadism by means of pity and sympathy. This step in development is also shown in the libretto of Ravel's opera: when the boy feels pity for the wounded squirrel and comes to its aid, the hostile world changes into a friendly one. The child has learnt to love and believes in love. The animals conclude: 'That is a good child – a very well-behaved child.' The profound psychological insight of the author of the libretto – her name is Colette – is shown in the way in which the conversion in the child's attitude takes place. As he cares for the wounded squirrel, he whispers: 'Mama.' The animals round him repeat this word. It is this redeeming word which has given the opera its title: *Das Zauberwort* (*The Magic Word*) [French: *L'Enfant et les sortilèges*. Ed.]. But we also learn from the text what is the factor which has ministered to the child's sadism. He says: 'I want to go for a walk

in the park! I want most of all to eat up all the cakes in the world!'
But his mother threatens to give him tea without sugar and dry
bread. The oral frustration which turns the indulgent 'good mother'
into the 'bad mother' stimulates his sadism.

I think we can now understand why the child, instead of
peaceably doing his homework, has become involved in such an
unpleasant situation. It *had* to be so, for he was driven to it by the
pressure of the old anxiety situation which he had never mastered.
The anxiety enhances the repetition compulsion, and the need for
punishment ministers to the compulsion (now grown very strong)
to secure for itself actual punishment in order that the anxiety
may be allayed by a chastisement less severe than that which the
anxiety situation causes him to anticipate. We are quite familiar
with the fact that children are naughty because they wish to be
punished, but it seems of the greatest importance to find out what
part anxiety plays in this craving for punishment and what is the
ideational content at the bottom of this urgent anxiety.

I will now illustrate from another literary example the anxiety
which I have found connected with the earliest danger situation in
a girl's development.

In an article entitled 'The Empty Space' Karin Michaelis gives
an account of the development of her friend, the painter Ruth Kjär.
Ruth Kjär possessed remarkable artistic feeling, which she
employed specially in the arrangement of her house, but she had no
pronounced creative talent. Beautiful, rich and independent, she
spent a great part of her life travelling, and was constantly leaving
the house upon which she had expended so much care and taste.
She was subject at times to fits of deep depression, which Karin
Michaelis describes as follows: 'There was only one dark spot in
her life. In the midst of the happiness which was natural to her,
and seemed so untroubled, she would suddenly be plunged into the
deepest melancholy. A melancholy that was suicidal. If she tried to
account for this, she would say something to this effect: "There is
an empty space in me, which I can never fill!" '

The time came when Ruth Kjär married and she seemed perfectly
happy. But after a short time the fits of melancholy recurred. In
Karin Michaelis's words: 'The accursed empty space was once more
empty.' I will let the writer speak for herself:

Have I already told you that her home was a gallery of modern art? Her husband's brother was one of the greatest painters in the country, and his best pictures decorated the walls of the room. But before Christmas this brother-in-law took away one picture, which he had only lent to her. The picture was sold. This left an empty space on the wall, which in some inexplicable way seemed to coincide with the empty space within her. She sank into a state of the most profound sadness. The blank space on the wall caused her to forget her beautiful home, her happiness, her friends, everything. Of course, a new picture could be got, and would be got, but it took time; one had to look about to find just the right one.

The empty space grinned hideously down at her.

The husband and wife were sitting opposite one another at the breakfast-table. Ruth's eyes were clouded with hopeless despair. Suddenly, however, her face was transfigured with a smile: 'I'll tell you what! I think I will try to daub a little on the wall myself, until we get a new picture!' 'Do, my darling,' said her husband. It was quite certain that whatever daub she made would not be too monstrously ugly.

He had hardly left the room when, in a perfect fever, she had rung up the colour-shop to order the paints which her brother-in-law generally used, brushes, palette, and all the rest of the 'gear', to be sent up at once. She herself had not the remotest idea how to begin. She had never squeezed paint out of a tube, laid the ground-colour on a canvas or mixed colours on a palette. Whilst the things were coming, she stood before the empty wall with a piece of black chalk in her hand and made strokes at random as they came into her head. Should she have the car and rush wildly to her brother-in-law to ask how one paints? No, she would rather die!

Towards evening her husband returned, and she ran to meet him with a hectic brilliance in her eyes. She was not going to be ill, was she? She drew him with her saying: 'Come, you will see!' And he saw. He could not take his eyes from this sight; could not take it in, did not believe it, *could* not believe it. Ruth threw herself on a sofa in a state of deadly exhaustion: 'Do you think it at all possible?'

The same evening they sent for the brother-in-law. Ruth palpitated with anxiety as to the verdict of the connoisseur. But the artist exclaimed immediately: 'You don't imagine you can persuade me that you painted that! What a damned lie! This picture was painted by an old and experienced artist. Who the devil is he? I don't know him!'

Ruth could not convince him. He thought they were making game of him. And when he went, his parting words were: 'If *you* painted that, *I* will go and conduct a Beethoven Symphony in the Chapel Royal tomorrow, though I don't know a note of music!'

That night Ruth could not sleep much. The picture on the wall had been painted, that was certain – it was not a dream. But how had it happened? And what next?

She was on fire, devoured by ardour within. She must prove to herself that the divine sensation, the unspeakable sense of happiness that she had felt could be repeated.

Karin Michaelis then adds that after this first attempt, Ruth Kjär painted several masterly pictures, and had exhibited them to the critics and the public.

Karin Michaelis anticipates one part of my interpretation of the anxiety relating to the empty space on the wall when she says: 'On the wall there was an empty space, which in some inexplicable way seemed to coincide with the empty space within her.' Now, what is the meaning of this empty space within Ruth, or rather, to put it more exactly, of the feeling that there was something lacking in her body?

Here there has come into consciousness one of the ideas connected with that anxiety which, in the paper I read at the last Congress (1927), I described as the most profound anxiety experienced by girls. It is the equivalent of castration anxiety in boys. The little girl has a sadistic desire, originating in the early stages of the Oedipus conflict, to rob the mother's body of its contents, namely, the father's penis, faeces, children, and to destroy the mother herself. This desire gives rise to anxiety lest the mother should in her turn rob the little girl herself of the contents of her body (especially of children) and lest her body should be destroyed or mutilated. In my view, this anxiety, which I have found in the analyses of girls and women to be the deepest anxiety of all, represents the little girl's earliest danger situation. I have come to realize that the dread of being alone, of the loss of love and of the love object, which Freud holds to be the basic infantile danger situation in girls, is a modification of the anxiety situation I have just described. When the little girl who fears the mother's assault upon her body cannot *see* her mother, it intensifies the anxiety. The presence of the real, loving mother diminishes the dread of the terrifying mother, whose image is introjected into the child's mind. At a later stage of development the content of the dread changes from that of an attacking mother to the dread that the real, loving mother may be lost and that the girl will be left solitary and forsaken.

In seeking the explanation of these ideas, it is instructive to consider what sort of pictures Ruth Kjär has painted since her first attempt, when she filled the empty space on the wall with the life-sized figure of a naked negress. Apart from one picture of flowers, she has confined herself to portraits. She has twice painted her younger sister, whom she invited to visit and sit to her, and, further, the portrait of an old woman and one of her mother. The two last are described by Karin Michaelis as follows:

And now Ruth cannot stop. The next picture represents an old woman, bearing the mark of years and disillusionments. Her skin is wrinkled, her hair faded, her gentle, tired eyes are troubled. She gazes before her with the disconsolate resignation of old age, with a look that seems to say: 'Do not trouble about me any more. My time is so nearly at an end!'

This is not the impression we receive from Ruth's latest work – the portrait of her Irish-Canadian mother. This lady has a long time before her before she must put her lips to the cup of renunciation. Slim, imperious, challenging, she stands there with a moonlight-coloured shawl draped over her shoulders; she has the effect of a magnificent woman of primitive times, who could any day engage in combat with the children of the desert with her naked hands. What a chin! What force there is in the haughty gaze!

The blank space has been filled.

It is obvious that the desire to make reparation, to make good the injury psychologically done to the mother and also to restore herself was at the bottom of the compelling urge to paint these portraits of her relatives. That of the old woman, on the threshold of death, seems to be the expression of the primary, sadistic desire to destroy. The daughter's wish to destroy her mother, to see her old, worn out, marred, is the cause of the need to represent her in full possession of her strength and beauty. By so doing, a daughter can allay her own anxiety and can endeavour to restore her mother and make her new through the portrait. In the analyses of children, when the representation of destructive wishes is succeeded by an expression of reactive tendencies, we constantly find that drawing and painting are used as means to make people anew. The case of Ruth Kjär shows plainly that this anxiety of the little girl is of great importance in the ego development of women, and is one of the incentives to achievement. But, on the other hand, this anxiety may be the cause of serious illness and many inhibitions. As with the boy's castration dread, the effect of his anxiety on the ego development depends on the maintenance of a certain optimum and a satisfactory interplay between the separate factors.

CHAPTER FIVE

Two years before this essay was published, Klein's paper 'The Early Stages of the Oedipus Conflict' (Chapter 3) had followed immediately after the translation in the *International Journal* of Freud's essay 'On Fetishism' (*SE*, Vol. XXI, 152–7). In 'On Fetishism' Freud re-emphasizes the need for a theoretical distinction to be drawn between neuroses and psychoses. In July 1929, at the International Congress in Oxford, Klein read this paper, 'The Importance of Symbol Formation in the Development of the Ego'. It was published in the *International Journal* a year later (Vol. XI, Part 1, pp. 724–39, 1930). Until this point Klein had tended to talk of childhood 'neuroses'; here she presents her first fascinating account of a child, Dick, who is clearly psychotic. The essay is important for two reasons. In it, Klein consolidates her understanding of the early development of the ego and she signposts a direction that was to become particularly fruitful for her followers: the study of psychosis.

In her theory of symbolism and of ego development, Klein confirms the central importance of anxiety. The ego must be able to feel and eventually tolerate anxiety. Anxiety about sadistic impulses and about retaliation from the objects that have been attacked in phantasy makes the child move to ever new equations in order to escape the dangers with which it has endowed a previous object. This is the driving force of symbol formation. Klein's idea here, resembling those concepts of Jones and Ferenczi on which she builds, differs fundamentally from Freud's emphasis on the symbolic relationship not of objects but of words.

Today Dick, whom Klein thought of as schizophrenic in a new, extended sense of the term, would probably be diagnosed as autistic.

Discussing the themes of this paper, Hanna Segal, a leading Kleinian, writes: 'the first phase of [Klein's] work was nearing its end . . . she was ready for some more fundamental formulation of her theory' (see Selected Bibliography). In this connection it is interesting to note that, in the same issue of the journal in which this essay was published, Klein's fellow-psychoanalyst Edward Glover speaks of 'Klein and her School'.

THE IMPORTANCE OF SYMBOL FORMATION IN THE DEVELOPMENT OF THE EGO (1930)

My argument in this paper is based on the assumption that there is an early stage of mental development at which sadism becomes active at all the various sources of libidinal pleasure.[1] In my experience sadism reaches its zenith in this phase, which is ushered in by the oral-sadistic desire to devour the mother's breast (or the mother herself) and passes away with the earlier anal age. At the period of which I am speaking, the subject's dominant aim is to possess himself of the contents of the mother's body and to destroy her by means of every weapon which sadism can command. At the same time this phase forms the introduction to the Oedipus conflict. The genital is beginning to exercise an influence, but this is as yet not evident, for the pre-genital impulses hold the field. My whole argument depends on the fact that the Oedipus conflict begins at a period when sadism predominates.

The child expects to find within the mother (a) the father's penis, (b) excrement and (c) children, and these things it equates with edible substances. According to the child's earliest phantasies (or 'sexual theories') of parental coitus, the father's penis (or his whole body) becomes incorporated in the mother during the act. Thus the child's sadistic attacks have for their object both father and mother, who are in phantasy bitten, torn, cut or stamped to bits. The attacks give rise to anxiety lest the subject should be punished by the united parents, and this anxiety also becomes internalized in consequence of the oral-sadistic introjection of the objects and is thus already directed towards the budding super-ego. I have found these anxiety situations of the early phases of mental development to be the most profound and overwhelming. It is my experience that in the phantasied attack on the mother's body a considerable part is played by the urethral and anal sadism which is very soon added to the oral and muscular sadism. In phantasy the excreta are transformed into dangerous weapons: wetting is regarded as cutting, stabbing, burning, drowning, while the faecal mass is equated with weapons and missiles. At a later stage of the phase which I have described, these violent modes of attack give place to hidden assaults by the most refined methods which sadism can devise, and the excreta are equated with poisonous substances.

The excess of sadism gives rise to anxiety and sets in motion the ego's earliest modes of defence. Freud writes:[2] 'It may well be that, before ego and id have become sharply differentiated and before a super-ego has been developed, the mental apparatus employs different modes of defence from those which it practises after these levels of organization have been reached.' According to what I have found in analysis the earliest defence set up by the ego has reference to two sources of danger: the subject's own sadism and the object which is attacked. This defence, in conformity with the degree of the sadism, is of a violent character and differs fundamentally from the later mechanism of repression. In relation to the subject's own sadism the defence implies expulsion, whereas in relation to the object it implies destruction. The sadism becomes a source of danger because it offers an occasion for the liberation of anxiety and also because the weapons employed to destroy the object are felt by the subject to be levelled at his own person also. The object of the attack becomes a source of danger because the subject fears similar, retaliatory attacks from it. Thus, the wholly undeveloped ego is faced with a task which at this stage is quite beyond it – the task of mastering the severest anxiety.

Ferenczi holds that identification, the forerunner of symbolism, arises out of the baby's endeavour to rediscover in every object his own organs and their functioning. In Jones's view the pleasure principle makes it possible for two quite different things to be equated because of a similarity marked by pleasure or interest. Some years ago I wrote a paper, based on these statements, in which I drew the conclusion that symbolism is the foundation of all sublimation and of every talent, since it is by way of symbolic equation that things, activities and interests become the subject of libidinal phantasies.

I can now add to what I said then[3] and state that, side by side with the libidinal interest, it is the anxiety arising in the phase that I have described which sets going the mechanism of identification. Since the child desires to destroy the organs (penis, vagina, breast) which stand for the objects, he conceives a dread of the latter. This anxiety contributes to make him equate the organs in question with other things; owing to this equation these in their turn become objects of anxiety, and so he is impelled constantly to make other and new equations, which form the basis of his interest in the new objects and of symbolism.

Thus, not only does symbolism come to be the foundation of all phantasy and sublimation but, more than that, upon it is built up the subject's relation to the outside world and to reality in general. I pointed out that the object of sadism at its zenith, and of the epistemophilic impulse arising and coexisting with sadism, is the mother's body with its phantasied contents. The sadistic phantasies directed against the inside of her body constitute the first and basic relation to the outside world and to reality. Upon the degree of success with which the subject passes through this phase will depend the extent to which he can subsequently acquire an external world corresponding to reality. We see then that the child's earliest reality is wholly phantastic; he is surrounded with objects of anxiety, and in this respect excrement, organs, objects, things animate and inanimate are to begin with equivalent to one another. As the ego develops, a true relation to reality is gradually established out of this unreal reality. Thus, the development of the ego and the relation to reality depend on the degree of the ego's capacity at a very early period to tolerate the pressure of the earliest anxiety situations. And, as usual, it is a question of a certain optimum amount of the factors concerned. A sufficient quantity of anxiety is the necessary basis for an abundance of symbol formation and of phantasy; an adequate capacity on the part of the ego to tolerate anxiety is necessary if it is to be satisfactorily worked over and if this basic phase is to have a favourable issue and the development of the ego to be successful.

I have arrived at these conclusions from my general analytical experience, but they are confirmed in a remarkably striking way by a case in which there was an unusual inhibition of ego development.

This case, of which I will now give some details, is that of a four-year-old boy who, as regards the poverty of his vocabulary and of his intellectual attainments, was on the level of a child of about fifteen or eighteen months. Adaptation to reality and emotional relations to his environment were almost entirely lacking. This child, Dick, was largely devoid of affects, and he was indifferent to the presence or absence of mother and nurse. From the very beginning he had only rarely displayed anxiety, and that in an abnormally small degree. With the exception of one particular interest, to which I will return presently, he had almost no interests, did not play, and had no contact with his environment. For the most part he simply strung sounds together in a meaningless way, and certain noises he constantly repeated. When he did speak he generally used his meagre vocabulary incorrectly. But it was not only that he was unable to make himself intelligible: he had no wish to do so. More than that, one could clearly perceive that Dick was antagonistic to his mother, an attitude which expressed itself in the fact that he often did the very *opposite* of what was expected of him. For instance, if she succeeded in getting him to say different words after her, he often entirely altered them, though at other times he could pronounce the same words perfectly. Again, sometimes he would repeat the words correctly, but would go on repeating them in an incessant, mechanical way until everyone round him was sick and tired of them. Both these modes of behaviour are different from that of a neurotic child. When the neurotic child expresses opposition in the form of defiance and when he expresses obedience (even accompanied by an excess of anxiety), he does so with a certain understanding and some sort of reference to the thing or person concerned. But Dick's opposition and obedience lacked both affect and understanding. Then too, when he hurt himself, he displayed very considerable insensibility to pain and felt nothing of the desire, so universal with little children, to be comforted and petted. His physical awkwardness, also, was quite remarkable. He could not grip knives or scissors, but it was noteworthy that he could handle quite normally the spoon with which he ate.

The impression his first visit left on me was that his behaviour was quite different from that which we observe in neurotic children. He had let his nurse go without manifesting any emotion, and had followed me into the room with complete indifference. There he ran to and fro in an aimless, purposeless way, and several times he also ran round me, just as if I were a piece of furniture, but he showed no interest in any of the objects in the room. His movements as he ran to and fro seemed to be without co-ordination. The expression of his eyes and face was fixed, far-away and lacking in interest. Compare once more the behaviour of children with severe neuroses. I have in mind children who, without actually having an anxiety attack, would on their first visit to me withdraw shyly and stiffly into a corner or sit motionless before the little table with toys on it or, without playing, lift up one object or another, only to put it down again. In all these modes of behaviour the great latent anxiety is unmistakable. The corner or the little table is a place of refuge from me. But Dick's behaviour had no meaning or purpose, nor was any affect or anxiety associated with it.

I will now give some details of his previous history. He had had an exceptionally unsatisfactory and disturbed time as a sucking infant, for his mother kept up for some weeks a fruitless attempt to nurse him, and he nearly died of starvation. Artificial foods were then resorted to. At last, when he was seven weeks old, a wet-nurse was found for him, but by then he did not thrive on breast-feeding. He suffered from indigestion, *prolapsus ani* and, later, from haemorrhoids. Undoubtedly his development was affected by the fact that, though he had every care, no real love was lavished on him, his mother's feeling for him being from the very beginning cold.[4]

As, moreover, neither his father nor his nurse gave him any tenderness, Dick grew up in an environment unusually poor in love. When he was two years old he had a new nurse, who was skilful and affectionate, and, shortly afterwards, he was for a considerable time with his grandmother, who was very loving to him. The influence of these changes was observable in his development. He had learnt to walk at about the normal age, but there was a difficulty in training him to control his excretory functions. Under the new nurse's influence he acquired habits of cleanliness much more readily. At the age of about three he had mastered them, and on this point he actually showed a certain amount of ambition and apprehensiveness. In one other respect he showed himself in his fourth year sensitive to blame. The nurse had found out that he practised masturbation and had told him it was 'naughty' and he must not do it. This prohibition clearly gave rise to apprehension and to a sense of guilt. Moreover, in his fourth year Dick did in general make a greater attempt at adaptation, but principally in relation to external things, especially to the mechanical learning of a number of new words. From his earliest days the question of feeding had been abnormally difficult. When he had the wet-nurse he showed no desire at all to suck, and his disinclination persisted. Next, he would not drink from a bottle. When the time came for him to have more solid food, he refused to bite it up and absolutely rejected everything that was not of the consistency of pap; even this he had almost to be forced to take. Another good effect of the new nurse's influence was an improvement in Dick's willingness to eat, but even so, the main difficulties persisted.[5]

Thus, although the kindly nurse had made a difference to his development in certain respects, the fundamental defects remained untouched. With her, as with everyone else, Dick had failed to establish friendly contact. Thus neither her tenderness nor that of his grandmother had succeeded in setting in train the lacking object relation.

I found from Dick's analysis that the reason for the unusual inhibition in his development was the failure of those earliest steps of which I spoke at the beginning of this paper. In Dick there was a complete and apparently constitutional incapacity of the ego to tolerate anxiety. The genital had begun to play its part very early; this caused a premature and exaggerated identification with the object attacked and had contributed to an equally premature defence against sadism. The ego had ceased to develop phantasy life and to establish a relation with reality. After a feeble beginning, symbol formation in this child had come to a standstill. The early attempts had left their mark in one interest, which, isolated and unrelated to reality, could not form the basis for further sublimations. The child was indifferent to most of the objects and playthings around him, and did not even grasp their purpose or meaning. But he was interested in trains and stations and also in door-handles, doors and the opening and shutting of them.

The interest in these things and actions had a single source: it really had to do with the penetration of the penis into the mother's body. Doors and locks stood for the ways in and out of her body, while the door-handles represented the father's penis and his own. Thus what had brought symbol formation to a standstill was the dread of what would be done to him (particularly by the father's penis) after he had penetrated into the mother's body. Moreover, his defences against his destructive impulses proved to be a fundamental impediment to his development. He was absolutely incapable of any act of aggression, and the basis of this incapacity was clearly indicated at a very early period in his refusal to bite up food. At four years old he could not hold scissors, knives or tools, and was remarkably clumsy in all his movements. The defence against the sadistic impulses directed against the mother's body and its contents – impulses connected with phantasies of coitus – had resulted in the cessation of the phantasies and the standstill of symbol formation. Dick's further development had come to grief because he could not bring into phantasy the sadistic relation to the mother's body.

The peculiar difficulty I had to contend with in the analysis was not his defective capacity for speech. In the play technique, which follows the child's symbolic representations and gives access to his anxiety and sense of guilt, we can, to a great extent, dispense with verbal associations. But this technique is not restricted to an analysis of the child's play. Our material can be derived (as it has to be in the case of children inhibited in play) from the symbolism revealed in details of his general behaviour.[6] But in Dick symbolism had not developed. This was partly because of the lack of any affective relation to the things around him, to which he was almost entirely indifferent. He had practically no special relations with particular objects, such as we usually find in even severely inhibited children. Since no affective or symbolic relation to them existed in his mind, any chance actions of his in relation to them were not coloured by phantasy, and it was thus impossible to regard them as having the character of symbolic representations. His lack of interest in his environment and the difficulty of making contact with his mind were, as I could perceive from certain points in which his behaviour differed from that of other children, only the effect of his lack of a symbolic relation to things. The analysis, then, had to begin with this, the *fundamental*, obstacle to establishing contact with him.

The first time Dick came to me, as I said before, he manifested no sort of affect when his nurse handed him over to me. When I showed him the toys I had put ready, he looked at them without the faintest interest. I took a big train and put it beside a smaller one and called them 'Daddy-train' and 'Dick-train'. Thereupon he picked up the train I called 'Dick' and made it roll to the window and said 'Station'. I explained: 'The station is mummy; Dick is going into mummy.' He left the train, ran into the space between the outer and inner doors of the room, shut himself in, saying 'dark' and ran out again directly. He went through this performance several times. I explained to him: 'It is dark inside mummy. Dick is inside dark mummy.' Meantime he picked up the train again, but soon ran back into the space between the doors. While I was saying that he was going into dark mummy, he said twice in a questioning way: 'Nurse?' I answered: 'Nurse is soon coming', and this he repeated and used the words later quite correctly, retaining them in his mind. The next time he came, he behaved in just the same way. But this time he ran right out of the room into the dark entrance hall. He put the 'Dick' train there too and insisted on its staying there. He kept constantly asking: 'Nurse coming?' In the third analytic hour he behaved in the same way, except that besides running into the hall and between the doors, he also ran behind the chest of drawers. There he was seized with anxiety, and for the first time called me to him. Apprehension was now evident in the way in which he repeatedly asked for his nurse, and, when the hour was over, he greeted her with quite unusual delight. We see that simultaneously with the appearance of anxiety there had emerged a sense of dependence, first on me and then on the nurse, and that at the same time he had begun to be interested in the words I used to soothe him and, contrary to his usual behaviour, had repeated and remembered them. During the third hour, however, he also, for the first time, looked at the toys with interest, in which an aggressive tendency was evident. He pointed to a little coal-cart and said: 'Cut.' I gave him a pair of scissors, and he tried to scratch the little pieces of black wood which represented coal, but he could not hold the scissors. Acting on a glance which he gave me, I cut the pieces of wood out of the cart, whereupon he threw the damaged cart and its contents into a drawer and said, 'Gone.' I told him that this meant that Dick was cutting faeces out of his mother. He then ran into the space between the doors and scratched on the doors a little with his nails, thus showing that he identified the space with the cart and both with the mother's body, which he was attacking. He immediately ran back from the space between the doors, found the cupboard and crept into it. At the beginning of the next analytic hour he cried when the nurse left him – an unusual thing for him to do. But he soon calmed down. This time he avoided the space between the doors, the cupboard and the corner, but concerned himself with the toys, examining them more closely and with obviously dawning curiosity. Whilst doing this he came across the cart which had been damaged the last time he came and upon its contents. He quickly pushed both aside and covered them with other toys. After I had explained that the damaged cart represented his mother, he fetched it and the little bits of coal out again and took them into the space between the doors. As his analysis progressed it became clear that in thus throwing them out of the room he was indicating an expulsion, both of the damaged object and of his own sadism (or the means employed by it), which was in this manner projected into the external world. Dick had also discovered the wash-basin as symbolizing the mother's body, and he displayed an extraordinary dread of being wetted with water. He anxiously wiped it off his hand and mine, which he had dipped in as well as his own, and immediately afterwards he showed the same anxiety when urinating. Urine and faeces represented to him injurious and dangerous substances.[7]

It became clear that in Dick's phantasy faeces, urine and penis stood for objects with which to attack the mother's body, and were therefore felt to be a source of injury to himself as well. These phantasies contributed to his dread of the contents of his mother's body, and especially of his father's penis which he phantasied as being in her womb. We came to recognize the father's penis and a growing feeling of aggression against it in many forms, the desire to eat and destroy it being specially prominent. For example, on one occasion, Dick lifted a little toy man to his mouth, gnashed his teeth and said 'Tea daddy', by which he meant 'Eat daddy'. He then asked for a drink of water. The introjection of the father's penis proved to be associated with the dread both of it, as of a primitive, harm-inflicting super-ego, and of being punished by the mother thus robbed: dread, that is, of the external and the introjected objects. And at this point there came into prominence the fact which I have already mentioned, and which was a determining factor in his development, namely, that the genital phase had become active in Dick prematurely. This was shown in the circumstance that such representations as I have just spoken of were followed not by anxiety only, but by remorse, pity and a feeling that he must make restitution. Thus he would proceed to place the little toy men on my lap or in my hand, put everything back in the drawer, and so on. The early operation of the reactions originating on the genital level was a result of premature ego development but further ego development was only inhibited by it. This early identification with the object could not as yet be brought into relation with reality. For instance, once when Dick saw some pencil shavings on my lap he said, 'Poor Mrs Klein.' But on a similar occasion he said in just the same way, 'Poor curtain.' Side by side with his incapacity for tolerating anxiety, this premature *empathy* became a decisive factor in his warding-off of all destructive impulses. Dick cut himself off from reality and brought his phantasy life to a standstill by taking refuge in the phantasies of a dark, empty, vague womb. He had thus succeeded in withdrawing his attention also from the different objects in the outside world which represented the contents of the mother's womb – the father's penis, faeces, children. His own penis, as the organ of sadism, and his own excreta were to be got rid of (or denied) as being dangerous and aggressive.

It had been possible for me, in Dick's analysis, to gain access to his unconscious by getting into contact with such rudiments of phantasy life and symbol formation as he displayed. The result was a diminution of his latent anxiety, so that it was possible for a certain amount of anxiety to become manifest. But this implied that the working-over of this anxiety was beginning by way of the establishment of a symbolic relation to things and objects, and at the same time his epistemophilic and aggressive impulses were set in action. Every advance was followed by the releasing of fresh quantities of anxiety and led to his turning away to some extent from the things with which he had already established an affective relation and which had therefore become objects of anxiety. As he turned away from these he turned towards new objects, and his aggressive and epistemophilic impulses were directed to these new affective relations in their turn. Thus, for instance, for some time Dick altogether avoided the cupboard, but thoroughly investigated the wash-basin and the electric radiator, which he examined in every detail, again manifesting destructive impulses against these objects. He then transferred his interest from them to fresh things or, again, to things with which he was already familiar and which he had given up earlier. He occupied himself once more with the cupboard, but this time his interest in it was accompanied by a far greater activity and curiosity and a stronger tendency to aggression of all kinds. He beat on it with a spoon, scratched and hacked it with a knife, and sprinkled water on it. He then briskly investigated the hinges of the door, the way in which it opened and shut, the lock, etc., climbed up inside the cupboard and asked what the different parts were called. Thus as his interests developed he at the same time enlarged his vocabulary, for he now began to take more and more interest not only in the things themselves but in their names. The words which before he had heard and disregarded he now remembered and applied correctly.

Hand in hand with this development of interests and an increasingly strong transference to myself, the hitherto lacking object relation has made its appearance. During these months his attitude to his mother and nurse has become affectionate and normal. He now desires their presence, wants them to take notice of him and is distressed when they leave him. With his father, too, his relation shows increasing indications of the normal Oedipus attitude, and there is an increasingly firm relation to objects in general. The desire to make himself intelligible, which was lacking before, is now in full force. Dick tries to make himself understood by means of his still meagre, but growing, vocabulary which he diligently endeavours to enlarge. There are many indications, moreover, that his relation to reality is becoming established.

So far we have spent six months over his analysis, and his development, which has begun to take place at all the fundamental points during this period, justifies a favourable prognosis. Several of the peculiar problems which arose in his case have proved soluble. It has been possible to get into contact with him with the help of quite a few words, to activate anxiety in a child in whom interest and affect were wholly lacking, and it has further been possible gradually to resolve and to regulate the anxiety released. I would emphasize the fact that in Dick's case I have modified my usual technique. In general I do not interpret the material until it has found expression in various representations. In this case, however, where the capacity to represent it was almost entirely lacking, I found myself obliged to make my interpretations on the basis of my general knowledge, the representations in Dick's behaviour being relatively vague. Finding access in this way to his unconscious, I succeeded in activating anxiety and other affects. The representations then became fuller and I soon acquired a more solid foundation for the analysis, and so was able gradually to pass over to the technique that we generally employ in analysing little children.

I have already described how I succeeded in causing the anxiety to become manifest by diminishing it in its latent state. When it did manifest itself, I was able to resolve part of it by interpretation. At the same time, however, it became possible for it to be worked over in a better way, namely, by its distribution amongst new things and interests; in this manner it became so far mitigated as to be tolerable for the ego. Whether, if the quantities of anxiety are thus regulated, the ego can become capable of tolerating and working over normal quantities, only the further course of the treatment can show. In Dick's case, therefore, it is a question of modifying a fundamental factor in his development by means of analysis.

The only possible thing to do in analysing this child, who could not make himself intelligible and whose ego was not open to influence, was to try to gain access to his unconscious and, by diminishing the unconscious difficulties, to open up a way for the development of the ego. Of course, in Dick's case as in every other, access to the unconscious had to be by way of the ego. Events proved that even this very imperfectly developed ego was adequate for establishing connection with the unconscious. From the theoretical point of view I think it is important to note that, even in so extreme a case of defective ego-development, it was possible to develop both ego and libido simply by analysing the unconscious conflicts, without bringing any educational influence to bear upon the ego. It seems plain that, if even the imperfectly developed ego of a child who had no relation at all with reality can tolerate the removal of repressions by the aid of analysis, without being overwhelmed by the id, we need not fear that in neurotic children (i.e. in very much less extreme cases) the ego might succumb to the id. It is also noteworthy that, whereas the educational influence exercised by those about him previously glided off Dick without any effect, now, when owing to analysis his ego is developing, he is increasingly amenable to such influence, which can keep pace with the instinctual impulses mobilized by analysis and quite suffices to deal with them.

There still remains the question of diagnosis. Dr Forsyth diagnosed the case as one of dementia praecox and thought it a suitable one in which to attempt analysis. His diagnosis would seem to be corroborated by the fact that the clinical picture agreed in many important points with that of advanced dementia praecox in adults. To summarize it once again: it was characterized by an almost complete absence of affect and anxiety, a very considerable degree of withdrawal from reality and of inaccessibility, a lack of emotional rapport, negativistic behaviour alternating with signs of automatic obedience, indifference to pain, perseveration – all symptoms which are characteristic of dementia praecox. Moreover, this diagnosis is further corroborated by the fact that the presence of any organic disease can be certainly excluded, firstly, because Dr Forsyth's examination revealed none and, secondly, because the case has proved amenable to psychological treatment. The analysis showed me that the idea of a psycho-neurosis could be definitely dismissed.

Against the diagnosis of dementia praecox is the fact that the essential feature of Dick's case was an inhibition in development and not a regression. Further, dementia praecox is of extraordinarily rare occurrence in early childhood, so that many psychiatrists hold that it does not occur at all at that period.

From the standpoint of clinical psychiatry I will not commit myself on the subject of diagnosis, but my general experience in analysing children enables me to make some observations of a general nature on psychosis in childhood. I have become convinced that schizophrenia is much commoner in childhood than is usually supposed. I will give some of the reasons why it is not in general recognized: (1) Parents, especially in the lower classes, mostly consult a psychiatrist only when the case is desperate, that is, when they can do nothing with the child themselves. Thus a considerable number of cases never come under medical observation. (2) In the patients whom the physician does see, it is often impossible for him in a single rapid examination to establish the presence of schizophrenia, so that many cases of this sort are classified under indefinite headings, such as 'arrested development', 'mental deficiency', 'psychopathic condition', 'asocial tendency', etc. (3) Above all, in children schizophrenia is less obvious and striking than in adults. Traits which are characteristic of this disease are less noticeable in a child because, in a lesser degree, they are natural in the development of normal children. Such things, for instance, as a marked severance from reality, a lack of emotional rapport, an incapacity to concentrate on any occupation, silly behaviour and talking nonsense do not strike us as so remarkable in children and we do not judge of them as we should if they occurred in adults. An excess of activity and stereotyped movements are quite common in children and differ only in degree from the hyperkinesis and stereotypy of schizophrenia. Automatic obedience must be very marked indeed for the parents to regard it as anything but 'docility'. Negativistic behaviour is usually looked upon as 'naughtiness', and dissociation is a phenomenon which generally escapes observation in a child altogether. That the phobic anxiety of children often contains ideas of persecution which are of a paranoiac character[8] and hypochondriacal fears is a fact which requires very close observation and can often be revealed only through analysis. (4) Even more commonly than psychoses we meet in children with psychotic character traits which, in unfavourable circumstances, lead to disease in later life.

Thus, in my opinion fully developed schizophrenia is more common and, especially, the occurrence of schizophrenic traits is a far more general phenomenon, in childhood than is usually supposed. I have come to the conclusion – for which I must give my full reasons elsewhere – that the concept of schizophrenia in particular and of psychosis in general as occurring in childhood must be extended, and I think that one of the chief tasks of the children's analyst is to discover and cure psychoses in children. The theoretical knowledge thus acquired would doubtless be a valuable contribution to our understanding of the structure of the psychoses and would also help us to reach a more accurate differential diagnosis between the various diseases.

If we extend the use of the term in the manner which I propose, I think we shall be justified in classifying Dick's illness under the heading schizophrenia. It is true that it differs from the typical schizophrenia of childhood in that in him the trouble was an inhibition in development, whereas in most cases there has been regression after a certain stage of development has been successfully reached.[9] Moreover the severity of the case adds to the unusual character of the clinical picture. Nevertheless, I have reason to think that even so it is not an isolated one, for recently I have become acquainted with two analogous cases in children of about Dick's age. One is therefore inclined to conjecture that, if we observed with a more penetrating eye, more cases of the kind would come to our knowledge.

I will now sum up my theoretical conclusions. I have drawn them not from Dick's case only but from other, less extreme, cases of schizophrenia in children between the ages of five and thirteen and from my general analytic experience.

The early stages of the Oedipus conflict are dominated by sadism. They take place during a phase of development which is inaugurated by oral sadism (with which urethral, muscular and anal sadism associate themselves) and terminates when the ascendancy of anal sadism comes to an end.

It is only in the later stages of the Oedipus conflict that the defence against the libidinal impulses makes its appearance; in the earlier stages it is against the accompanying *destructive* impulses that the defence is directed. The earliest defence set up by the ego is directed against the subject's own sadism and the object attacked, both of these being regarded as sources of danger. This defence is of a violent character, different from the mechanism of repression. In boys this violent defence is also directed against his penis as the executive organ of his sadism and it is one of the deepest sources of all disturbances of potency.

Such are my hypotheses with regard to the development of normal persons and neurotics; let us now turn to the genesis of the psychoses.

The first part of the phase when sadism is at its zenith is that in which the attacks are conceived of as being made by violence. This I have come to recognize as the fixation point in dementia praecox. In the second part of this phase the attacks are imagined as being made by poisoning, and the urethral and anal-sadistic impulses predominate. This I believe to be the fixation point in paranoia.[10] I may recall that Abraham maintained that in paranoia the libido regresses to the earlier anal stage. My conclusions are in agreement with Freud's hypotheses, according to which the fixation points of dementia praecox and paranoia are to be sought in the narcissistic stage, that of dementia praecox preceding that of paranoia.

The ego's exaggerated and premature defence against sadism checks the establishing of a right relation to reality and the development of phantasy. The further sadistic appropriation and exploration of the mother's body and of the outside world (the mother's body in an extended sense) are brought to a standstill, and this causes the more or less complete suspension of the symbolic relation to the things and objects representing the contents of the mother's body and, hence, of the relation to the subject's environment and to reality. This withdrawal becomes the basis of the lack of affect and anxiety, which is one of the symptoms of dementia praecox. In this disease, therefore, the regression would go right back to the early phase of development in which the sadistic appropriation and destruction of the interior of the mother's body, as conceived of by the subject in phantasy, together with the establishing of the relation to reality, was prevented or checked owing to anxiety.

KLEIN'S THEORY
AND THE
FOUNDATION
OF A
KLEINIAN SCHOOL

CHAPTER SIX

In 1932, Klein had published her volume *The Psycho-Analysis of Children*. It collected and re-presented her ideas to date. In England it was most favourably received.

During the mid-1930s Klein was in her professional hey-day. Disagreements between London and Vienna were coming to a head. Joan Riviere, one of Klein's staunchest supporters, gave a lecture 'On the Genesis of Psychical Conflict in Earliest Infancy' as the second of a series of exchange lectures aimed at sorting out the differences between the two psychoanalytic capitals – Vienna and London. Riviere claimed that, 'directly or indirectly', Klein had influenced most British psychoanalysts. In London Melanie Klein had strong support. In a review of her book, Edward Glover claimed that Chapter 8 of *The Psycho-Analysis of Children* was a landmark ranking with Freud's work. It appeared to many analysts as though Melanie Klein had put the first two years of life firmly on the mental map. Alternative readings to Freud's account of women, basing female sexuality on the first maternal relationship, abounded – Klein's among them. Klein's daughter, Melitta Schmideberg, encouraged by Glover and Joan Riviere, started to analyse adult psychotics. The concept of 'phantasy' so central to subsequent Kleinian thought, so crucial for Kleinian practice, was being debated at the 'Scientific Meetings' at the Institute of Psychoanalysis. A training in child analysis incorporating Klein's ideas was started in London.

In this major paper, which Hanna Segal (see Selected Bibliography) calls 'a watershed in the development of Melanie Klein's thought', Klein first formulates the concept of a depressive position – a concept that can truly be said to be the hallmark of Kleinian theory.

At about six months the baby who has hitherto been destructive of or attached to 'part-objects', such as the mother's breast, is now able to take in the whole mother. How the baby manages this position – whether or not it can identify with an internalized 'good' mother to the extent that it can repair the damage done by its destructive urges to the 'bad' mother, or whether it must flee the implications of the position – constitutes the nodal experience for the infant on which its subsequent relative normality or psychosis depends. For Klein, the depressive position comes to incorporate and replace the psychic centrality that Freud had accorded to the later Oedipus complex. In some ways, like Klein's later, even more explosive theory of envy, it held the same place among Kleinians that the Oedipus complex held among Freudians – acceptance of the concept of a depressive position distinguishes the Kleinian psychoanalyst. Retrospectively we can see that its introduction marked the beginning of disagreement among British analysts.

Melanie Klein first used the term 'position' in 1930 but its real deployment only starts in this essay. In place of the emphasis on libidinal stages – oral, anal, phallic, genital – deployed by Anna Freud and other analysts, Melanie Klein introduces a concept that presents the moment of ego organization – she substitutes a structural for a developmental notion. This facilitates the making of a connection between adult psychosis and infant development – a 'position' is an always available state, not something one passes through.

The paper was given to the British Society in 1935 after an abridged version had been read to the meeting of the International Congress of Psychoanalysis held at Lucerne in the summer of 1934.

A CONTRIBUTION TO THE PSYCHOGENESIS OF MANIC-DEPRESSIVE STATES (1935)

My earlier writings[1] contain the account of a phase of sadism at its zenith, through which children pass during the first year of life. In the very first months of the baby's existence it has sadistic impulses directed, not only against its mother's breast, but also against the inside of her body: scooping it out, devouring the contents, destroying it by every means which sadism can suggest. The development of the infant is governed by the mechanisms of introjection and projection. From the beginning the ego introjects objects 'good' and 'bad', for both of which its mother's breast is the prototype – for good objects when the child obtains it and for bad when it fails him. But it is because the baby projects its own aggression on to these objects that it feels them to be 'bad' and not only in that they frustrate its desires: the child conceives of them as actually dangerous – persecutors who it fears will devour it, scoop out the inside of its body, cut it to pieces, poison it – in short, compassing its destruction by all the means which sadism can devise. These imagos, which are a phantastically distorted picture of the real objects upon which they are based, are installed by it not only in the outside world but, by the process of incorporation, also within the ego. Hence, quite little children pass through anxiety situations (and react to them with defence mechanisms), the content of which is comparable to that of the psychoses of adults.

One of the earliest methods of defence against the dread of persecutors, whether conceived of as existing in the external world or internalized, is that of scotomization, the *denial of psychic reality*; this may result in a considerable restriction of the mechanisms of introjection and projection and in the denial of external reality, and it forms the basis of the most severe psychoses. Very soon, too, the ego tries to defend itself against internalized persecutors by the processes of expulsion and projection. At the same time, since the dread of internalized objects is by no means extinguished with their projection, the ego marshals against the persecutors inside the body the same forces as it employs against those in the outside world. These anxiety contents and defence mechanisms form the basis of paranoia. In the infantile dread of magicians, witches, evil beasts, etc. we detect something of this anxiety, but here it has already undergone projection and modification. One of my conclusions, moreover, was that infantile psychotic anxiety, in particular paranoid anxiety, is bound and modified by the obsessional mechanisms which make their appearance very early.

In the present paper I propose to deal with depressive states in their relation to paranoia on the one hand and to mania on the other. I have acquired the material upon which my conclusions are based from the analysis of depressive states in cases of severe neuroses, border-line cases and in patients, both adults and children, who displayed mixed paranoiac and depressive trends.

I have studied manic states in various degrees and forms, including the slightly hypomanic states which occur in normal persons. The analysis of depressive and manic features in normal children and adults also proved very instructive.

According to Freud and Abraham, the fundamental process in melancholia is the loss of the loved object. The real loss of a real object, or some similar situation having the same significance, results in the object becoming installed within the ego. Owing, however, to an excess of cannibalistic impulses in the subject, this introjection miscarries and the consequence is illness.

Now, why is it that the process of introjection is so specific for melancholia? I believe that the main difference between incorporation in paranoia and in melancholia is connected with changes in

n of the subject to the object, though it is also a question
e in the constitution of the introjecting ego. According to
lover, the ego, at first but loosely organized, consists of
rable number of ego nuclei. In his view, in the first place
an oral ego nucleus and later an anal ego nucleus predominates over
the others.[2] In this very early phase, in which oral sadism plays a
prominent part and which in my view is the basis of schizophrenia,[3]
the ego's power of identifying itself with its objects is as yet small,
partly because it is itself still unco-ordinated and partly because the
introjected objects are still mainly partial objects, which it equates
with faeces.

In paranoia the characteristic defences are chiefly aimed at
annihilating the 'persecutors', while anxiety on the ego's account
occupies a prominent place in the picture. As the ego becomes more
fully organized, the internalized imagos will approximate more
closely to reality and the ego will identify itself more fully with
'good' objects. The dread of persecution, which was at first felt on
the ego's account, now relates to the good object as well and from
now on preservation of the good object is regarded as synonymous
with the survival of the ego.

Hand in hand with this development goes a change of the highest
importance, namely, from a partial object relation to the relation to
a complete object. Through this step the ego arrives at a new
position, which forms the foundation of that situation called the
loss of the loved object. Not until the object is lived *as a whole* can
its loss be felt as a whole.

With this change in the relation to the object, new anxiety
contents make their appearance and a change takes place in the
mechanisms of defence. The development of the libido also is
decisively influenced. Paranoid anxiety lest the objects sadistically
destroyed should themselves be a source of poison and danger inside
the subject's body causes him, in spite of the vehemence of his oral
sadistic onslaughts, at the same time to be profoundly mistrustful
of them while yet incorporating them.

This leads to a weakening of oral fixations. One manifestation of
this may be observed in the difficulties very young children often
show in regard to eating which, I think, always have a paranoid
root. As a child (or an adult) identifies himself more fully with a
good object, the libidinal urges increase; he develops a greedy love

and desire to devour this object and the mechanism of introjection is reinforced. Besides, he finds himself constantly impelled to repeat the incorporation of a good object, partly because he dreads that he has forfeited it by his cannibalism – i.e. the repetition of the act is designed to test the reality of his fears and disprove them – and partly because he fears internalized persecutors against whom he requires a good object to help him. In this stage the ego is more than ever driven both by love and by need to introject the object.

Another stimulus for an increase of introjection is the phantasy that the loved object may be preserved in safety inside oneself. In this case the dangers of the inside are projected on to the external world.

If, however, consideration for the object increases, and a better acknowledgement of psychic reality sets in, the anxiety lest the object should be destroyed in the process of introjecting it leads – as Abraham has described – to various disturbances of the function of introjection.

In my experience there is, furthermore, a deep anxiety as to the dangers which await the object inside the ego. It could not be safely maintained there, as the inside is felt to be a dangerous and poisonous place in which the loved object would perish. Here we see one of the situations which I have described as being fundamental for 'the loss of the loved object', the situation, namely, when the ego becomes fully identified with its good, internalized objects, and at the same time becomes aware of its own incapacity to protect and preserve them against the internalized, persecuting objects and the id. This anxiety is psychologically justified.

For the ego, when it becomes fully identified with the object, does not abandon its earlier defence mechanisms. According to Abraham's hypothesis, the annihilation and expulsion of the object – processes characteristic of the earlier anal level – initiate the depressive mechanism. If this be so, it confirms my notion of the genetic connection between paranoia and melancholia. In my opinion, the paranoiac mechanism of destroying the objects (whether inside the body or in the outside world) by every means which oral, urethral and anal sadism can command, persists, but in a lesser degree and with a certain modification to the change in the subject's relation to his objects. As I have said, the dread lest the *good* object should be expelled along with the *bad* causes the mechanisms of expulsion and projection to lose value. We know that, at this stage, the ego makes a greater use of introjection of the *good* object as a mechanism of defence. This is associated with another important mechanism: that of making reparation to the object. In certain of my earlier works[4] I discussed in detail the concept of restoration and showed that it is far more than a mere reaction formation. The ego feels impelled (and I can now add, impelled by its identification with the good object) to make restitution for all the sadistic attacks that it has launched on that object. When a well-marked cleavage between good and bad objects has been attained, the subject attempts to restore the former, making good in the restoration every detail of his sadistic attacks. But the ego cannot as yet believe enough in the benevolence of the object and in its own capacity to make restitution. On the other hand, through its identification with a good object and through the other mental advances which this implies, the ego finds itself forced to a fuller recognition of psychic reality, and this exposes it to fierce conflicts. Some of its objects – an indefinite number – are persecutors to it, ready to devour and do violence to it. In all sorts of ways they endanger both the ego and the good object. Every injury inflicted in phantasy by the child upon its parents (primarily from hate and secondarily in self-defence), every act of violence committed by one object upon another (in particular the destructive, sadistic coitus of the parents, which it regards as yet another consequence of its own sadistic wishes) – all this is played out, both in the outside world and, since the ego is constantly absorbing into itself the whole external world, within the ego as well. Now, however, all these processes are viewed as a perpetual source of danger both to the good object and to the ego.

It is true that, now that good and bad objects are more clearly differentiated, the subject's hate is directed rather against the latter, while his love and his attempts at reparation are more focused on the former; but the excess of his sadism and anxiety acts as a check to this advance in his mental development. Every external or internal stimulus (e.g. every real frustration) is fraught with the utmost danger: not only bad objects but also the good ones are thus menaced by the id, for every access of hate or anxiety may temporarily abolish the differentiation and thus result in a 'loss of the loved object'. And it is not only the vehemence of the subject's uncontrollable hatred but that of his love too which imperils the object. For at this stage of his development loving an object and devouring it are very closely connected. A little child which believes, when its mother disappears, that it has eaten her up and destroyed her (whether from motives of love or of hate) is tormented by anxiety both for her and for the good mother which it has absorbed into itself.

It now becomes plain why, at this phase of development, the ego feels itself constantly menaced in its possession of internalized good objects. It is full of anxiety lest such objects should die. Both in children and adults suffering from depression, I have discovered the dread of harbouring dying or dead objects (especially the parents) inside one and an identification of the ego with objects in this condition.

From the very beginning of psychic development there is a constant correlation of real objects with those installed within the ego. It is for this reason that the anxiety which I have just described manifests itself in a child's exaggerated fixation to its mother or whoever looks after it.[5] The absence of the mother arouses in the child anxiety lest it should be handed over to bad objects, external and internalized, either because of her *death* or because of her return in the guise of a '*bad*' mother.

Both cases signify to it that it has lost its loved mother and I would particularly draw attention to the fact that dread of the loss of the 'good', internalized object becomes a perpetual source of anxiety lest the real mother should die. On the other hand, every experience which suggests the loss of the real loved object stimulates the dread of losing the internalized one too.

I have already stated that my experience has led me to conclude that the loss of the loved object takes place during that phase of development in which the ego makes the transition from partial to total incorporation of the object. Having now described the situation of the ego in that phase, I can express myself with greater precision on this point. The processes which subsequently become defined as 'loss of the loved object' are determined by the subject's sense of failure (during weaning and in the periods which precede and follow it) to secure his *good, internalized* object, i.e. to possess himself of it. One reason for his failure is that he has been unable to overcome his paranoid dread of internalized persecutors.

At this point we are confronted with a question of importance for our whole theory. My own observations and those of a number of my English colleagues have led us to conclude that the direct influence of the early processes of introjection upon both normal and pathological development is very much more momentous, and in some respects other, than has hitherto commonly been accepted in psycho-analytical circles.

According to our views, even the earliest incorporated objects form the basis of the super-ego and enter into its structure. The question is by no means a merely theoretical one. As we study the relations of the early infantile ego to its internalized objects and to the id, and come to understand the gradual changes these relations undergo, we obtain a deeper insight into the specific anxiety situations through which the ego passes and the specific defence mechanisms which it develops as it becomes more highly organized. Viewed from this standpoint in our experience we find that we arrive at a more complete understanding of the earliest phases of psychic development, of the structure of the super-ego and of the genesis of psychotic diseases. For where we deal with aetiology it seems essential to regard the libido disposition not merely as such, but also to consider it in connection with the subject's earliest relations to his internalized and external objects, a consideration which implies an understanding of the defence mechanisms developed by the ego gradually in dealing with its varying anxiety situations.

If we accept this view of the formation of the super-ego, its relentless severity in the case of the melancholic becomes more intelligible. The persecutions and demands of bad internalized objects; the attacks of such objects upon one another (especially that represented by the sadistic coitus of the parents); the urgent necessity to fulfil the very strict demands of the 'good objects' and to protect and placate them within the ego, with the resultant hatred of the id; the constant uncertainty as to the 'goodness' of a good object, which causes it so readily to become transformed into a bad one – all these factors combine to produce in the ego a sense of being a prey to contradictory and impossible claims from within, a condition which is felt as a bad conscience. That is to say: the earliest utterances of conscience are associated with persecution by bad objects. The very word 'gnawing of conscience' (*Gewissensbisse*) testifies to the relentless 'persecution' of conscience and to the fact that it is originally conceived of as devouring its victim.

Among the various internal demands which go to make up the severity of the super-ego in the melancholic, I have mentioned his urgent need to comply with the very strict demands of the 'good' objects. It is this part of the picture only – namely, the cruelty of the 'good', i.e. loved, objects within – which has been recognized hitherto by general analytic opinion, namely, in the relentless severity of the super-ego in the melancholic. But in my view it is only by looking at the whole relation of the ego to its phantastically bad objects as well as to its good objects, only by looking at the whole picture of the internal situation which I have tried to outline in this paper, that we can understand the slavery to which the ego submits when complying with the extremely cruel demands and admonitions of its loved object which has become installed within the ego. As I have mentioned before, the ego endeavours to keep the good apart from the bad, and the real from the phantastic objects. The result is a conception of extremely bad and *extremely perfect* objects, that is to say, its loved objects are in many ways intensely moral and exacting. At the same time, since the ego cannot really keep its good and bad objects apart in its mind,[6] some of the cruelty of the bad objects and of the id becomes related to the good objects and this then again increases the severity of their demands.[7] These strict demands serve the purpose of supporting the ego in its fight against its uncontrollable hatred and its bad attacking objects, with whom the ego is partly identified.[8] The stronger the anxiety is of losing the loved objects, the more the ego strives to save them, and the harder the task of restoration becomes the stricter will grow the demands which are associated with the super-ego.

I have tried to show that the difficulties which the ego experiences when it passes on to the incorporation of whole objects proceed from its as yet imperfect capacity for mastering, by means of its new defence mechanisms, the fresh anxiety contents arising out of this advance in its development.

I am aware how difficult it is to draw a sharp line between the anxiety contents and feelings of the paranoiac and those of the depressive, since they are so closely linked up with each other. But they can be distinguished one from the other if, as a criterion of differentiation, one considers whether the persecution anxiety is mainly related to the preservation of the ego – in which case it is paranoiac – or to the preservation of the good internalized objects with whom the ego is identified as a whole. In the latter case – which is the case of the depressive – the anxiety and feelings of suffering are of a much more complex nature. The anxiety lest the good objects and with them the ego should be destroyed, or that they are in a state of disintegration, is interwoven with continuous and desperate efforts to save the good objects both internalized and external.

It seems to me that only when the ego has introjected the object as a whole and has established a better relationship to the external world and to real people is it able fully to realize the disaster created through its sadism and especially through its cannibalism, and to feel distressed about it. This distress is related not only to the past but to the present as well, since at this early stage of development the sadism is in full swing. It needs a fuller identification with the loved object, and a fuller recognition of its value, for the ego to become aware of the state of disintegration to which it has reduced and is continuing to reduce its loved object. The ego then finds itself confronted with the psychical fact that its loved objects are in a state of dissolution – in bits – and the despair, remorse and anxiety deriving from this recognition are at the bottom of numerous anxiety situations. To quote only a few of them: there is anxiety how to put the bits together in the right way and at the right time; how to pick out the good bits and do away with the bad ones; how to bring the object to life when it has been put together; and there is the anxiety of being interfered with in this task by bad objects and by one's own hatred, etc.

Anxiety situations of this kind I have found to be at the bottom not only of depression, but of all inhibitions of work. The attempts to save the loved object, to repair and restore it, attempts which in the state of depression are coupled with despair, since the ego doubts its capacity to achieve this restoration, are determining factors for all sublimations and the whole of the ego development. In this connection I shall only mention the specific importance for sublimation of the bits to which the loved object has been reduced and the effort to put them together. It is a 'perfect' object which is in pieces; thus the effort to undo the state of disintegration to which it has been reduced presupposes the necessity to make it beautiful and 'perfect'. The idea of perfection is, moreover, so compelling because it disproves the idea of disintegration. In some patients who had turned away from their mother in dislike or hate, or used other mechanisms to get away from her, I have found that there existed in their minds nevertheless a beautiful picture of the mother, but one which was felt to be a *picture* of her only, not her real self. The real object was felt to be unattractive – really an injured, incurable and therefore dreaded person. The beautiful picture had been dissociated from the real object but had never been given up, and played a great part in the specific ways of their sublimations.

It appears that the desire for perfection is rooted in the depressive anxiety of disintegration, which is thus of great importance in all sublimations.

As I have pointed out before, the ego comes to a realization of its love for a good object, a whole object and in addition a real object, together with an overwhelming feeling of guilt towards it. Full identification with the object based on the libidinal attachment, first to the breast, then to the whole person, goes hand in hand with anxiety for it (of its disintegration), with guilt and remorse, with a sense of responsibility for preserving it intact against persecutors and the id, and with sadness relating to expectation of the impending loss of it. These emotions, whether conscious or unconscious, are in my view among the essential and fundamental elements of the feelings we call love.

In this connection I may say we are familiar with the self-reproaches of the depressive which represent reproaches against the object. But to my mind the ego's hate of the id, which is paramount in this phase, accounts even more for its feelings of unworthiness and despair than do its reproaches against the object. I have often found that these reproaches and the hatred against bad objects are secondarily increased as a defence against the hatred of the id, which is even more unbearable. In the last analysis it is the ego's unconscious knowledge that the hate is indeed also there, as well as the love, and that it may at any time get the upper hand (the ego's anxiety of being carried away by the id and so destroying the loved object), which brings about the sorrow, feelings of guilt and the despair which underlie grief. This anxiety is also responsible for the doubt of the goodness of the loved object. As Freud has pointed out, doubt is in reality a doubt of one's own love and 'a man who doubts his own love may, or rather *must*, doubt every lesser thing'.[9]

The paranoiac, I should say, has also introjected a whole and real object, but has not been able to achieve a full identification with it, or, if he has got as far as this, he has not been able to maintain it. To mention a few of the reasons which are responsible for this failure: the persecution anxiety is too great; suspicions and anxieties of a phantastic nature stand in the way of a full and stable introjection of a good object and a real one. In so far as it has been introjected, there is little capacity to maintain it as a good object, since doubts and suspicions of all kinds will soon turn the loved object again into a persecutor. Thus his relationship to whole objects and to the real world is still influenced by his early relation to internalized part-objects and faeces as persecutors and may again give way to the latter.

It seems to me characteristic of the paranoiac that, though, on account of his persecution anxiety and his suspicions, he develops a very strong and acute power of observation of the external world and of real objects, this observation and his sense of reality are nevertheless distorted, since his persecution anxiety makes him look at people mainly from the point of view of whether they are persecutors or not. Where the persecution anxiety for the ego is in the ascendant, a full and stable identification with another object, in the sense of looking at it and understanding it as it really is, and a full capacity for love, are not possible.

Another important reason why the paranoiac cannot maintain his whole-object relation is that while the persecution anxieties and the anxiety for himself are still so strongly in operation he cannot endure the additional burden of anxieties for a loved object and, besides, the feelings of guilt and remorse which accompany this depressive position. Moreover, in this position he can make far less use of projection, for fear of expelling his good objects and so losing them, and, on the other hand, for fear of injuring good external objects by expelling what is bad from within himself.

Thus we see that the sufferings connected with the depressive position thrust him back to the paranoiac position. Nevertheless, though he has retreated from it, the depressive position has been reached and therefore the liability to depression is always there.

This accounts, in my opinion, for the fact that we frequently meet depression along with severe paranoia as well as in milder cases.

If we compare the feelings of the paranoiac with those of the depressive in regard to disintegration, one can see that characteristically the depressive is filled with sorrow and anxiety for the object, which he would strive to unite again into a whole, while to the paranoiac the disintegrated object is mainly a multitude of persecutors, since each piece is growing again into a persecutor.[10] This conception of the dangerous fragments to which the object is reduced seems to me to be in keeping with the introjection of part-objects which are equated with faeces (Abraham), and with the anxiety of a multitude of internal persecutors to which, in my view,[11] the introjection of many part-objects and the multitude of dangerous faeces gives rise.

I have already considered the distinctions between the paranoiac and the depressive from the point of view of their different relations to loved objects. Let us take inhibitions and anxieties about food in this connection. The anxiety of absorbing dangerous substances destructive to one's inside will thus be paranoiac, while the anxiety of destroying the external good objects by biting and chewing, or of endangering the internal good object by introducing bad substances from outside into it will be depressive. Again, the anxiety of leading an external good object into danger within oneself by incorporating it is a depressive one. On the other hand, in cases with strong paranoiac features I have met phantasies of luring an external object into one's inside, which was regarded as a cave full of dangerous monsters, etc. Here we can see the paranoiac reasons for an intensification of the introjection mechanism, while the depressive employs this mechanism so characteristically, as we know, for the purpose of incorporating a *good* object.

Considering now hypochondriacal symptoms in this comparative way, the pains and other manifestations which in phantasy result from the attacks of internal bad objects within against the ego are typically paranoid.[12] The symptoms which derive, on the other hand, from the attacks of bad internal objects and the id against good ones, i.e. an internal warfare in which the ego is identified with the sufferings of the good objects, are typically depressive.

For instance, a patient who had been told as a child that he had tapeworms (which he himself never saw) connected the tapeworms inside him with his greediness. In his analysis he had phantasies that a tapeworm was eating its way through his body and a strong anxiety of cancer came to the fore. The patient, who suffered from hypochondriacal and paranoid anxieties, was very suspicious of me, and among other things, suspected me of being allied with people who were hostile towards him. At this time he dreamt that a detective was arresting a hostile and persecuting person and putting this person in prison. But then the detective proved unreliable and became the accomplice of the enemy. The detective stood for myself and the whole anxiety was internalized and was also connected with the tapeworm phantasy. The prison in which the enemy was kept was his own inside – actually the special part of his inside where the persecutor was to be confined. It became clear that the dangerous tapeworm (one of his associations was that the tapeworm is bisexual) represented the two parents in a hostile alliance (actually in intercourse) against him.

At the time when the tapeworm phantasies were being analysed the patient developed diarrhoea which – as he wrongly thought – was mixed with blood. This frightened him very much; he felt it as a confirmation of dangerous processes going on inside him. This feeling was founded on phantasies in which he attacked his bad united parents in his inside with poisonous excreta. The diarrhoea meant to him poisonous excreta, as well as the bad penis of his father. The blood which he thought was in his faeces represented me (this was shown by associations in which I was connected with blood). Thus the diarrhoea was felt to represent dangerous weapons with which he was fighting his bad internalized parents, as well as his poisoned and broken-up parents themselves – the tapeworm. In his early childhood he had in phantasy attacked his real parents with poisonous excreta and actually disturbed them in intercourse by defecating. Diarrhoea had always been something very frightening to him. Along with these attacks on his real parents this whole warfare became internalized and threatened his ego with destruction. I may mention that this patient remembered during his analysis that at about ten years of age he had definitely felt that he had a little man inside his stomach who controlled him and gave him orders, which he, the patient, had to execute, although they were always perverse and wrong (he had had similar feelings about his real father).

When the analysis progressed and distrust in me had diminished, the patient became very much concerned about me. He had always worried about his mother's health; but he had not been able to develop real love towards her, though he did his best to please her. Now, together with the concern for me, strong feelings of love and gratitude came to the fore, together with feelings of unworthiness, sorrow and depression. The patient had never felt really happy, his depression had been spread out, one might say, over his whole life, but he had not suffered from actual depressed states. In his analysis he went through phases of deep depression with all the symptoms characteristic of this state of mind. At the same time the feelings and phantasies connected with his hypochondriacal pains changed. For instance, the patient felt anxiety that the cancer would make its way through the lining of his stomach; but now it appeared that, while he feared for his stomach, he really wanted to protect 'me' inside him – actually the internalized mother – whom he felt was being attacked by the father's penis and by his own id (the cancer). Another time the patient had phantasies connected with physical discomfort about an internal haemorrhage from which he would die. It became clear that I was identified with the haemorrhage, the good blood representing me. We must remember that, when the paranoid anxieties dominated and I was mainly felt as a persecutor, I had been identified with the *bad* blood which was mixed with the diarrhoea (with the bad father). Now the precious *good* blood represented me – losing it meant my death, which would imply his death. It became clear now that the cancer which he made responsible for the death of his loved object, as well as for his own, and which stood for the bad father's penis, was even more felt to be his own sadism, especially his greed. That is why he felt so unworthy and so much in despair.

While the paranoid anxieties predominated and the anxiety of his bad united objects prevailed, he felt only hypochondriacal anxieties for his own body. When depression and sorrow had set in, the love and the concern for the good object came to the fore and the anxiety contents as well as the whole feelings and defences altered. In this case as well as in others, I have found that *paranoid fears and suspicions were reinforced as a defence against the depressive position* which was overlaid by them. I shall now quote another case with strong paranoiac and depressive features (the paranoia predominating) and with hypochondria. The complaints about manifold physical troubles, which occupied a large part of the hours, alternated with strong feelings of suspicion about people in his environment and often became directly related to them, since he made them responsible for his physical troubles in one way or another. When, after hard analytic work, distrust and suspicion diminished, his relation to me improved more and more. It became clear that, buried under the continuous paranoid accusations, complaints and criticisms of others, there existed an extremely deep love for his mother and concern for his parents as well as for other people. At the same time sorrow and deep depression came more and more to the fore. During this phase the hypochondriacal complaints altered, both in the way they were presented to me and in the content which underlay them. For instance, the patient complained about different physical troubles and then went on to say what medicines he had taken – enumerating what he had done for his chest, his throat, his nose, his ears, his intestines, etc. It sounded rather as if he were nursing these parts of his body and his organs. He went on to speak about his concern for some young people under his care (he is a teacher) and then about the worry he was feeling for some members of his family. It became quite clear that the different organs he was trying to cure were identified with his internalized brothers and sisters, about whom he felt guilty and whom he had to be perpetually keeping right. It was his *over-anxiousness* to put them right, because he had ruined them in phantasy, and his *excessive* sorrow and despair about it, which had led to such an increase of the paranoid anxieties and defences that love and concern for people and identification with them became buried under hate. In this case, too, when depression came to the fore in full force and the paranoid anxieties diminished, the hypochondriacal anxieties became related to the internalized loved objects and (thus) to the ego, while before they had been experienced in reference to the ego only.

After having attempted to differentiate between the anxiety contents, feelings and defences at work in paranoia and those in the depressive states, I must again make clear that in my view the depressive state is based on the paranoid state and genetically derived from it. I consider the depressive state as being the result of a mixture of paranoid anxiety and of those anxiety contents, distressed feelings and defences which are connected with the impending loss of the whole loved object. It seems to me that to introduce a term for those specific anxieties and defences might further the understanding of the structure and nature of paranoia as well as of the manic-depressive states.[13]

In my view, wherever a state of depression exists, be it in the normal, the neurotic, in manic-depressives or in mixed cases, there is always in it this specific grouping of anxieties, distressed feelings and different varieties of these defences, which I have here described at full length.

If this point of view proves correct, we should be able to understand those very frequent cases where we are presented with a picture of mixed paranoiac and depressive trends, since we could then isolate the various elements of which it is composed.

The considerations that I have brought forward in this paper about depressive states may lead us, in my opinion, to a better understanding of the still rather enigmatic reaction of suicide. According to the findings of Abraham and James Glover, a suicide is directed against the introjected object. But, while in committing suicide the ego intends to murder its bad objects, in my view at the same time it also always aims at saving its loved objects, internal or external. To put it shortly: in some cases the phantasies underlying suicide aim at preserving the internalized good objects and that part of the ego which is identified with good objects, and also at destroying the other part of the ego which is identified with the bad objects and the id. Thus the ego is enabled to become united with its loved objects.

In other cases, suicide seems to be determined by the same type of phantasies, but here they relate to the external world and real objects, partly as substitutes for the internalized ones. As already stated, the subject hates not only his 'bad' objects, but his id as well and that vehemently. In committing suicide, his purpose may be to make a clean breach in his relation to the outside world because he desires to rid some real object – or the 'good' object which that whole world represents and which the ego is identified with – of himself, or of that part of the ego which is identified with his bad objects and his id.[14] At bottom we perceive in such a step his reaction to his own sadistic attacks on his mother's body, which to a little child is the first representative of the outside world. Hatred and revenge against the real (good) objects also always play an important part in such a step, but it is precisely the uncontrollable dangerous hatred which is perpetually welling up in him from which the melancholic by his suicide is in part struggling to preserve his real objects.

Freud has stated that mania has for its basis the same contents as melancholia and is, in fact, a way of escape from that state. I would suggest that in mania the ego seeks refuge not only from melancholia but also from a paranoiac condition which it is unable to master. Its torturing and perilous dependence on its loved objects drives the ego to find freedom. But its identification with these objects is too profound to be renounced. On the other hand, the ego is pursued by its dread of bad objects and of the id and, in its effort to escape from all these miseries, it has recourse to many different mechanisms, some of which, since they belong to different phases of development, are mutually incompatible.

The *sense of omnipotence*, in my opinion, is what first and foremost characterizes mania and, further (as Helene Deutsch has stated),[15] mania is based on the mechanism of *denial*. I differ, however, from Helene Deutsch in the following point. She holds that this 'denial' is connected with the phallic phase and the castration complex (in girls it is a denial of the lack of the penis); while my observations have led me to conclude that this mechanism of denial originates in that very early phase in which the undeveloped ego endeavours to defend itself from the most overpowering and profound anxiety of all, namely, its dread of internalized persecutors and of the id. That is to say, that which is *first of all denied is psychic reality* and the ego may then go on to deny a great deal of external reality.

We know that scotomization may lead to the subject's becoming entirely cut off from reality, and to his complete inactivity. In mania, however, denial is associated with an over-activity, although this excess of activity, as Helene Deutsch points out, often bears no relation to any actual results achieved. I have explained that in this state the source of the conflict is that the ego is unwilling and unable to renounce its good internal objects and yet endeavours to escape from the perils of dependence on them as well as from its bad objects. Its attempt to detach itself from an object without at the same time completely renouncing it seems to be conditioned by an increase in the ego's own strength. It succeeds in this compromise by *denying the importance* of its good objects and also of the dangers with which it is menaced from its bad objects and the id. At the same time, however, it endeavours ceaselessly to *master and control* all its objects, and the evidence of this effort is its hyperactivity.

What to my view is quite specific for mania is the *utilization of the sense of omnipotence for* the purpose of *controlling and mastering* objects. This is necessary for two reasons: (*a*) in order to deny the dread of them which is being experienced, and (*b*) so that the mechanism (acquired in the previous – the depressive position) of making reparation to the object may be carried through.[16] By mastering his objects the manic person imagines he will prevent them not only from injuring himself but from being a danger to one another. His mastery is to enable him particularly to prevent dangerous coitus between the parents[17] he has internalized and their death within him. The manic defence assumes so many forms that it is, of course, not easy to postulate a general mechanism. But I believe that we really have such a mechanism (though its varieties are infinite) in this mastery of the internalized parents, while at the same time the existence of this internal world is being depreciated and denied. Both in children and in adults I have found that, where obsessional neurosis was the most powerful factor in the case, such mastery betokened a forcible separation of two (or more) objects; whereas, where mania was in the ascendant, the patient had recourse to methods more violent. That is to say, the objects were killed but, since the subject was omnipotent, he supposed he could also immediately call them to life again. One of my patients spoke of this process as 'keeping them in suspended animation'. The killing corresponds to the defence mechanism (retained from the earliest phase) of destruction of the object; the resuscitation corresponds to the reparation made to the object. In this position the ego effects a similar compromise in its relation to real objects. The hunger for objects, so characteristic of mania, indicates that the ego has retained one defence mechanism of the depressive position: the introjection of good objects. The manic subject *denies* the different form of anxiety associated with this introjection (anxiety, that is to say, lest either he should introject bad objects or else destroy his good objects by the process of introjection); his denial relates not merely to the impulses of the id but to his own concern for the object's safety. Thus we may suppose that the process by which ego and ego ideal come to coincide (as Freud has shown that they do in mania) is as follows. The ego incorporates the object in a cannibal-istic way (the 'feast', as Freud calls it in his account of mania) but denies that it feels any concern for it. 'Surely,' argues the ego, 'it is not a matter of such great importance if this particular object is destroyed. There are so many others to be incorporated.' This *disparagement of the object's importance and the contempt for it* is, I think, a specific characteristic of mania and enables the ego to effect that partial detachment which we observe side by side with its hunger for objects. Such detachment, which the ego cannot achieve in the depressive position, represents an advance, a fortifying of the ego in relation to its objects. But this advance is counteracted by the regressive mechanisms described which the ego at the same time employs in mania.

Before I go on to make a few suggestions about the part which the paranoid, depressive and manic positions play in normal devel-opment, I shall speak about two dreams of a patient which illustrate some of the points I have put forward in connection with the psychotic positions. Different symptoms and anxieties, of which I shall only mention severe depressions and paranoid and hypochon-driacal anxieties, had induced the patient C. to come for analysis. At the time he dreamt these dreams his analysis was well advanced. He dreamt that he was travelling with his parents in a railway-carriage, probably without a roof, since they were in the open air. The patient felt that he was 'managing the whole thing', taking care of the parents, who were much older and more in need of his care than in reality. The parents were lying in bed, not side by side, as they usually did, but with the ends of the beds joined together. The patient found it difficult to keep them warm. Then the patient urinated, while his parents were watching him, into a basin in the middle of which there was a cylindrical object. The urination seemed complicated, since he had to take special care not to urinate into the cylindrical part. He felt this would not have mattered had he been able to aim exactly into the cylinder and not to splash anything about. When he had finished urinating he noticed that the basin was overflowing and felt this as unsatisfactory. While urinating he noticed that his penis was very large and he had an uncomfortable feeling about this – as if his father ought not to see it, since he would feel beaten by him and he did not want to humiliate his father. At the same time he felt that by urinating he was sparing his father the trouble of getting out of bed and urinating himself. Here the patient stopped, and then said that he really felt as if his parents were a part of himself. In the dream the basin with the cylinder was supposed to be a Chinese vase, but it was not right, because the stem was not underneath the basin, as it should have been, it was 'in the wrong place', since it was above the basin – really inside it. The patient then associated the basin to a glass bowl, as used for gas-burners in his grandmother's house, and the cylindrical part reminded him of a gas mantle. He then thought of a dark passage, at the end of which there was a low-burning gas-light, and said that this picture evoked in him sad feelings. It made him think of poor and dilapidated houses, where there seemed to be nothing alive but this low-burning gas-light. It is true, one had only to pull the string and then the light would burn fully. This reminded him that he had always been frightened of gas and that the flames of a gas-ring made him feel that they were jumping out at him, biting him, as if they were a lion's head. Another thing which frightened him about gas was the 'pop' noise it made, when it was put out. After my interpretation that the cylindrical part in the basin and the gas mantle were the same thing and that he was afraid to urinate into it because he did not want for some reason to put the flame out, he replied that of course one cannot extinguish a gas flame in this way, as then poison remains behind – it is not like a candle which one can simply blow out.

The night after this the patient had the following dream: He heard the frizzling sound of something which was frying in an oven. He could not see what it was, but he thought of something brown, probably a kidney which was frying in a pan. The noise he heard was like the squeaking or crying of a tiny voice and his feeling was that a live creature was being fried. His mother was there and he tried to draw her attention to this, and to make her understand that to fry something alive was much the worst thing to do, worse than boiling or cooking it. It was more torturing since the hot fat prevented it from burning altogether and kept it alive while skinning it. He could not make his mother understand this and she did not seem to mind. This worried him, but in a way it reassured him, as he thought it could not be so bad after all if she did not mind. The oven, which he did not open in the dream – he never saw the kidney and the pan – reminded him of a refrigerator. In a friend's flat he had repeatedly mixed up the refrigerator door with the oven door. He wonders whether heat and cold are, in a way, the same thing for him. The torturing hot fat in the pan reminds him of a book about tortures which he had read as a child; he was especially excited by beheadings and by tortures with hot oil. Beheading reminded him of King Charles. He had been very excited over the story of his execution and later on developed a sort of devotion towards him. As regards tortures with hot oil, he used to think a great deal about them, imagining himself in such a situation (especially his legs being burnt), and trying to find out how, if it had to be done, it could be done so as to cause the least possible pain.

On the day the patient told me this second dream, he had first remarked on the way I struck my match for lighting a cigarette. He said it was obvious that I did not strike the match in the right way as a bit of the top had flown towards him. He meant I did not strike it at the right angle, and then went on to say, 'like his father, who served the balls the wrong way at tennis'. He wondered how often it had happened before in his analysis that the top of the match had flown towards him. (He had remarked once or twice before that I must have silly matches, but now the criticism applied to my way of striking them.) He did not feel inclined to talk, complaining that he had developed a heavy cold in the last two days; his head felt very heavy and his ears were blocked up, the mucus was thicker than it had been at other times when he had a cold. Then he told me the dream which I have already given, and in the course of the associations once again mentioned the cold and that it made him so disinclined to do anything.

Through the analysis of these dreams a new light was thrown on some fundamental points in the patient's development. These had already come out and been worked through before in his analysis, but now they appeared in new connections and then became fully clear and convincing to him. I shall now single out only the points bearing on the conclusions arrived at in this paper; I must mention that I have no space to quote the most important associations given.

The urination in the dream led on to the early aggressive phantasies of the patient towards his parents, especially directed against their sexual intercourse. He had phantasied biting them and eating them up, and, among other attacks, urinating on and into his father's penis, in order to skin and burn it and to make his father set his mother's inside on fire in their intercourse (the torturing with hot oil). These phantasies extended to babies inside his mother's body, which were to be killed (burnt). The kidney burnt alive stood both for his father's penis – equated to faeces – and for the babies inside his mother's body (the stove which he did not open). Castration of the father is expressed by the associations about beheading. Appropriation of the father's penis was shown by the feeling that his penis was so large and that he urinated both for himself and for his father (phantasies of having his father's penis inside his own or joined on to his own had come out a great deal in his analysis). The patient's urinating into the bowl meant also his sexual intercourse with his mother (whereby the bowl and the mother in the dream represented both her as a real and as an internalized figure). The impotent castrated father was made to look on at the patient's intercourse with his mother – the reverse of the situation the patient had gone through in phantasy in his childhood. The wish to humiliate his father is expressed by his feeling that he ought not to do so. These (and other sadistic phantasies) had given rise to different anxiety contents: the mother could not be made to understand that she was endangered by the burning and biting penis inside her (the burning and biting lion's head, the gas-ring which he had lit), and that her babies were in danger of being burnt, at the same time being a danger to herself (the kidney in the oven). The patient's feeling that the cylindrical stem was 'in the wrong place' (inside the bowl instead of outside) expressed not only his early hate and jealousy that his mother took his father's penis into herself, but also his anxiety about this dangerous happening. The phantasy of keeping the kidney and the penis alive while they were being tortured expressed both the destructive tendencies against the father and the babies, and, to a certain degree the wish to preserve them. The special position of the beds – different from the one in the actual bedroom – in which the parents were lying showed, not only the primary aggressive and jealous drive to separate them in their intercourse, but also the anxiety lest they should be injured or killed by intercourse which in his phantasies the son had arranged to be so dangerous. The death wishes against the parents had led to an overwhelming anxiety of their death. This is shown by the associations and feelings about the low-burning gas-light, the advanced age of the parents in the dream (older than in reality), their helplessness and the necessity for the patient to keep them warm.

One of the defences against his feelings of guilt and his responsibility for the disaster he had arranged was brought out by the association of the patient that I am striking the matches and that his father serves tennis balls in the wrong way. Thus he makes the parents responsible for their own wrong and dangerous intercourse, but the fear of retaliation based on projection (my burning him) is expressed by his remark that he wondered how often during his analysis tops of my matches had flown towards him, and all the other anxiety contents related to attacks against him (the lion's head, the burning oil).

The fact that he had internalized (introjected) his parents is shown in the following: (1) The railway-carriage, in which he was travelling with his parents, continuously taking care of them, 'managing the whole thing', represented his own body. (2) The carriage was open, in contrast to his feeling, representing their internalization, that he could not free himself from his internalized objects, but its being open was a denial of this. (3) That he had to do everything for his parents, even to urinate for his father. (4) The definite expression of a feeling that they were a part of himself.

But through the internalization of his parents all the anxiety situations which I have mentioned before in regard to the real parents became internalized and thus multiplied, intensified and, partly, altered in character. His mother containing the burning penis and the dying children (the oven with frying pan) is inside him. There is his anxiety of his parents having dangerous intercourse inside him and the necessity to keep them separated. This necessity became the source of many anxiety situations and was found in his analysis to be at the bottom of his obsessional symptoms. At any time the parents may have dangerous intercourse, burn and eat each other and, since his ego has become the place where all these danger situations are acted out, destroy him as well. Thus he has at the same time to bear great anxiety both for them and for himself. He is full of sorrow about the impending death of the internalized parents, but at the same time he dare not bring them back to full life (he dare not pull the string of the gas-burner), since intercourse would be implied in their coming fully to life and this would then result in their death and his.

Then there are the dangers threatening from the id. If jealousy and hate stirred by some real frustration are welling up in him, he will again in his phantasy attack the internalized father with his burning excreta, and disturb their intercourse, which gives rise to renewed anxiety. Either external or internal stimuli may increase his paranoid anxieties of internalized persecutors. If he then kills his father inside him altogether, the dead father becomes a persecutor of a special kind. We see this from the patient's remark (and the following associations) that if gas is extinguished by liquid, poison remains behind. Here the paranoid position comes to the fore and the dead object within becomes equated with faeces and flatus.[18] However, the paranoid position, which had been very strong in the patient at the beginning of his analysis, but is now greatly diminished, does not appear much in the dreams.

What dominates the dreams are the distressed feelings which are connected with anxiety for his loved objects and, as I have pointed out before, are characteristic for the depressive position. In the dreams the patient deals with the depressive position in different ways. He uses the sadistic manic control over his parents by keeping them separated from each other and thus stopping them in pleasurable as well as in dangerous intercourse. At the same time, the way in which he takes care of them is indicative of obsessional mechanisms. But his main way of overcoming the depressive position is restoration. In the dream he devotes himself entirely to his parents in order to keep them alive and comfortable. His concern for his mother goes back to his earliest childhood, and the drive to put her right and to restore her as well as his father, and to make babies grow, plays an important part in all his sublimations. The connection between the dangerous happenings in his inside and his hypochondriacal anxieties is shown by the patient's remarks about the cold he had developed at the time he had the dreams. It appeared that the mucus, which was so extraordinarily thick, was identified with the urine in the bowl – with the fat in the pan – at the same time with his semen, and that in his head, which he felt so heavy, he carried the genitals of his parents (the pan with the kidney). The mucus was supposed to preserve his mother's genital from contact with that of his father and at the same time it implied sexual intercourse with his mother within. The feeling which he had in his head was that of its being blocked up, a feeling which corresponded to the blocking off of one parent's genital from the other, and to separating his internal objects. One stimulus for the dream had been a real frustration which the patient experienced shortly before he had these dreams, though this experience did not lead to a depression, but it influenced his emotional balance deep down, a fact which became clear from the dreams. In the dreams the strength of the depressive position appears increased and the effectiveness of the patient's strong defences is, to a certain amount, reduced. This is not so in his actual life. It is interesting that another stimulus for the dreams was of a very different kind. It was already after the painful experience that he went recently with his parents on a short journey which he very much enjoyed. Actually the dream started in a way which reminded him of this pleasant journey, but then the depressive feelings overshadowed the gratifying ones. As I pointed out before, the patient used formerly to worry a great deal about his mother, but this attitude has changed during his analysis, and he has now quite a happy and carefree relation to his parents.

The points which I stressed in connection with the dreams seem to me to show that the process of internalization, which sets in in the earliest stage of infancy, is instrumental for the development of the psychotic positions. We see how, as soon as the parents become internalized, the early aggressive phantasies against them lead to the paranoid fear of external and, still more, internal persecutions, produce sorrow and distress about the impending death of the incorporated objects, together with hypochondriacal anxieties, and give rise to an attempt to master in an omnipotent manic way the unbearable sufferings within, which are imposed on the ego. We also see how the masterful and sadistic control of the internalized parents becomes modified as the tendencies to restoration increase.

Space does not permit me to deal here in detail with the ways in which the normal child works through the depressive and manic positions, which in my view make up a part of normal development.[19] I shall confine myself therefore to a few remarks of a general nature.

In my former work I have brought forward the view which I referred to at the beginning of this paper, that in the first few months of its life the child goes through paranoid anxieties related to the 'bad' denying breasts, which are felt as external and internalized persecutors.[20] From this relation to part-objects, and from their equation with faeces, springs at this stage the phantastic and unrealistic nature of the child's relation to all other things: parts of its own body, people and things around it, which are at first but dimly perceived. The object-world of the child in the first two or three months of its life could be described as consisting of hostile and persecuting, or else of gratifying parts and portions of the real world. Before long the child perceives more and more of the whole person of the mother, and this more realistic perception extends to the world beyond the mother. The fact that a good relation to its mother and to the external world helps the baby to overcome its early paranoid anxieties throws a new light on the importance of its earliest experiences. From its inception analysis has always laid stress on the importance of the child's early experiences, but it seems to me that only since we know more about the nature and contents of its early anxieties, and the continuous interplay between its actual experiences and its phantasy life, are we able fully to understand *why* the external factor is so important. But when this happens its sadistic phantasies and feelings, especially its cannibalistic ones, are at their height. At the same time it now experiences a change in its emotional attitude towards its mother. The child's libidinal fixation to the breast develops into feelings towards her as a person. Thus feelings both of a destructive and of a loving nature are experiences towards one and the same object and this gives rise to deep and disturbing conflicts in the child's mind.

In the normal course of events the ego is faced at this point of its development – roughly between four to five months of age – with the necessity to acknowledge psychic reality as well as the external reality to a certain degree. It is thus made to realize that the loved object is at the same time the hated one, and in addition to this that the real objects and the imaginary figures, both external and internal, are bound up with each other. I have pointed out elsewhere that in the quite small child there exists, side by side with its relations to real objects – but on a different plane, as it were – relations to its unreal imagos, both as excessively good and excessively bad figures,[21] and that these two kinds of object relations intermingle and colour each other to an ever-increasing degree in the course of development.[22] The first important steps in this direction occur, in my view, when the child comes to know its mother as a whole person and becomes identified with her as a whole, real and loved person. It is then that the depressive position – the characteristics of which I have described in this paper – come to the fore. This position is stimulated and reinforced by the 'loss of the loved object' which the baby experiences over and over again when the mother's breast is taken away from it, and this loss reaches its climax during weaning. Sándor Radó has pointed out[23] that 'the deepest fixation-point in the depressive disposition is to be found in the situation of threatened loss of love (Freud), more especially in the hunger situation of the suckling baby'. Referring to Freud's statement that in mania the ego is once more merged with the super-ego in unity, Radó comes to the conclusion that 'this process is the faithful intrapsychic repetition of the experience of that fusing with the mother that takes place during drinking at her breast'. I agree with these statements, but my views differ in important points from the conclusions which Radó arrives at, especially about the indirect and circuitous way in which he thinks that guilt becomes connected with these early experiences. I have pointed out before that, in my view, already during the sucking period, when it comes to know its mother as a whole person and when it progresses from the introjection of part-objects to the introjection of the whole object, the infant experiences some of the feelings of guilt and remorse, some of the pain which results from the conflict between love and uncontrollable hatred, some of the anxieties of the impending death of the loved internalized and external objects – that is to say, in a lesser and milder degree the sufferings and feelings which we find fully developed in the adult melancholic. Of course these feelings are experienced in a different setting. The whole situation and the defences of the baby, which obtains reassurance over and over again in the love of the mother, differ greatly from those in the adult melancholic. But the important point is that these sufferings, conflicts, and feelings of remorse and guilt, resulting from the relation of the ego to its internalized object, are already active in the baby. The same applies, as I suggested, to paranoid and manic positions. If the infant at this period of life fails to establish its loved object within – if the introjection of the 'good' object miscarries – then the situation of the 'loss of the loved object' arises already in the same sense as it is found in the adult melancholic. This first and fundamental external loss of a real loved object, which is experienced through the loss of the breast before and during weaning, will only then result later on in a depressive state if at this early period of development the infant has failed to establish its loved object within its ego. In my view it is also at this early stage of development that the manic phantasies, first of controlling the breast and, very soon after, of controlling the internalized parents as well as the external ones, set in, with all the characteristics of the manic position which I have described, and are made use of to combat the depressive position. At any time that the child finds the breast again, after having lost it, the manic process by which the ego and ego ideal come to coincide (Freud) is set going; for the child's gratification of being fed is not only felt to be a cannibalistic incorporation of external objects (the 'feast' in mania, as Freud calls it), but also sets going cannibalistic phantasies relating to the internalized loved objects and connects with the control over these objects. No doubt, the more the child can at this stage develop a happy relationship to its real mother, the more will it be able to overcome the depressive position. But all depends on how it is able to find its way out of the conflict between love and uncontrollable hatred and sadism. As I have pointed out before, in the earliest phase the persecuting and the good objects (breasts) are kept wide apart in the child's mind. When, along with the introjection of the whole and real object, they come closer together, the ego has over and over again recourse to that mechanism – so important for the development of the relations to objects – namely, a splitting of its imagos into loved and hated, that is to say, into good and dangerous ones.

One might think that it is actually at this point that ambivalence which, after all, refers to object relations – that is to say, to whole and real objects – sets in. Ambivalence, carried out in a splitting of the imagos, enables the small child to gain more trust and belief in its real objects and thus in its internalized ones – to love them more and to carry out in an increasing degree its phantasies of restoration on the loved object. At the same time the paranoid anxieties and defences are directed towards the 'bad' objects. The support which the ego gets from a real 'good' object is increased by a flight mechanism, which alternates between its external and internal good objects.

It seems that at this stage of development the unification of external and internal, loved and hated, real and imaginary objects is carried out in such a way that each step in the unification leads again to a renewed splitting of the imagos. But as the adaptation to the external world increases, this splitting is carried out on planes which gradually become increasingly nearer and nearer to reality. This goes on until love for the real and the internalized objects and trust in them are well established. Then ambivalence, which is partly a safeguard against one's own hate and against the hated and terrifying objects, will in normal development again diminish in varying degrees.

Along with the increase in love for one's good and real objects goes a greater trust in one's capacity to love and a lessening of the paranoid anxiety of the bad objects – changes which lead to a decrease of sadism and again to better ways of mastering aggression and working it off. The reparation tendencies which play an all-important part in the normal process of overcoming the infantile depressive position are set going by different methods, of which I shall just mention two fundamental ones: the manic and the obsessional positions and mechanisms.

It would appear that the step from the introjection of part-objects to whole loved objects with all its implications is of the most crucial importance in development. Its success – it is true – depends largely on how the ego has been able to deal with its sadism and its anxiety in the preceding stage of development and whether or not it has developed a strong libidinal relation to part-objects. But once the ego has made this step it has, as it were, arrived at a crossroad from which the ways determining the whole mental make-up radiate in different directions.

I have already considered at some length how a failure to maintain the identification with both internalized and real loved objects may result in the psychotic disorders of the depressive states, or of mania, or of paranoia.

I shall now mention one or two other ways by which the ego attempts to make an end to all the sufferings which are connected with the depressive position, namely: (*a*) by a 'flight to the "good", internalized object', a mechanism to which Melitta Schmideberg has drawn attention in connection with schizophrenia.[24] The ego has introjected a whole loved object, but owing to its immoderate dread of internalized persecutors, which are projected on to the external world, the ego takes refuge in an extravagant belief in the benevolence of his internalized objects. The result of such a flight may be denial of psychic and external reality and the deepest psychosis.

(*b*) By a flight to external 'good' objects as a means to disprove all anxieties – internal as well as external. This is a mechanism which is characteristic for neurosis and may lead to a slavish dependence on objects and to a weakness of the ego.

These defence mechanisms, as I pointed out before, play their part in the normal working-through of the infantile depressive position. Failure to work successfully through this position may lead to predominance of one or another of the flight mechanisms referred to and thus to a severe psychosis or a neurosis.

I have emphasized in this paper that, in my view, the infantile depressive position is the central position in the child's development. The normal development of the child and its capacity for love would seem to rest largely on how the ego works through this nodal position. This again depends on the modification undergone by the earliest mechanisms (which remain at work in the normal person also) in accordance with the changes in the ego's relations to its objects, and especially on a successful interplay between the depressive, the manic and the obsessional positions and mechanisms.

CHAPTER SEVEN

'Mourning and Its Relation to Manic-Depressive States' can be read almost as a sequel to the previous essay. In 1934, Klein's eldest son had been killed in a climbing accident. In childhood, Klein had suffered some severe bereavements – a sister and then a brother. Now, too, she experienced another kind of loss – the harsh desertion of her daughter from her group of supporters. It is as though the personal experience of terrible loss confirmed all Klein's observations of the development of her child patients.

In 'Mourning and Its Relation to Manic-Depressive States', Melanie Klein links mourning as it occurs at any age with a normal infantile developmental position – the depressive position.

Although, as is often the case, Klein embeds her theoretical development in Freud's seminal essay 'Mourning and Melancholia' (SE, Vol. XIV), in fact the terrain she explores is somewhat different. Freud stresses the severance of the subject's ego from the dead, loved object; Klein emphasizes the complexity of the inner world in which eventually the dead person is restored as a good object within. To show how this is achieved, she traces the interplay of destructive and reparative, aggressive and loving feelings towards the object and the need for the mourner to re-live the constant threat of the loss of the mother in infancy. There is the need to know that the good mother and the good feelings towards her have survived the bad ones and, in phantasy, can do so again in the crisis of a present death.

Melanie Klein read 'Mourning and Its Relation to the Manic-Depressive States' at the International Congress in Paris in the summer of 1938 and to the British Society in the autumn. She expanded and revised the essay for a special edition of the *International Journal of Psycho-Analysis* issued as a tribute to Ernest Jones on his sixtieth birthday (*Int. J. Psycho-Anal.*, Vol. XX, Pts 3 and 4, 1939).

MOURNING AND ITS RELATION TO
MANIC-DEPRESSIVE STATES
(1940)

An essential part of the work of mourning is, as Freud points out in 'Mourning and Melancholia', the testing of reality. He says that 'in grief this period of time is necessary for detailed carrying out of the behest imposed by the testing of reality, and . . . by accomplishing this labour the ego succeeds in freeing its libido from the lost object'.[1] And again: 'Each single one of the memories and hopes which bound the libido to the object is brought up and hyper-cathected, and the detachment of the libido from it accomplished. Why this process of carrying out the behest of reality bit by bit, which is in the nature of a compromise, should be so extraordinarily painful is not at all easy to explain in terms of mental economics. It is worth noting that this pain seems natural to us.'[2] And, in another passage: 'We do not even know by what economic measures the work of mourning is carried through; possibly, however, a conjecture may help us here. Reality passes its verdict – that the object no longer exists – upon each single one of the memories and hopes through which the libido was attached to the lost object, and the ego, confronted as it were with the decision whether it will share this fate, is persuaded by the sum of its narcissistic satisfactions in being alive to sever its attachment to the non-existent object. We may imagine that, because of the slowness and the gradual way in which this severance is achieved, the expenditure of energy necessary for it becomes somehow dissipated by the time the task is carried through.'[3]

In my view there is a close connection between the testing of reality in normal mourning and early processes of the mind. My contention is that the child goes through states of mind comparable to the mourning of the adult, or rather, that this early mourning is revived whenever grief is experienced in later life. The most important of the methods by which the child overcomes his states of mourning, is, in my view, the testing of reality; this process, however, as Freud stresses, is part of the work of mourning.

In my paper 'A Contribution to the Psychogenesis of Manic-Depressive States',[4] I introduced the conception of the *infantile depressive position*, and showed the connection between that position and manic-depressive states. Now in order to make clear the relation between the infantile depressive position and normal mourning I must first briefly refer to some statements I made in that paper, and shall then enlarge on them. In the course of this exposition I also hope to make a contribution to the further understanding of the connection between normal mourning, on the one hand, and abnormal mourning and manic-depressive states, on the other.

I said there that the baby experiences depressive feelings which reach a climax just before, during and after weaning. This is the state of mind in the baby which I termed the 'depressive position', and I suggested that it is a melancholia in *statu nascendi*. The object which is being mourned is the mother's breast and all that the breast and the milk have come to stand for in the infant's mind: namely, love, goodness and security. All these are felt by the baby to be lost, and lost as a result of his own uncontrollable greedy and destructive phantasies and impulses against his mother's breasts. Further distress about impending loss (this time of both parents) arises out of the Oedipus situation, which sets in so early and in such close connection with breast frustrations that in its beginnings it is dominated by oral impulses and fears. The circle of loved objects who are attacked in phantasy and whose loss is therefore feared widens owing to the child's ambivalent relations to his brothers and sisters. The aggression against phantasied brothers and sisters, who are attacked inside the mother's body, also gives rise to feelings of guilt and loss. The sorrow and concern about the feared loss of the 'good' objects, that is to say, the depressive position, is, in my experience, the deepest source of the painful conflicts in the Oedipus situation, as well as in the child's relations to people in general. In normal development these feelings of grief and fears are overcome by various methods.

Along with the child's relation, first to his mother and soon to his father and other people, go those processes of internalization on which I have laid so much stress in my work. The baby, having incorporated his parents, feels them to be live people inside his body in the concrete way in which deep unconscious phantasies are experienced – they are, in his mind, 'internal' or 'inner' objects, as I have termed them. Thus an inner world is being built up in the child's unconscious mind, corresponding to his actual experiences and the impression he gains from people and the external world, and yet altered by his own phantasies and impulses. If it is a world of people predominantly at peace with each other and with the ego, inner harmony, security and integration ensue.

There is a constant interaction between anxieties relating to the 'external' mother – as I will call her here in contrast to the 'internal' one – and those relating to the 'internal' mother, and the methods used by the ego for dealing with these two sets of anxieties are closely inter-related. In the baby's mind, the 'internal' mother is bound up with the 'external' one, of whom she is a 'double', though one which at once undergoes alterations in his mind through the very process of internalization; that is to say, her image is influenced by his phantasies, and by internal stimuli and internal experiences of all kinds. When external situations which he lives through become internalized – and I hold that they do, from the earliest days onwards – they follow the same pattern: they also become 'doubles' of real situations, and are again altered for the same reasons. The fact that by being internalized, people, things, situations and happenings – the whole inner world which is being built up – become inaccessible to the child's accurate observation and judgement, and cannot be verified by the means of perception which are available in connection with the tangible and palpable object-world, has an important bearing on the phantastic nature of this inner world. The ensuing doubts, uncertainties and anxieties act as a continuous incentive to the young child to observe and make sure about the external object-world,[5] from which this inner world springs, and by these means to understand the internal one better. The visible mother thus provides continuous proofs of what the 'internal' mother is like, whether she is loving or angry, helpful or revengeful. The extent to which external reality is able to disprove anxieties and sorrow relating to the internal reality varies with each individual, but could be taken as one of the criteria for normality. In children who are so much dominated by their internal world that their anxieties cannot be sufficiently disproved and counteracted even by the pleasant aspects of their relationships with people, severe mental difficulties are unavoidable. On the other hand, a certain amount even of unpleasant experiences is of value in this testing of reality by the child if, through overcoming them, he feels that he can retain his objects as well as their love for him and his love for them, and thus preserve or re-establish internal life and harmony in face of dangers.

All the enjoyments which the baby lives through in relation to his mother are so many proofs to him that the loved object *inside as well as outside* is not injured, is not turned into a vengeful person. The increase of love and trust, and the diminishing of fears through happy experiences, help the baby step by step to overcome his depression and feeling of loss (mourning). They enable him to test his inner reality by means of outer reality. Through being loved and through the enjoyment and comfort he has in relation to people his confidence in his own as well as in other people's goodness becomes strengthened, his hope that his 'good' objects and his own ego can be saved and preserved increases, at the same time as his ambivalence and acute fears of internal destruction diminish.

Unpleasant experiences and the lack of enjoyable ones, in the young child, especially lack of happy and close contact with loved people, increase ambivalence, diminish trust and hope and confirm anxieties about inner annihilation and external persecution; moreover they slow down and perhaps permanently check the beneficial processes through which in the long run inner security is achieved.

In the process of acquiring knowledge, every new piece of experience has to be fitted into the patterns provided by the psychic reality which prevails at the time; whilst the psychic reality of the child is gradually influenced by every step in his progressive knowledge of external reality. Every such step goes along with his more and more firmly establishing his inner 'good' objects, and is used by the ego as a means of overcoming the depressive position.

In other connections I have expressed the view that every infant experiences anxieties which are psychotic in content,[6] and that the infantile neurosis[7] is the normal means of dealing with and modifying these anxieties. This conclusion I can now state more precisely, as a result of my work on the infantile depressive position, which has led me to believe that it is the central position in the child's development. In the infantile neurosis the early depressive position finds expression, is worked through and gradually overcome; and this is an important part of the process of organization and integration which, together with his sexual development,[8] characterizes the first years of life. Normally the child passes through his infantile neurosis, and among other achievements arrives step by step at a good relation to people and to reality. I hold that this satisfactory relation to people depends upon his having succeeded in his struggles against the chaos inside him (the depressive position) and having securely established his 'good' internal objects.

Let us now consider more closely the methods and mechanisms by which this development comes about.

In the baby, processes of introjection and projection, since they are dominated by aggression and anxieties which reinforce each other, lead to fears of persecution by terrifying objects. To such fears are added those of losing his loved objects; that is to say, the depressive position has arisen. When I first introduced the conception of the depressive position I put forward the suggestion that the introjection of the whole loved object gives rise to concern and sorrow lest that object should be destroyed (by the 'bad' objects and the id), and that these distressed feelings and fears, in addition to the paranoid set of fears and defences, constitute the depressive position. There are thus two sets of fears, feelings and defences, which, however varied in themselves and however intimately linked together, can in my view, for purposes of theoretical clearness, be isolated from each other. The first set of feelings and phantasies are the persecutory ones, characterized by fears relating to the destruction of the ego by internal persecutors. The defences against these fears are predominantly the destruction of the persecutors by violent or secretive and cunning methods. With these fears and defences I have dealt in detail in other contexts. The second set of feelings which go to make up the depressive position I formerly described without suggesting a term for them. I now propose to use for these feelings of sorrow and concern for the loved objects, the fears of losing them and the longing to regain them, a simple word derived from everyday language – namely the 'pining' for the loved object. In short – persecution (by 'bad' objects) and the characteristic defences against it, on the one hand, and pining for the loved ('good') object, on the other, constitute the depressive position.

When the depressive position arises, the ego is forced (in addition to earlier defences) to develop methods of defence which are essentially directed against the 'pining' for the loved object. These are fundamental to the whole ego organization. I formerly termed some of these methods *manic defences*, or the *manic position*, because of their relationship to the manic-depressive illness.[9]

The fluctuations between the depressive and the manic position are an essential part of normal development. The ego is driven by depressive anxieties (anxiety lest the loved objects as well as itself should be destroyed) to build up omnipotent and violent phantasies, partly for the purpose of controlling and mastering the 'bad', dangerous objects, partly in order to save and restore the loved ones. From the very beginning, these omnipotent phantasies, both the destructive and the reparative ones, stimulate and enter into all the activities, interests and sublimations of the child. In the infant, the extreme character both of his sadistic and of his constructive phantasies is in line with the extreme frightfulness of his persecutors – and, at the other end of the scale, the extreme perfection of his 'good' objects.[10] Idealization is an essential part of the manic position and is bound up with another important element of that position, namely denial. Without partial and temporary denial of psychic reality the ego cannot bear the disaster by which it feels itself threatened when the depressive position is at its height. Omnipotence, denial and idealization, closely bound up with ambivalence, enable the early ego to assert itself to a certain degree against its internal persecutors and against a slavish and perilous dependence upon its loved objects, and thus to make further advances in development. I will here quote a passage from my former paper:

In the earliest phase the persecuting and the good objects (breasts) are kept wide apart in the child's mind. When, along with the introjection of the whole and real object, they come closer together, the ego has over and over again recourse to that mechanism – so important for the development of the relations to objects – namely, a splitting of its imagos into loved and hated, that is to say, into good and dangerous ones.

One might think that it is actually at this point that ambivalence which, after all, refers to object relations – that is to say, to whole and real objects – sets in. Ambivalence, carried out in a splitting of the imagos, enables the small child to gain more trust and belief in its real objects and thus in its internalized ones – to love them more and to carry out in an increasing degree its phantasies of restoration on the loved object. At the same time the paranoid anxieties and defences are directed towards the 'bad' objects. The support which the ego gets from a real 'good' object is increased by a flight mechanism, which alternates between its external and internal good objects. [Idealization.]

It seems that at this stage of development the unification of external and internal, loved and hated, real and imaginary objects is carried out in such a way that each step in the unification leads again to a renewed splitting of the imagos. But as the adaptation to the external world increases, this splitting is carried out on planes which gradually become increasingly nearer and nearer to reality. This goes on until love for the real and the internalized objects and trust in them are well established. Then ambivalence, which is partly a safeguard against one's own hate and against the hated and terrifying objects, will in normal development again diminish in varying degrees.[11]

As has already been stated, omnipotence prevails in the early phantasies, both the destructive and the reparative ones, and influences sublimations as well as object relations. Omnipotence, however, is so closely bound up in the unconscious with the sadistic impulses with which it was first associated that the child feels again and again that his attempts at reparation have not succeeded, or will not succeed. His sadistic impulses, he feels, may easily get the better of him. The young child, who cannot sufficiently trust his reparative and constructive feelings, as we have seen, resorts to manic omnipotence. For this reason, in an early stage of development the ego has not adequate means at its disposal to deal sufficiently with guilt and anxiety. All this leads to the need in the child – and for that matter to some extent in the adult also – to repeat certain actions obsessionally (this, in my view, is part of the repetition compulsion);[12] or – the contrasting method – omnipotence and denial are resorted to. When the defences of a manic nature fail, defences in which dangers from various sources are in an omnipotent way denied or minimized, the ego is driven alternately or simultaneously, to combat the fears of deterioration and disintegration by attempted reparations carried out in obsessional ways. I have described elsewhere[13] my conclusion that the obsessional mechanisms are a defence against paranoid anxieties as well as a means of modifying them, and here I will only show briefly the connection between obsessional mechanisms and manic defences in relation to the depressive position in normal development.

The very fact that manic defences are operating in such close connection with the obsessional ones contributes to the ego's fear that the reparation attempted by obsessional means has also failed. The desire to control the object, the sadistic gratification of overcoming and humiliating it, of getting the better of it, the *triumph* over it, may enter so strongly into the act of reparation (carried out by thoughts, activities or sublimations) that the benign circle started by this act becomes broken. The objects which were to be restored change again into persecutors, and in turn paranoid fears are revived. These fears reinforce the paranoid defence mechanisms (of destroying the object) as well as the manic mechanisms (of controlling it or keeping it in suspended animation, and so on). The reparation which was in progress is thus disturbed or even nullified – according to the extent to which these mechanisms are activated. As a result of the failure of the act of reparation, the ego has to resort again and again to obsessional and manic defences.

When in the course of normal development a relative balance between love and hate is attained, and the various aspects of objects are more unified, then also a certain equilibrium between these contrasting and yet closely related methods is reached, and their intensity is diminished. In this connection I wish to stress the importance of *triumph*, closely bound up with contempt and omnipotence, as an element of the manic position. We know the part rivalry plays in the child's burning desire to equal the achievement of the grown-ups. In addition to rivalry, his wish, mingled with fears, to 'grow out' of his deficiencies (ultimately to overcome his destructiveness and his bad inner objects and to be able to control them) is an incentive to achievements of all kinds. In my experience, the desire to reverse the child–parent relation, to get power over the parents and to triumph over them, is always to some extent associated with the impulse towards the attainment of success. A time will come, the child phantasies, when he will be strong, tall and grown up, powerful, rich and potent, and father and mother will have changed into helpless children, or again, in other phantasies, will be very old, weak, poor and rejected. The triumph over the parents in such phantasies, through the guilt to which it gives rise, often cripples endeavours of all kinds. Some people are obliged to remain unsuccessful, because success always implies to them the humiliation or even the damage of somebody else, in the first place the triumph over parents, brothers and sisters. The efforts by which they seek to achieve something may be of a highly constructive nature, but the implicit triumph and the ensuing harm and injury done to the object may outweigh these purposes, in the subject's mind, and therefore prevent their fulfilment. The effect is that the reparation to the loved objects, which in the depths of the mind are the same as those over which he triumphs, is again thwarted, and therefore guilt remains unrelieved. The subject's triumph over his objects necessarily implies to him their wish to triumph over him, and therefore leads to distrust and feelings of persecution. Depression may follow, or an increase in manic defences and more violent control of his objects, since he has failed to reconcile, restore or improve them, and therefore feelings of being persecuted by them again have the upper hand. All this has an important bearing on the infantile depressive position and the ego's success or failure in overcoming it. The triumph over his internal objects which the young child's ego controls, humiliates and tortures is a part of the destructive aspect of the manic position which disturbs the reparation and re-creating of his inner world and of internal peace and harmony; and thus triumph impedes the work of early mourning.

To illustrate these developmental processes let us consider some features which can be observed in hypomanic people. It is characteristic of the hypomanic person's attitude towards people, principles and events that he is inclined to exaggerated valuations: over-admiration (idealization) or contempt (devaluation). With this goes his tendency to conceive of everything on a large scale, to think in *large numbers*, all this in accordance with the greatness of his omnipotence, by which he defends himself against his fear of losing the one irreplaceable object, his mother, whom he still mourns at bottom. His tendency to minimize the importance of details and small numbers, and a frequent casualness about details and contempt of conscientiousness contrast sharply with the very meticulous methods, the concentration on the smallest things (Freud), which are part of the obsessional mechanisms.

This contempt, however, is also based to some extent on denial. He must deny his impulse to make extensive and detailed reparation because he has to deny the cause for the reparation, namely the injury to the object and his consequent sorrow and guilt.

Returning to the course of early development, we may say that every step in emotional, intellectual and physical growth is used by the ego as a means of overcoming the depressive position. The child's growing skills, gifts and arts increase his belief in the psychical reality of his constructive tendencies, in his capacity to master and control his hostile impulses as well as his 'bad' internal objects. Thus anxieties from various sources are relieved, and this results in a diminution of aggression and, in turn, of his suspicions of 'bad' external and internal objects. The strengthened ego, with its greater trust in people, can then make still further steps towards unification of its imagos – external, internal, loved and hated – and towards further mitigation of hatred by means of love, and thus to a general process of integration.

When the child's belief and trust in his capacity to love, in his reparative powers and in the integration and security of his good inner world increase as a result of the constant and manifold proofs and counter-proofs gained by the testing of external reality, manic omnipotence decreases and the obsessional nature of the impulses towards reparation diminishes, which means in general that the infantile neurosis has passed.

We have now to connect the infantile depressive position with normal mourning. The poignancy of the actual loss of a loved person is, in my view, greatly increased by the mourner's unconscious phantasies of having lost his *internal* 'good' objects as well. He then feels that his internal 'bad' objects predominate and his inner world is in danger of disruption. We know that the loss of a loved person leads to an impulse in the mourner to reinstate the lost loved object in the ego. (Freud and Abraham.) In my view, however, he not only takes into himself (re-incorporates) the person whom he has just lost, but also reinstates his internalized good objects (ultimately his loved parents), who became part of his inner world from the earliest stages of his development onwards. These too are felt to have gone under, to be destroyed, whenever the loss of a loved person is experienced. Thereupon the early depressive position, and with it anxieties, guilt and feelings of loss and grief derived from the breast situation, the Oedipus situation and all other such sources, are reactivated. Among all these emotions, the fears of being robbed and punished by both dreaded parents – that is to say, feelings of persecution – have also been revived in deep layers of the mind.

If, for instance, a woman loses her child through death, along with sorrow and pain, her early dread of being robbed by a 'bad' retaliating mother is reactivated and confirmed. Her own early aggressive phantasies of robbing her mother of babies gave rise to fears and feelings of being punished, which strengthened ambivalence and led to hatred and distrust of others. The reinforcing of feelings of persecution in the state of mourning is all the more painful because, as a result of an increase in ambivalence and distrust, friendly relations with people, which might at that time be so helpful, become impeded.

The pain experienced in the slow process of testing reality in the work of mourning thus seems to be partly due to the necessity, not only to renew the links to the external world and thus continuously to re-experience the loss, but at the same time and by means of this to rebuild with anguish the inner world, which is felt to be in danger of deteriorating and collapsing.[14] Just as the young child passing through the depressive position is struggling, in his unconscious mind, with the task of establishing and integrating his inner world, so the mourner goes through the pain of re-establishing and re-integrating it.

In normal mourning early psychotic anxieties are reactivated; the mourner is in fact ill, but, because this state of mind is so common and seems so natural to us, we do not call mourning an illness. (For similar reasons, until recent years, the infantile neurosis of the normal child was not recognized as such.) To put my conclusions more precisely: I should say that in mourning the subject goes through a modified and transitory manic-depressive state and over-comes it, thus repeating, though in different circumstances and with different manifestations, the processes which the child normally goes through in his early development.

The greatest danger for the mourner comes from the turning of his hatred against the lost loved person himself. One of the ways in which hatred expresses itself in the situation of mourning is in feelings of triumph over the dead person. I refer in an earlier part of this paper to triumph as part of the manic position in infantile development. Infantile death wishes against parents, brothers and sisters are actually fulfilled whenever a loved person dies, because he is necessarily to some extent a representative of the earliest important figures, and therefore takes over some of the feelings pertaining to them. Thus his death, however shattering for other reasons, is to some extent also felt as a victory, and gives rise to triumph, and therefore all the more to guilt.

At this point I find that my view differs from that of Freud, who stated: 'First, then: in normal grief too the loss of the object is undoubtedly surmounted, and this process too absorbs all the energies of the ego while it lasts. Why then does it not set up the economic condition for a phase of triumph after it has run its course or at least produce some slight indication of such a state? I find it impossible to answer this objection off-hand.'[15] In my experience, feelings of triumph are inevitably bound up even with normal mourning, and have the effect of retarding the work of mourning, or rather they contribute much to the difficulties and pain which the mourner experiences. When hatred of the lost loved object in its various manifestations gets the upper hand in the mourner, this not only turns the loved lost person into a persecutor, but shakes the mourner's belief in his good inner objects as well. The shaken belief in the good objects disturbs most painfully the process of idealization, which is an essential intermediate step in mental development. With the young child, the idealized mother is the safeguard against a retaliating or a dead mother and against all bad objects, and therefore represents security and life itself. As we know, the mourner obtains great relief from recalling the lost person's kindness and good qualities, and this is partly due to the reassurance he experiences from keeping his loved object for the time being as an idealized one.

The passing states of elation[16] which occur between sorrow and distress in normal mourning are manic in character and are due to the feeling of possessing the perfect loved object (idealized) inside. At any time, however, when hatred against the loved person wells up in the mourner, his belief in him breaks down and the process of idealization is disturbed. (His hatred of the loved person is increased by the fear that by dying the loved one was seeking to inflict punishment and deprivation upon him, just as in the past he felt that his mother, whenever she was away from him and he wanted her, had died in order to inflict punishment and deprivation upon him.) Only gradually, by regaining trust in external objects and values of various kinds, is the normal mourner able once more to strengthen his confidence in the lost loved persons. Then he can again bear to realize that this object was not perfect, and yet not lose trust and love for him, nor fear his revenge. When this stage is reached, important steps in the work of mourning and towards overcoming it have been made.

To illustrate the ways in which a normal mourner re-established connections with the external world I shall now give an instance. Mrs A., in the first few days after the shattering loss of her young son, who had died suddenly while at school, took to sorting out letters, keeping his and throwing others away. She was thus unconsciously attempting to restore him and keep him safe inside herself, and throwing out what she felt to be indifferent, or rather hostile – that is to say, the 'bad' objects, dangerous excreta and bad feelings.

Some people in mourning tidy the house and rearrange furniture, actions which spring from an increase of the obsessional mechanisms which are a repetition of one of the defences used to combat the infantile depressive position.

In the first week after the death of her son she did not cry much, and tears did not bring her the relief which they did later on. She felt numbed and closed up, and physically broken. It gave her some relief, however, to see one or two intimate people. At this stage Mrs A., who usually dreamed every night, had entirely stopped dreaming because of her deep unconscious denial of her actual loss. At the end of the week she had the following dream:

She saw two people, a mother and son. The mother was wearing a black dress. The dreamer knew that this boy had died, or was going to die. No sorrow entered into her feelings, but there was a trace of hostility towards the two people.

The associations brought up an important memory. When Mrs A. was a little girl, her brother, who had difficulties in his school work, was going to be tutored by a school-fellow of his own age (I will call him B.). B.'s mother had come to see Mrs A.'s mother to arrange about the coaching, and Mrs A. remembered this incident with very strong feelings. B.'s mother behaved in a patronizing way, and her own mother appeared to her to be rather dejected. She herself felt that a fearful disgrace had fallen upon her very much admired and beloved brother and the whole family. This brother, a few years older than herself, seemed to her full of knowledge, skill and strength – a paragon of all the virtues, and her ideal was shattered when his deficiencies at school came to light. The strength of her feelings about this incident as being an irreparable misfortune, which persisted in her memory, was, however, due to her unconscious feelings of guilt. She felt it to be the fulfilment of her own harmful wishes. Her brother himself was very much chagrined by the situation, and expressed great dislike and hatred of the other boy. Mrs A. at the time identified herself strongly with him in these resentful feelings. In the dream, the two people whom Mrs A. saw were B. and his mother, and the fact that the boy was dead expressed Mrs A.'s early death wishes against him. At the same time, however, the death wishes against her own brother and the wish to inflict punishment and deprivation upon her mother through the loss of her son – very deeply repressed wishes – were part of her dream thoughts. It now appeared that Mrs A., with all her admiration and love for her brother, had been jealous of him on various grounds, envying his greater knowledge, his mental and physical superiority, and also his possession of a penis. Her jealousy of her much beloved mother for possessing such a son had contributed towards her death wishes against her brother. One dream thought, therefore, ran: 'A mother's son has died, or will die. It is this unpleasant woman's son, who hurt my mother and brother, who should die.' But in deeper layers, the death wish against her brother had also been reactivated, and this dream thought ran: 'My mother's son died, and not my own.' (Both her mother and her brother were in fact already dead.) Here a contrasting feeling came in – sympathy with her mother and sorrow for herself. She felt: 'One death of the kind was enough. My mother lost her son; she should not lose her grandson also.' When her brother died, besides great sorrow, she unconsciously felt triumph over him, derived from her early jealousy and hatred, and corresponding feelings of guilt. She had carried over some of her feelings for her brother into her relation to her son. In her son, she also loved her brother; but at the same time, some of the ambivalence towards her brother, though modified through her strong motherly feelings, was also transferred on to her son. The mourning for her brother, together with the sorrow, the triumph and the guilt experienced in relation to him, entered into her present grief, and was shown in the dream.

Let us now consider the interplay of defences as they appeared in this material. When the loss occurred, the manic position became reinforced, and denial in particular came especially into play. Unconsciously, Mrs A. strongly rejected the fact that her son had died. When she could no longer carry on this denial so strongly, but was not yet able to face the pain and sorrow, triumph, one of the other elements of the manic position, became reinforced. 'It is not at all painful,' the thought seemed to run, as the associations showed, 'if *a* boy dies. It is even satisfactory. Now I get my revenge against this unpleasant boy who injured my brother.' The fact that triumph over her brother had also been revived and strengthened became clear only after hard analytic work. But this triumph was associated with control of the *internalized* mother and brother, and triumph over them. At this stage the *control* over her internal objects was reinforced, the misfortune and grief were *displaced* from herself on to her internalized mother. Here denial again came into play – denial of the psychical reality that she and her internal mother were one and suffered together. Compassion and love for the internal mother were denied, feelings of revenge and triumph over the internalized objects and control of them were reinforced, partly because, through her own revengeful feelings, they had turned into persecuting figures.

In the dream there was only one slight hint of Mrs A.'s growing unconscious knowledge (indicating that the denial was lessening) that it was she *herself* who lost her son. On the day preceding the dream she was wearing a black dress with a white collar. The woman in the dream had something white around her neck on her black dress.

Two nights after this dream she dreamt again:

She was flying with her son, and he disappeared. She felt that this meant his death – that he was drowned. She felt as if, she, too, were to be drowned – but then she made an effort and drew away from the danger, back to life.

The associations showed that in the dream she had decided that she would not die with her son, but would survive. It appeared that even in the dream, she felt that it was good to be alive and bad to be dead. In this dream the unconscious knowledge of her loss is much more accepted than in the one of two days earlier. Sorrow and guilt had drawn closer. The feeling of triumph had apparently gone, but it became clear that it had only diminished. It was still present in her satisfaction about remaining alive – in contrast to her son's being dead. The feelings of guilt which already made themselves felt were partly due to this element of triumph.

I am reminded here of a passage in Freud's 'Mourning and Melancholia':[17] 'Reality passes its verdict – that the object no longer exists – upon each single one of the memories and hopes through which the libido was attached to the lost object, and the ego, confronted as it were with the decision whether it will share this fate, is persuaded by the sum of its narcissistic satisfactions in being alive to sever its attachment to the non-existent object.' In my view, this 'narcissistic satisfaction' contains in a milder way the element of triumph which Freud seemed to think does not enter into normal mourning.

In the second week of her mourning Mrs A. found some comfort in looking at nicely situated houses in the country, and in wishing to have such a house of her own. But this comfort was soon interrupted by bouts of despair and sorrow. She now cried abundantly, and found relief in tears. The solace she found in looking at houses came from her rebuilding her inner world in her phantasy by means of this interest and also getting satisfaction from the knowledge that other people's houses and good objects existed. Ultimately this stood for re-creating her good parents, internally and externally, unifying them and making them happy and creative. In her mind she made reparation to her parents for having, in phantasy, killed their children, and by this she anticipated their wrath. Thus her fear that the death of her son was a punishment inflicted on her by retaliating parents lost in strength, and also the feeling that her son frustrated and punished her by his death was lessened. The diminution of hatred and fear all round allowed the sorrow itself to come out in full strength. Increase of distrust and fears had intensified her feeling of being persecuted and mastered by her internal objects and strengthened her need to master them. All this had expressed itself by a hardening in her internal relationships and feelings – that is to say, in an increase in manic defences. (This was shown in the first dream.) If these again diminish through the strengthening of the subject's belief in goodness – his own and others' – and fears decrease, the mourner is able to surrender to his own feelings, and to cry out his sorrow about the actual loss.

It seems that the processes of projecting and ejecting, which are closely connected with giving vent to feelings, are held up in certain stages of grief by an extensive manic control, and can again operate more freely when that control relaxes. Through tears, which in the unconscious mind are equated to excrement, the mourner not only expresses his feelings and thus eases tension, but also expels his 'bad' feelings and his 'bad' objects, and this adds to the relief obtained through crying. This greater freedom in the inner world implies that the internalized objects, being less controlled by the ego, are also allowed more freedom: that these objects themselves are allowed, in particular, greater freedom of feeling. In the mourner's situation, the feelings of his internalized objects are also sorrowful. In his mind, they share his grief, in the same way as actual kind parents would. The poet tells us that 'Nature mourns with the mourner.' I believe that 'Nature' in this connection represents the internal good mother. This experience of mutual sorrow and sympathy in internal relationships, however, is again bound up with external ones. As I have already stated, Mrs A.'s greater trust in actual people and things and help received from the external world contributed to a relaxing of the manic control over her inner world. Thus introjection (as well as projection) could operate still more freely, more goodness and love could be taken in from without, and goodness and love increasingly experienced within. Mrs A., who at an earlier stage of her mourning had to some extent felt that her loss was inflicted on her by revengeful parents, could now in phantasy experience the sympathy of these parents (dead long since), their desire to support and to help her. She felt that they also suffered a severe loss and shared her grief, as they would have done had they lived. In her internal world harshness and suspicion had diminished, and sorrow had increased. The tears which she shed were also to some extent the tears which her internal parents shed, and she also wanted to comfort them as they – in her phantasy – comforted her.

If greater security in the inner world is gradually regained, and feelings and inner objects are therefore allowed to come more to life again, re-creative processes can set in and hope return.

As we have seen, this change is due to certain movements in the two sets of feelings which make up the depressive position: persecution decreases and the pining for the lost loved object is experienced in full force. To put it in other words: hatred has receded and love is freed. It is inherent in the feeling of persecution that it is fed by hatred and at the same time feeds hatred. Furthermore, the feeling of being persecuted and watched by internal 'bad' objects, with the consequent necessity for constantly watching them, leads to a kind of dependence which reinforces the manic defences. These defences, in so far as they are used predominantly against persecutory feelings (and not so much against the pining for the loved object), are of a very sadistic and forceful nature. When persecution diminishes, the hostile dependence on the object, together with hatred, also diminishes, and the manic defences relax. The pining for the lost loved object also implies dependence on it, but dependence of a kind which becomes an incentive to reparation and preservation of the object. It is creative because it is dominated by love, while the dependence based on persecution and hatred is sterile and destructive.

Thus, while grief is experienced to the full and despair is at its height, the love for the object wells up and the mourner feels more strongly that life inside and outside will go on after all, and that the lost loved object can be preserved within. At this stage in mourning, suffering can become productive. We know that painful experiences of all kinds sometimes stimulate sublimations, or even bring out quite new gifts in some people, who may take to painting, writing or other productive activities under the stress of frustrations and hardships. Others become more productive in a different way – more capable of appreciating people and things, more tolerant in their relation to others – they become wiser. Such enrichment is in my view gained through processes similar to those steps in mourning which we have just investigated. That is to say, any pain caused by unhappy experiences, whatever their nature, has something in common with mourning. It reactivates the infantile depressive position, and encountering and overcoming adversity of any kind entails mental work similar to mourning.

It seems that every advance in the process of mourning results in a deepening in the individual's relation to his inner objects, in the happiness of regaining them after they were felt to be lost ('Paradise Lost and Regained'), in an increased trust in them and love for them because they proved to be good and helpful after all. This is similar to the way in which the young child step by step builds up his relations to external objects, for he gains trust not only from pleasant experiences, but also from the ways in which he overcomes frustrations and unpleasant experiences, nevertheless retaining his good objects (externally and internally). The phases in the work of mourning when manic defences relax and a renewal of life inside sets in, with a deepening in internal relationships, are comparable to the steps which in early development lead to greater independence from external as well as internal objects.

To return to Mrs A. Her relief in looking at pleasant houses was due to the setting in of some hope that she could re-create her son as well as her parents; life started again inside herself and in the outer world. At this time she could dream again and unconsciously begin to face her loss. She now felt a stronger wish to see friends again, but only one at a time and only for a short while. These feelings of greater comfort, however, again alternated with distress. (In mourning as well as in infantile development, inner security comes about not by a straightforward movement but in waves.) After a few weeks of mourning, for instance, Mrs A. went for a walk with a friend through the familiar streets, in an attempt to re-establish old bonds. She suddenly realized that the number of people in the street seemed overwhelming, the houses strange, and the sunshine artificial and unreal. She had to retreat into a quiet restaurant. But there she felt as if the ceiling were coming down, and the people in the place became vague and blurred. Her own house suddenly seemed the only secure place in the world. In analysis it became clear that the frightening indifference of these people was reflected from her internal objects, who in her mind had turned into a multitude of 'bad' persecuting objects. The external world was felt to be artificial and unreal, because real trust in inner goodness had gone.

Many mourners can only make slow steps in re-establishing the bonds with the external world because they are struggling against the chaos inside; for similar reasons the baby develops his trust in the object-world first in connection with a few loved people. No doubt other factors as well, e.g., his intellectual immaturity, are partly responsible for this gradual development in the baby's object relations, but I hold that this also is due to the chaotic state of his inner world.

One of the differences between the early depressive position and normal mourning is that when the baby loses the breast or bottle, which has come to represent to him a 'good', helpful, protective object inside him, and experiences grief, he does this in spite of his mother being there. With the grown-up person however the grief is brought about by the actual loss of an actual person; yet help comes to him against this overwhelming loss through his having established in his early life his 'good' mother inside himself. The young child, however, is at the height of his struggles with fears of losing her internally and externally, for he has not yet succeeded in establishing her securely inside himself. In this struggle, the child's relation to his mother, her actual presence, is of the greatest help. Similarly, if the mourner has people whom he loves and who share his grief, and if he can accept their sympathy, the restoration of the harmony in his inner world is promoted, and his fears and distress are more quickly reduced.

Having described some of the processes which I have observed at work in mourning and in depressive states, I wish now to link up my contribution with the work of Freud and Abraham.

Following Freud's and his own discoveries about the nature of the archaic processes at work in melancholia, Abraham found that such processes also operate in the work of normal mourning. He concluded that in this work the individual succeeds in establishing the lost loved person in his ego, while the melancholic has failed to do so. Abraham also described some of the fundamental factors upon which that success or failure depends.

My experience leads me to conclude that, while it is true that the characteristic feature of normal mourning is the individual's setting up the lost loved object inside himself, he is not doing so for the first time but, through the work of mourning, is reinstating that object as well as all his loved *internal* objects which he feels he has lost. He is therefore *recovering* what he had already attained in childhood.

In the course of his early development, as we know, he establishes his parents within his ego. (It was the understanding of the processes of introjection in melancholia and in normal mourning which, as we know, led Freud to recognize the existence of the super-ego in normal development.) But, as regards the nature of the super-ego and the history of its individual development, my conclusions differ from those of Freud. As I have often pointed out, the processes of introjection and projection from the beginning of life lead to the institution inside ourselves of loved and hated objects, who are felt to be 'good' and 'bad', and who are interrelated with each other, and with the self: that is to say, they constitute an inner world. This assembly of internalized objects becomes organized, together with the organization of the ego, and in the higher strata of the mind it becomes discernible as the super-ego. Thus, the phenomenon which was recognized by Freud, broadly speaking, as the voices and the influence of the actual parents established in the ego is, according to my findings, a complex object-world, which is felt by the individual, in deep layers of the unconscious, to be concretely inside himself, and for which I and some of my colleagues therefore use the term 'internalized', or an internal (inner) world. This inner world consists of innumerable objects taken into the ego, corresponding partly to the multitude of varying aspects, good and bad, in which the parents (and other people) appeared to the child's unconscious mind through-out various stages of his development. Further, they also represent all the real people who are continually becoming internalized in a variety of situations provided by the multitude of ever-changing external experiences as well as phantasied ones. In addition, all these objects are in the inner world in an infinitely complex relation both with each other and with the self.

If I now apply this conception of the super-ego organization as compared with Freud's super-ego to the process of mourning, the nature of my contribution to the understanding of this process becomes clear. In normal mourning the individual re-introjects and reinstates, as well as the actual lost person, his loved parents – who are felt to be his 'good' inner objects. His inner world, the one which he has built up from his earliest days onwards, in his phantasy was destroyed when the actual loss occurred. The rebuilding of this inner world characterizes the successful work of mourning.

An understanding of this complex inner world enables the analyst to find and resolve a variety of early anxiety situations which were formerly unknown, and is therefore theoretically and therapeutically of an importance so great that it cannot yet be fully estimated. I believe that the problem of mourning also can only be more fully understood by taking account of these early anxiety situations.

I shall now illustrate in connection with mourning one of these anxiety situations which I have found to be of crucial importance also in manic-depressive states. I refer to the anxiety about the internalized parents in destructive sexual intercourse; they as well as the self are felt to be in constant danger of violent destruction. In the following material I shall give extracts from a few dreams of a patient, D., a man in his early forties, with strong paranoid and depressive traits. I am not going into details about the case as a whole: but am here concerned only to show the ways in which these particular fears and phantasies were stirred in this patient by the death of his mother. She had been in failing health for some time, and was, at the time to which I refer, more or less unconscious.

One day in analysis, D. spoke of his mother with hatred and bitterness, accusing her of having made his father unhappy. He also referred to a case of suicide and one of madness which had occurred in his mother's family. His mother, he said, had been 'muddled' for some time. Twice he applied the term 'muddled' to himself and then said: 'I know you are going to drive me mad and then lock me up.' He spoke about an animal being locked up in a cage. I interpreted that his mad relative and his muddled mother were now felt to be inside himself, and that the fear of being locked up in a cage partly implied his deeper fear of containing these mad people inside himself and thus of going mad himself. He then told me a dream of the previous night:

He saw a bull lying in a farmyard. It was not quite dead, and looked very uncanny and dangerous. He was standing on one side of the bull, his mother on the other. He escaped into a house, feeling that he was leaving his mother behind in danger and that he should not do so; but he vaguely hoped that she would go away.

To his own astonishment, my patient's first association to the dream was of the blackbirds which had disturbed him very much by waking him up that morning. He then spoke of buffaloes in America, the country where he was born. He had always been interested in them and attracted by them when he saw them. He now said that one could shoot them and use them for food, but that they are dying out and should be preserved. Then he mentioned the story of a man who had been kept lying on the ground, with a bull standing over him for hours, unable to move for fear of being crushed. There was also an association about an actual bull on a friend's farm; he had lately seen this bull, and he said it looked ghastly. This farm had associations for him by which it stood for his own home. He had spent most of his childhood on a large farm his father owned. In between, there were associations about flower seeds spreading from the country and taking root in town gardens. D. saw the owner of this farm again the same evening and urgently advised him to keep the bull under control. (D. had learnt that the bull had recently damaged some buildings on the farm.) Later that evening he received the news of his mother's death.

In the following hour, D. did not at first mention his mother's death, but expressed his hatred of me – my treatment was going to kill him. I then reminded him of the dream of the bull, interpreting that in his mind his mother had become mixed up with the attacking bull father – half dead himself – and had become uncanny and dangerous. I myself and the treatment were at the moment standing for this combined parent figure. I pointed out that the recent increase of hatred against his mother was a defence against his sorrow and despair about her approaching death. I referred to his aggressive phantasies by which, in his mind, he had changed his father into a dangerous bull which would destroy his mother; hence his feeling of responsibility and guilt about this impending disaster. I also referred to the patient's remark about eating buffaloes, and explained that he had incorporated the combined parent figure and so felt afraid of being crushed internally by the bull. Former material had shown his fear of being controlled and attacked internally by dangerous beings, fears which had resulted among other things in his taking up at times a very rigid and immobile posture. His story of the man who was in danger of being crushed by the bull, and who was kept immobile and controlled by it, I interpreted as a representation of the dangers by which he felt threatened internally.[18]

I now showed the patient the sexual implications of the bull's attacking his mother, connecting this with his exasperation about the birds waking him that morning (this being his first association to the bull dream). I reminded him that in his associations birds often stood for people, and that the noise the birds made – a noise to which he was quite accustomed – represented to him the dangerous sexual intercourse of his parents, and was so unendurable on this particular morning because of the bull dream, and owing to his acute state of anxiety about his dying mother. Thus his mother's death meant to him her being destroyed by the bull inside him, since – the work of mourning having already started – he had internalized her in this most dangerous situation.

I also pointed out some hopeful aspects of the dream. His mother might save herself from the bull. Blackbirds and other birds he is actually fond of. I showed him also the tendencies to reparation and re-creation present in the material. His father (the buffaloes) should be preserved, i.e. protected against his – the patient's – own greed. I reminded him, among other things, of the seeds which he wanted to spread from the country he loved to the town, and which stood for new babies being created by him and by his father as a reparation to his mother – these live babies being also a means of keeping her alive.

It was only after this interpretation that he was actually able to tell me that his mother had died the night before. He then admitted, which was unusual with him, his full understanding of the internalization processes which I had interpreted to him. He said that after he had received the news of his mother's death he felt sick, and that he thought, even at the time, that there could be no physical reason for this. It now seemed to him to confirm my interpretation that he had internalized the whole imagined situation of his fighting and dying parents.

During this hour he had shown great hatred, anxiety and tension, but scarcely any sorrow; towards the end, however, after my interpretation, his feelings softened, some sadness appeared, and he experienced some relief.

The night after his mother's funeral, D. dreamt that X. (a father figure) and another person (who stood for me) were trying to help him, but actually he had to fight for his life against us; as he put it: 'Death was claiming me.' In this hour he again spoke bitterly about his analysis, as disintegrating him. I interpreted that he felt the helpful external parents to be at the same time the fighting, disintegrating parents, who would attack and destroy him – the half-dead bull and the dying mother inside him – and that I myself and analysis had come to stand for the dangerous people and happenings inside himself. That his father was also internalized by him as dying or dead was confirmed when he told me that at his mother's funeral he had wondered for a moment whether his father was not dead. (In reality the father was still alive.)

Towards the end of this hour, after a decrease of hatred and anxiety, he again became more co-operative. He mentioned that the day before, looking out of the window of his father's house into the garden and feeling lonely, he disliked a jay he saw on a bush. He thought that this nasty and destructive bird might possibly interfere with another bird's nest with eggs in it. Then he associated that he had seen, some time previously, bunches of wild flowers thrown on the ground – probably picked and thrown away by children. I again interpreted his hatred and bitterness as being in part a defence against sorrow, loneliness and guilt. The destructive bird, the destructive children – as often before – stood for himself, who had, in his mind, destroyed his parents' home and happiness and killed his mother by destroying her babies inside her. In this connection his feelings of guilt related to his *direct* attacks in phantasy on his mother's body; whilst in connection with the bull dream the guilt was derived from his *indirect* attacks on her, when he changed his father into a dangerous bull who was thus carrying into effect his – the patient's – own sadistic wishes.

On the third night after his mother's funeral, D. had another dream:

He saw a bus coming towards him in an uncontrolled way – apparently driving itself. It went towards a shed. He could not see what happened to the shed, but knew definitely that the shed 'was going to blazes'. Then two people, coming from behind him, were opening the roof of the shed and looking into it. D. did not 'see the point of their doing this', but they seemed to think it would help.

Besides showing his fear of being castrated by his father through a homosexual act which he at the same time desired, this dream expressed the same internal situation as the bull dream – the death of his mother inside him and his own death. The shed stood for his mother's body, for himself, and also for his mother inside him. The dangerous sexual intercourse represented by the bus destroying the shed happened in his mind to his mother as well as to himself; but in addition, and that is where the predominant anxiety lay, to his mother inside him.

His not being able to see what happened in the dream indicated that in his mind the catastrophe was happening internally. He also knew, without seeing it, that the shed was 'going to blazes'. The bus 'coming towards him', besides standing for sexual intercourse and castration by his father, also meant 'happening inside him'.[19]

The two people opening the roof from behind (he had pointed to my chair) were himself and myself, looking into his inside and into his mind (psycho-analysis). The two people also meant myself as the 'bad' combined parent figure, myself containing the dangerous father – hence his doubts whether looking into the shed (analysis) could help him. The uncontrolled bus represented also himself in dangerous sexual intercourse with his mother, and expressed his fears and guilt about the badness of his own genitals. Before his mother's death, at a time when her fatal illness had already begun, he accidentally ran his car into a post – without serious consequences. It appeared that this was an unconscious suicidal attempt, meant to destroy the internal 'bad' parents. This accident also represented his parents in dangerous sexual intercourse inside him, and was thus an acting out as well as an externalization of an internal disaster.

The phantasy of the parents combined in 'bad' intercourse – or rather, the accumulation of emotions of various kinds, desires, fears and guilt, which go with it – had very much disturbed his relation to both parents, and had played an important part not only in his illness but in his whole development. Through the analysis of these emotions referring to the actual parents in sexual intercourse, and particularly through the analysis of these internalized situations, the patient became able to experience real mourning for his mother. All his life, however, he had warded off the depression and sorrow about losing her, which were derived from his infantile depressive feelings, and had denied his very great love for her. In his mind he had reinforced his hatred and feelings of persecution, because he could not bear the fe of losing his loved mother. When his anxieties about his own destructiveness decreased and confidence in his power to restore and preserve her became strengthened, persecution lessened and love for her came gradually to the fore. But together with this he increasingly experienced the grief and longing for her which he had repressed and denied from his early days onward. While he was going through this mourning with sorrow and despair, his deeply buried love for his mother came more and more into the open, and his relation to both parents altered. On one occasion he spoke of them, in connection with a pleasant childhood memory, as 'my dear old parents' – a new departure in him.

I have described here and in my former paper the deeper reasons for the individual's incapacity to overcome successfully the infantile depressive position. Failure to do so may result in depressive illness, mania or paranoia. I pointed out one or two other methods by which the ego attempts to escape from the sufferings connected with the depressive position, namely either the flight to internal good objects (which may lead to severe psychosis) or the flight to external good objects (with the possible outcome of neurosis). There are, however, many ways, based on obsessional, manic and paranoid defences, varying from individual to individual in their relative proportion, which in my experience all serve the same purpose, that is, to enable the individual to escape from the sufferings connected with the depressive position. (All these methods, as I have pointed out, have a part in normal development also.) This can be clearly observed in the analyses of people who fail to experience mourning. Feeling incapable of saving and securely reinstating their loved objects inside themselves, they must turn away from them more than hitherto and therefore deny their love for them. This may mean that their emotions in general become more inhibited; in other cases it is mainly feelings of love which become stifled and hatred is increased. At the same time, the ego uses various ways of dealing with paranoid fears (which will be the stronger the more hatred is reinforced). For instance, the internal 'bad' objects are manically subjugated, immobilized and at the same time denied, as well as strongly projected into the external world. Some people who fail to experience mourning may escape from an outbreak of manic-depressive illness or paranoia only by a severe restriction of their emotional life which impoverishes their whole personality.

Whether some measure of mental balance can be maintained in people of this type often depends on the ways in which these various methods interact, and on their capacity to keep alive in other directions some of the love which they deny to their lost objects. Relations to people who do not in their minds come too close to the lost object, and interest in things and activities, may absorb some of this love which belonged to the lost object. Though these relations and sublimations will have some manic and paranoid qualities, they may nevertheless offer some reassurance and relief from guilt, for through them the lost loved object which has been rejected and thus again destroyed is to some extent restored and retained in the unconscious mind.

If, in our patients, analysis diminishes the anxieties of destructive and persecuting internal parents, it follows that hate and thus in turn anxieties decrease, and the patients are enabled to revise their relation to their parents – whether they be dead or alive – and to rehabilitate them to some extent even if they have grounds for actual grievances. This greater tolerance makes it possible for them to set up 'good' parent figures more securely in their minds, alongside the 'bad' internal objects, or rather to mitigate the fear of these 'bad' objects by the trust in 'good' objects. This means enabling them to experience emotions – sorrow, guilt and grief, as well as love and trust – to go through mourning, but to overcome it, and ultimately to overcome the infantile depressive position, which they have failed to do in childhood.

To conclude. In normal mourning, as well as in abnormal mourning and in manic-depressive states, the infantile depressive position is reactivated. The complex feelings, phantasies and anxieties included under this term are of a nature which justifies my contention that the child in his early development goes through a transitory manic-depressive state as well as a state of mourning, which become modified by the infantile neurosis. With the passing of the infantile neurosis, the infantile depressive position is overcome.

The fundamental difference between normal mourning, on the one hand, and abnormal mourning and manic-depressive states, on the other, is this. The manic-depressive and the person who fails in the work of mourning, though their defences may differ widely from each other, have this in common, that they have been unable in early childhood to establish their internal 'good' objects and to feel secure in their inner world. They have never really overcome the infantile depressive position. In normal mourning, however, the early depressive position, which had become revived through the loss of the loved object, becomes modified again, and is overcome by methods similar to those used by the ego in childhood. The individual is reinstating his actually lost loved object; but he is also at the same time re-establishing inside himself his first loved objects – ultimately the 'good' parents – whom, when the actual loss occurred, he felt in danger of losing as well. It is by reinstating inside himself the 'good' parents as well as the recently lost person, and by rebuilding his inner world, which was disintegrated and in danger, that he overcomes his grief, regains security, and achieves true harmony and peace.

CHAPTER EIGHT

In 1938 Freud and his family came as refugees to England. Hitherto, to an extent, in the twenties and thirties, the intense disagreements between Anna Freud and Melanie Klein can be seen as part of a more general divergence between psychoanalysts in Vienna and London. By the second half of the thirties there was growing division within the British Society itself. Analysts who had developed ideas independently of Freud's main tenets were not willing to follow Klein as a new leader into what they saw emerging as a new dogmatism. In 1943 and 1944 a critical series of substantive and angry debates took place in the British Society. These 'Controversial Discussions' were finally resolved by a division into two distinct but co-operating groups – the 'A' group, followers of Klein; the 'B' group, adherents of Anna Freud. British analysts who did not follow Klein distinguished themselves as a third, or 'middle' group: the 'Independents'.

Already in the thirties, Edward Glover had referred to 'Klein and her School' but after the resolution of the Controversial Discussions, Klein not only had old friends (and enemies) of her own generation but young adherents to (and opponents of) her theory that was by now a clearly cohesive position which one could espouse or oppose.

In this paper we can see a new emphasis on understanding how normal infantile positions underlie psychoses. The ideas in this and the two preceding papers offer the core concepts of much of the later Kleinian work with psychosis.

Where earlier Klein had emphasized the projective mechanisms that characterize paranoia, here she expands her ideas on the effects of splitting which underlie schizoid conditions. Both defences are the chief feature of the paranoid-schizoid position which must be overcome if the greater integration of the depressive position is to be reached. It is in this paper that Klein explicitly introduces the notion of the mechanism she calls 'projective identification'.

One of Freud's very last, unfinished papers had been on 'The Splitting of the Ego in the Process of Defence' (1938), and clearly Klein has this in mind in this essay. In an appendix, she reopens a discussion of Freud's case of Schreber (*SE*, XII).

'Notes on Some Schizoid Mechanisms' was read to the British Society at the end of 1946. Klein added some footnotes in 1952. The essay printed here is the revised version taken from *CW*, Vol. III.

NOTES ON SOME SCHIZOID
MECHANISMS[1]
(1946)

INTRODUCTION

The present paper is concerned with the importance of early paranoid and schizoid anxieties and mechanisms. I have given much thought to this subject for a number of years, even before clarifying my views on the depressive processes in infancy. In the course of working out my concept of the infantile depressive position, however, the problems of the phase preceding it again forced themselves on my attention. I now wish to formulate some hypotheses at which I have arrived regarding the earlier anxieties and mechanisms.[2]

The hypotheses I shall put forward, which relate to very early stages of development, are derived by inference from material gained in the analyses of adults and children, and some of these hypotheses seem to tally with observations familiar in psychiatric work. To substantiate my contentions would require an accumulation of detailed case material for which there is no room in the framework of this paper, and I hope in further contributions to fill this gap.

At the outset it will be useful to summarize briefly the conclusions regarding the earliest phases of development which I have already put forward.[3]

In early infancy anxieties characteristic of psychosis arise which drive the ego to develop specific defence mechanisms. In this period the fixation points for all psychotic disorders are to be found. This hypothesis led some people to believe that I regarded all infants as psychotic; but I have already dealt sufficiently with this misunderstanding on other occasions. The psychotic anxieties, mechanisms and ego defences of infancy have a profound influence on development in all its aspects, including the development of the ego, super-ego and object relations.

I have often expressed my view that object relations exist from the beginning of life, the first object being the mother's breast which to the child becomes split into a good (gratifying) and bad (frustrating) breast; this splitting results in a severance of love and hate. I have further suggested that the relation to the first object implies its introjection and projection, and thus from the beginning object relations are moulded by an interaction between introjection and projection, between internal and external objects and situations. These processes participate in the building up of the ego and super-ego and prepare the ground for the onset of the Oedipus complex in the second half of the first year.

From the beginning the destructive impulse is turned against the object and is first expressed in phantasied oral-sadistic attacks on the mother's breast, which soon develop into onslaughts on her body by all sadistic means. The persecutory fears arising from the infant's oral-sadistic impulses to rob the mother's body of its good contents, and from the anal-sadistic impulses to put his excrements into her (including the desire to enter her body in order to control her from within) are of great importance for the development of paranoia and schizophrenia.

I enumerated various typical defences of the early ego, such as the mechanisms of splitting the object and the impulses, idealization, denial of inner and outer reality and the stifling of emotions. I also mentioned various anxiety contents, including the fear of being poisoned and devoured. Most of these phenomena – prevalent in the first few months of life – are found in the later symptomatic picture of schizophrenia.

This early period (first described as the 'persecutory phase') I later termed 'paranoid position',[4] and held that it precedes the depressive position. If persecutory fears are very strong, and for this reason (among others) the infant cannot work through the paranoid-schizoid position, the working through of the depressive position is in turn impeded. This failure may lead to a regressive reinforcing of persecutory fears and strengthen the fixation points for severe psychoses (that is to say, the group of schizophrenias). Another outcome of serious difficulties arising during the period of the depressive position may be manic-depressive disorders in later life. I also concluded that in less severe disturbances of development the same factors strongly influence the choice of neurosis.

While I assumed that the outcome of the depressive position depends on the working through of the preceding phase, I neverthe-less attributed to the depressive position a central role in the child's early development. For with the introjection of the object as a whole the infant's object relation alters fundamentally. The synthesis between the loved and hated aspects of the complete object gives rise to feelings of mourning and guilt which imply vital advances in the infant's emotional and intellectual life. This is also a crucial juncture for the choice of neurosis or psychosis. To all these conclusions I still adhere.

SOME NOTES ON FAIRBAIRN'S RECENT PAPERS

In a number of recent papers[5] W. R. D. Fairbairn has given much attention to the subject matter with which I am now dealing. I therefore find it helpful to clarify some essential points of agreement and disagreement between us. It will be seen that some of the conclusions which I shall present in this paper are in line with Fairbairn's conclusions, while others differ fundamentally. Fairbairn's approach was largely from the angle of ego development in relation to objects, while mine was predominantly from the angle of anxieties and their vicissitudes. He called the earliest phase the 'schizoid position': he stated that it forms part of normal development and is the basis for adult schizoid and schizophrenic illness. I agree with this contention and consider his description of developmental schizoid phenomena as significant and revealing, and of great value for our understanding of schizoid behaviour and of schizophrenia. I also think that Fairbairn's view that the group of schizoid or schizophrenic disorders is much wider than has been acknowledged is correct and important; and the particular emphasis he laid on the inherent relation between hysteria and schizophrenia deserves full attention. His term 'schizoid position' would be appropriate if it is understood to cover both persecutory fear and schizoid mechanisms.

I disagree – to mention first the most basic issues – with his revision of the theory of mental structure and instincts. I also disagree with his view that to begin with only the bad object is internalized – a view which seems to me to contribute to the important differences between us regarding the development of object relations as well as of ego development. For I hold that the introjected good breast forms a vital part of the ego, exerts from the beginning a fundamental influence on the process of ego development and affects both ego structure and object relations. I also differ from Fairbairn's view that 'the great problem of the schizoid individual is how to love without destroying by love, whereas the great problem of the depressive individual is how to love without destroying by hate'.[6] This conclusion is in line not only with his rejecting Freud's concept of primary instincts but also with his underrating the role which aggression and hatred play from the beginning of life. As a result of this approach, he does not give enough weight to the importance of early anxiety and conflict and their dynamic effects on development.

CERTAIN PROBLEMS OF THE EARLY EGO

In the following discussion I shall single out one aspect of ego development and I shall deliberately not attempt to link it with the problems of ego development as a whole. Nor can I here touch on the relation of the ego to the id and super-ego.

So far, we know little about the structure of the early ego. Some of the recent suggestions on this point have not convinced me: I have particularly in mind Glover's concept of ego nuclei and Fairbairn's theory of a central ego and two subsidiary egos. More helpful in my view is Winnicott's emphasis on the unintegration of the early ego.[7] I would also say that the early ego largely lacks cohesion, and a tendency towards integration alternates with a tendency towards disintegration, a falling into bits.[8] I believe that these fluctuations are characteristic of the first few months of life.

We are, I think, justified in assuming that some of the functions which we know from the later ego are there at the beginning. Prominent amongst these functions is that of dealing with anxiety. I hold that anxiety arises from the operation of the death instinct within the organism, is felt as fear of annihilation (death) and takes the form of fear of persecution. The fear of the destructive impulse seems to attach itself at once to an object – or rather it is experienced as the fear of an uncontrollable overpowering object. Other important sources of primary anxiety are the trauma of birth (separation anxiety) and frustration of bodily needs; and these experiences too are from the beginning felt as being caused by objects. Even if these objects are felt to be external, they become through introjection internal persecutors and thus reinforce the fear of the destructive impulse within.

The vital need to deal with anxiety forces the early ego to develop fundamental mechanisms and defences. The destructive impulse is partly projected outwards (deflection of the death instinct) and, I think, attaches itself to the first external object, the mother's breast. As Freud has pointed out, the remaining portion of the destructive impulse is to some extent bound by the libido within the organism. However, neither of these processes entirely fulfils its purpose, and therefore the anxiety of being destroyed from within remains active. It seems to me in keeping with the lack of cohesiveness, that under the pressure of this threat the ego tends to fall to pieces.[9] This falling to pieces appears to underlie states of disintegration in schizophrenics.

The question arises whether some active splitting processes within the ego may not occur even at a very early stage. As we assume, the early ego splits the object and the relation to it in an active way, and this may imply some active splitting of the ego itself. In any case, the result of splitting is a dispersal of the destructive impulse which is felt as the source of danger. I suggest that the primary anxiety of being annihilated by a destructive force within, with the ego's specific response of falling to pieces or splitting itself, may be extremely important in all schizophrenic processes.

SPLITTING PROCESSES IN RELATION TO THE OBJECT

The destructive impulse projected outwards is first experienced as oral aggression. I believe that oral-sadistic impulses towards the mother's breast are active from the beginning of life, though with the onset of teething the cannibalistic impulses increase in strength – a factor stressed by Abraham.

In states of frustration and anxiety the oral-sadistic and cannibalistic desires are reinforced, and then the infant feels that he has taken in the nipple and the breast *in bits*. Therefore in addition to the divorce between a good and a bad breast in the young infant's phantasy, the frustrating breast – attacked in oral-sadistic phantasies – is felt to be in fragments; the gratifying breast, taken in under the dominance of the sucking libido, is felt to be complete. This first internal good object acts as a focal point in the ego. It counteracts the processes of splitting and dispersal, makes for cohesiveness and integration, and is instrumental in building up the ego.[10] The infant's feeling of having inside a good and complete breast may, however, be shaken by frustration and anxiety. As a result, the divorce between the good and bad breast may be difficult to maintain, and the infant may feel that the good breast too is in pieces.

I believe that the ego is incapable of splitting the object – internal and external – without a corresponding splitting taking place within the ego. Therefore the phantasies and feelings about the state of the internal object vitally influence the structure of the ego. The more sadism prevails in the process of incorporating the object, and the more the object is felt to be in pieces, the more the ego is in danger of being split in relation to the internalized object fragments.

The processes I have described are, of course, bound up with the infant's phantasy life; and the anxieties which stimulate the mechanism of splitting are also of a phantastic nature. It is in phantasy that the infant splits the object and the self, but the effect of this phantasy is a very real one, because it leads to feelings and relations (and later on, thought processes) being in fact cut off from one another.[11]

SPLITTING IN CONNECTION WITH PROJECTION AND INTROJECTION

So far, I have dealt particularly with the mechanism of splitting as one of the earliest ego mechanisms and defences against anxiety. Introjection and projection are from the beginning of life also used in the service of this primary aim of the ego. Projection, as Freud described, originates from the deflection of the death instinct outwards and in my view it helps the ego to overcome anxiety by ridding it of danger and badness. Introjection of the good object is also used by the ego as a defence against anxiety.

Closely connected with projection and introjection are some other mechanisms. Here I am particularly concerned with the connection between splitting, idealization and denial. As regards splitting of the object, we have to remember that in states of gratification love feelings turn towards the gratifying breast, while in states of frustration hatred and persecutory anxiety attach themselves to the frustrating breast.

Idealization is bound up with the splitting of the object, for the good aspects of the breast are exaggerated as a safeguard against the fear of the persecuting breast. While idealization is thus the corollary of persecutory fear, it also springs from the power of the instinctual desires which aim at unlimited gratification and therefore create the picture of an inexhaustible and always bountiful breast – an ideal breast.

We find an instance of such a cleavage in infantile hallucinatory gratification. The main processes which come into play in idealization are also operative in hallucinatory gratification, namely, splitting of the object and denial both of frustration and of persecution. The frustrating and persecuting object is kept widely apart from the idealized object. However, the bad object is not only kept apart from the good one but its very existence is denied, as is the whole situation of frustration and the bad feelings (pain) to which frustration gives rise. This is bound up with denial of psychic reality. The denial of psychic reality becomes possible only through strong feelings of omnipotence – an essential characteristic of early mentality. Omnipotent denial of the existence of the bad object and of the painful situation is in the unconscious equal to annihilation by the destructive impulse. It is, however, not only a situation and an object that are denied and annihilated – *it is an object relation* which suffers this fate; and therefore a part of the ego, from which the feelings towards the object emanate, is denied and annihilated as well.

In hallucinatory gratification, therefore, two interrelated processes take place: the omnipotent conjuring up of the ideal object and situation, and the equally omnipotent annihilation of the bad persecutory object and the painful situation. These processes are based on splitting both the object and the ego.

In passing I would mention that in this early phase splitting, denial and omnipotence play a role similar to that of repression at a later stage of ego development. In considering the importance of the processes of denial and omnipotence at a stage which is characterized by persecutory fear and schizoid mechanisms, we may remember the delusions both of grandeur and of persecution in schizophrenia.

So far, in dealing with persecutory fear, I have singled out the oral element. However, while the oral libido still has the lead, libidinal and aggressive impulses and phantasies from other sources come to the fore and lead to a confluence of oral, urethral and anal desires, both libidinal and aggressive. Also the attacks on the mother's breast develop into attacks of a similar nature on her body, which comes to be felt as it were as an extension of the breast, even before the mother is conceived of as a complete person. The phantasied onslaughts on the mother follow two main lines: one is the predominantly oral impulse to suck dry, bite up, scoop out and rob the mother's body of its good contents. (I shall discuss the bearing of these impulses on the development of object relations in connection with introjection.) The other line of attack derives from the anal and urethral impulses and implies expelling dangerous substances (excrements) out of the self and into the mother. Together with these harmful excrements, expelled in hatred, split-off parts of the ego are also projected on to the mother or, as I would rather call it, *into* the mother.[12] These excrements and bad parts of the self are meant not only to injure but also to control and to take possession of the object. In so far as the mother comes to contain the bad parts of the self, she is not felt to be a separate individual but is felt to be *the* bad self.

Much of the hatred against parts of the self is now directed towards the mother. This leads to a particular form of identification which establishes the prototype of an aggressive object relation. I suggest for these processes the term 'projective identification'. When projection is mainly derived from the infant's impulse to harm or to control the mother,[13] he feels her to be a persecutor. In psychotic disorders this identification of an object with the hated parts of the self contributes to the intensity of the hatred directed against other people. As far as the ego is concerned the excessive splitting off and expelling into the outer world of part of itself considerably weaken it. For the aggressive component of feelings and of the personality is intimately bound up in the mind with power, potency, strength, knowledge and many other desired qualities.

It is, however, not only the bad parts of the self which are expelled and projected, but also good parts of the self. Excrements then have the significance of gifts; and parts of the ego which, together with excrements, are expelled and projected into the other person represent the good, i.e. the loving parts of the self. The identification based on this type of projection again vitally influences object relations. The projection of good feelings and good parts of the self into the mother is essential for the infant's ability to develop good object relations and to integrate his ego. However, if this projective process is carried out excessively, good parts of the personality are felt to be lost, and in this way the mother becomes the ego ideal; this process too results in weakening and impoverishing the ego. Very soon such processes extend to other people,[14] and the result may be an over-strong dependence on these external representatives of one's own good parts. Another consequence is a fear that the capacity to love has been lost because the loved object is felt to be loved predominantly as a representative of the self.

The processes of splitting off parts of the self and projecting them into objects are thus of vital importance for normal development as well as for abnormal object relations.

The effect of introjection on object relations is equally important. The introjection of the good object, first of all the mother's breast, is a precondition for normal development. I have already described that it comes to form a focal point in the ego and makes for cohesiveness of the ego. One characteristic feature of the earliest relation to the good object – internal and external – is the tendency to idealize it. In states of frustration or increased anxiety, the infant is driven to take flight to his internal idealized object as a means of escaping from persecutors. From this mechanism various serious disturbances may result: when persecutory fear is too strong, the flight to the idealized object becomes excessive, and this severely hampers ego development and disturbs object relations. As a result the ego may be felt to be entirely subservient to and dependent on the internal object – only a shell for it. With an unassimilated idealized object there goes a feeling that the ego has no life and no value of its own.[15] I would suggest that the condition of flight to the unassimilated idealized object necessitates further splitting processes within the ego. For parts of the ego attempt to unite with the ideal object, while other parts strive to deal with the internal persecutors.

The various ways of splitting the ego and internal objects result in the feeling that the ego is in bits. This feeling amounts to a state of disintegration. In normal development, the states of disintegration which the infant experiences are transitory. Among other factors, gratification by the external good object[16] again and again helps to break through these schizoid states. The infant's capacity to overcome temporary schizoid states is in keeping with the strong elasticity and resilience of the infantile mind. If states of splitting and therefore of disintegration, which the ego is unable to overcome, occur too frequently and go on for too long, then in my view they must be regarded as a sign of schizophrenic illness in the infant, and some indications of such illness may already be seen in the first few months of life. In adult patients, states of depersonalization and of schizophrenic dissociation seem to be a regression to these infantile states of disintegration.[17]

In my experience, excessive persecutory fears and schizoid mechanisms in early infancy may have a detrimental effect on intellectual development in its initial stages. Certain forms of mental deficiency would therefore have to be regarded as belonging to the group of schizophrenias. Accordingly, in considering mental deficiency in children at any age one should keep in mind the possibility of schizophrenic illness in early infancy.

I have so far described some effects of excessive introjection and projection on object relations. I am not attempting to investigate here in any detail the various factors which in some cases make for a predominance of introjective and in other cases for a predominance of projective processes. As regards normal personality, it may be said that the course of ego development and object relations depends on the degree to which an optimal balance between introjection and projection in the early stages of development can be achieved. This in turn has a bearing on the integration of the ego and the assimilation of internal objects. Even if the balance is disturbed and one or the other of these processes in excessive, there is some interaction between introjection and projection. For instance the projection of a predominantly hostile inner world which is ruled by persecutory fears leads to the introjection – in taking-back – of a hostile external world; and vice versa, the introjection of a distorted and hostile external world reinforces the projection of a hostile inner world.

Another aspect of projective processes, as we have seen, concerns the forceful entry into the object and control of the object by parts of the self. As a consequence, introjection may then be felt as a forceful entry from the outside into the inside, in retribution for violent projection. This may lead to the fear that not only the body but also the mind is controlled by other people in a hostile way. As a result there may be a severe disturbance in introjecting good objects

– a disturbance which would impede all ego functions as well as sexual development and might lead to an excessive withdrawal to the inner world. This withdrawal is, however, caused not only by the fear of introjecting a dangerous external world but also by the fear of internal persecutors and an ensuing flight to the idealized internal object.

I have referred to the weakening and impoverishment of the ego resulting from excessive splitting and projective identification. This weakened ego, however, becomes also incapable of assimilating its internal objects, and this leads to the feeling that it is ruled by them. Again, such a weakened ego feels incapable of taking back into itself the parts which it projected into the external world. These various disturbances in the interplay between projection and introjection, which imply excessive splitting of the ego, have a detrimental effect on the relation to the inner and outer world and seem to be at the root of some forms of schizophrenia.

Projective identification is the basis of many anxiety situations, of which I shall mention a few. The phantasy of forcefully entering the object gives rise to anxieties relating to the dangers threatening the subject from within the object. For instance, the impulses to control an object from within it stir up the fear of being controlled and persecuted inside it. By introjecting and reintrojecting the forcefully entered object, the subject's feelings of inner persecution are strongly reinforced; all the more since the reintrojected object is felt to contain the dangerous aspects of the self. The accumulation of anxieties of this nature, in which the ego is, as it were, caught between a variety of external and internal persecution-situations, is a basic element in paranoia.[18]

I have previously described[19] the infant's phantasies of attacking and sadistically entering the mother's body as giving rise to various anxiety situations (particularly the fear of being imprisoned and persecuted within her) which are at the bottom of paranoia. I also showed that the fear of being imprisoned (and especially of the penis being attacked) inside the mother is an important factor in later disturbances of male potency (impotence) and also underlies claustrophobia.[20]

SCHIZOID OBJECT RELATIONS

To summarize now some of the disturbed object relations which are found in schizoid personalities: the violent splitting of the self and excessive projection have the effect that the person towards whom this process is directed is felt as a persecutor. Since the destructive and hated part of the self which is split off and projected is felt as a danger to the loved object and therefore gives rise to guilt, this process of projection in some ways also implies a deflection of guilt from the self on to the other person. Guilt has, however, not been done away with, and the deflected guilt is felt as an unconscious responsibility for the people who have become representatives of the aggressive part of the self.

Another typical feature of schizoid object relations is their narcissistic nature which derives from the infantile introjective and projective processes. For, as I suggested earlier, when the ego ideal is projected into another person, this person becomes predominantly loved and admired because he contains the good parts of the self. Similarly, the relation to another person on the basis of projecting bad parts of the self into him is of a narcissistic nature, because in this case as well the object strongly represents one part of the self. Both these types of a narcissistic relation to an object often show strong obsessional features. The impulse to control other people is, as we know, an essential element in obsessional neurosis. The need to control others can to some extent be explained by a deflected drive to control parts of the self. When these parts have been projected excessively into another person, they can only be controlled by controlling the other person. One root of obsessional mechanisms may thus be found in the particular identification which results from infantile projective processes. This connection may also throw some light on the obsessional element which so often enters into the tendency for reparation. For it is not only an object about whom guilt is experienced but also parts of the self which the subject is driven to repair or restore.

All these factors may lead to a compulsive tie to certain objects or – another outcome – to a shrinking from people in order to prevent both a destructive intrusion into them and the danger of retaliation by them. The fear of such dangers may show itself in various negative attitudes in object relations. For instance, one of my patients told me that he dislikes people who are too much influenced by him, for they seem to become too much like himself and therefore he gets tired of them.

Another characteristic of schizoid object relations is a marked artificiality and lack of spontaneity. Side by side with this goes a severe disturbance of the feeling of the self or, as I would put it, of the relation to the self. This relation, too, appears to be artificial. In other words psychic reality and the relation to external reality are equally disturbed.

The projection of split-off parts of the self into another person essentially influences object relations, emotional life and the personality as a whole. To illustrate this contention I will select as an instance two universal phenomena which are interlinked: the feeling of loneliness and fear of parting. We know that one source of the depressive feelings accompanying parting from people can be found in the fear of the destruction of the object by the aggressive impulses directed against it. But it is more specifically the splitting and projective processes which underlie this fear. If aggressive elements in relation to the object are predominant and strongly aroused by the frustration of parting, the individual feels that the split-off components of his self, projected into the object, control his object in an aggressive and destructive way. At the same time the internal object is felt to be in the same danger of destruction as the external one in whom one part of the self is felt to be left. The result is an excessive weakening of the ego, a feeling that there is nothing to sustain it, and a corresponding feeling of loneliness. While this description applies to neurotic individuals, I think that in some degree it is a general phenomenon.

One need hardly elaborate the fact that some other features of schizoid object relations, which I described earlier, can also be found in minor degrees and in a less striking form in normal people – for instance shyness, lack of spontaneity or, on the other hand, a particularly intense interest in people.

In similar ways normal disturbances in thought-processes link up with the developmental paranoid-schizoid position. For all of us are liable at times to a momentary impairment of logical thinking which amounts to thoughts and associations being cut off from one another and situations being split off from one another; in fact, the ego is temporarily split.

THE DEPRESSIVE POSITION IN RELATION TO
THE PARANOID-SCHIZOID POSITION

I now wish to consider further steps in the infant's development. So far I have described the anxieties, mechanisms and defences which are characteristic of the first few months of life. With the introjection of the complete object in about the second quarter of the first year marked steps in integration are made. This implies important changes in the relation to objects. The loved and hated aspects of the mother are no longer felt to be so widely separated, and the result is an increased fear of loss, states akin to mourning and a strong feeling of guilt, because the aggressive impulses are felt to be directed against the loved object. The depressive position has come to the fore. The very experience of depressive feelings in turn has the effect of further integrating the ego, because it makes for an increased understanding of psychic reality and better perception of the external world, as well as for a greater synthesis between inner and external situations.

The drive to make reparation, which comes to the fore at this stage, can be regarded as a consequence of greater insight into psychic reality and of growing synthesis, for it shows a more realistic response to the feelings of grief, guilt and fear of loss resulting from the aggression against the loved object. Since the drive to repair or protect the injured object paves the way for more satisfactory object relations and sublimations, it in turn increases synthesis and contributes to the integration of the ego.

During the second half of the first year the infant makes some fundamental steps towards working through the depressive position. However, schizoid mechanisms still remain in force, though in a modified form and to a lesser degree, and early anxiety situations are again and again experienced in the process of modification. The working through of the persecutory and depressive positions extends over the first few years of childhood and plays an essential part in the infantile neurosis. In the course of this process, anxieties lose in strength; objects become both less idealized and less terrifying, and the ego becomes more unified. All this is interconnected with the growing perception of reality and adaptation to it.

If development during the paranoid-schizoid position has not proceeded normally and the infant cannot – for internal or external reasons – cope with the impact of depressive anxieties a vicious circle arises. For if persecutory fear, and correspondingly schizoid mechanisms, are too strong, the ego is not capable of working through the depressive position. This forces the ego to regress to the paranoid-schizoid position and reinforces the earlier persecutory fears and schizoid phenomena. Thus the basis is established for various forms of schizophrenia in later life; for when such a regression occurs, not only are the fixation points in the schizoid position reinforced, but there is a danger of greater states of disintegration setting in. Another outcome may be the strengthening of depressive features.

External experiences are, of course, of great importance in these developments. For instance, in the case of a patient who showed depressive and schizoid features, the analysis brought up with great vividness his early experiences in babyhood, to such an extent that in some sessions physical sensations in the throat or digestive organs occurred. The patient had been weaned suddenly at four months of age because his mother fell ill. In addition, he did not see his mother for four weeks. When she returned, she found the child greatly changed. He had been a lively baby, interested in his surroundings, and he seemed to have lost this interest. He had become apathetic. He had accepted the substitute food fairly easily and in fact never refused food. But he did not thrive on it any more, lost weight and had a good deal of digestive trouble. It was only at the end of the first year, when other food was introduced, that he again made good physical progress.

Much light was thrown in the analysis on the influence these experiences had on his whole development. His outlook and attitudes in adult life were based on the patterns established in this early stage. For instance, we found again and again a tendency to be influenced by other people in an unselective way – in fact to take in greedily whatever was offered – together with great distrust during the process of introjection. This process was constantly disturbed by anxieties from various sources, which also contributed to an increase of greed.

Taking the material of this analysis as a whole, I came to the conclusion that at the time when the sudden loss of the breast and of the mother occurred, the patient had already to some extent established a relation to a complete good object. He had no doubt already entered the depressive position but could not work through it successfully and the paranoid-schizoid position became regressively reinforced. This expressed itself in the 'apathy' which followed a period when the child had already shown a lively interest in his surroundings. The fact that he had reached the depressive position and had introjected a complete object showed in many ways in his personality. He had actually a strong capacity for love and a great longing for a good and complete object. A characteristic feature of his personality was the desire to love people and trust them, unconsciously to regain and build up again the good and complete breast which he had once possessed and lost.

CONNECTION BETWEEN SCHIZOID AND MANIC-DEPRESSIVE PHENOMENA

Some fluctuations between the paranoid-schizoid and the depressive positions always occur and are part of normal development. No clear division between the two stages of development can therefore be drawn; moreover, modification is a gradual process and the phenomena of the two positions remain for some time to some extent intermingled and interacting. In abnormal development this interaction influences, I think, the clinical picture both of some forms of schizophrenia and of manic-depressive disorders.

To illustrate this connection I shall briefly refer to some case-material. I do not intend to present a case-history here and am therefore only selecting some parts of material relevant to my topic. The patient I have in mind was a pronounced manic-depressive case (diagnosed as such by more than one psychiatrist) with all the characteristics of that disorder: there was the alternation between depressive and manic states, strong suicidal tendencies leading repeatedly to suicidal attempts, and various other characteristic manic and depressive features. In the course of her analysis a stage was reached in which a real and great improvement was achieved. Not only did the cycle stop but there were fundamental changes in her personality and her object relations. Productivity on various lines developed, as well as actual feelings of happiness (not of a manic type). Then, partly owing to external circumstances, another phase set in. During this last phase, which continued for several months, the patient co-operated in the analysis in a particular way. She came regularly to the analytic sessions, associated fairly freely, reported dreams and provided material for the analysis. There was, however, no emotional response to my interpretations and a good deal of contempt of them. There was very seldom any conscious confirmation of what I suggested. Yet the material by which she responded to the interpretations reflected their unconscious effect. The powerful resistance shown at this stage seemed to come from one part of the personality only, while at the same time another part responded to the analytic work. It was not only that parts of her personality did not co-operate with me; they did not seem to co-operate with each other, and at the time the analysis was unable to help the patient to achieve synthesis. During this stage she decided to bring the analysis to an end. External circumstances contributed strongly to this decision and she fixed a date for the last session.

On that particular date she reported the following dream: there was a blind man who was very worried about being blind; but he seemed to comfort himself by touching the patient's dress and finding out how it was fastened. The dress in the dream reminded her of one of her frocks which was buttoned high up to the throat. The patient gave two further associations to this dream. She said, with some resistance, that the blind man was herself; and when referring to the dress fastened up to the throat, she remarked that she had again gone into her 'hide'. I suggested to the patient that she unconsciously expressed in the dream that she was blind to her own difficulties, and that her decisions with regard to the analysis as well as to various circumstances in her life were not in accordance with her unconscious knowledge. This was also shown by her admitting that she had gone into her 'hide', meaning by it that she was shutting herself off, an attitude well known to her from previous stages in her analysis. Thus the unconscious insight, and even some co-operation of the conscious level (recognition that *she* was the blind man and that she had gone into her 'hide'), derived from isolated parts of her personality only. Actually, the interpretation of this dream did not produce any effect and did not alter the patient's decision to bring the analysis to an end in that particular hour.[21]

The nature of certain difficulties encountered in this analysis as well as in others had revealed itself more clearly in the last few months before the patient broke off the treatment. It was the mixture of schizoid and manic-depressive features which determined the nature of her illness. For at times throughout her analysis – even in the early stage when depressive and manic states were at their height – depressive and schizoid mechanisms sometimes appeared simultaneously. There were, for instance, hours when the patient was obviously deeply depressed, full of self-reproaches and feelings of unworthiness; tears were running down her cheeks and her gestures expressed despair; and yet she said, when I interpreted these emotions, that she did not feel them at all. Whereupon she reproached herself for having no feelings at all, for being completely empty. In such sessions there was also a flight of ideas, the thoughts seemed to be broken up, and their expression was disjointed.

Following the interpretation of the unconscious reasons underlying such states, there were sometimes sessions in which the emotions and depressive anxieties came out fully, and at such times thoughts and speech were much more coherent.

This close connection between depressive and schizoid phenomena appeared, though in different forms, throughout her analysis but became very pronounced during the last stage preceding the break just described.

I have already referred to the developmental connection between the paranoid-schizoid and depressive positions. The question now arises whether this developmental connection is the basis for the mixture of these features in manic-depressive disorders and, as I would suggest, in schizophrenic disorders as well. If this tentative hypothesis could be proved, the conclusion would be that the groups of schizophrenic and manic-depressive disorders are more closely connected developmentally with one another than has been assumed. This would also account for the cases in which, I believe, the differential diagnosis between melancholia and schizophrenia is exceedingly difficult. I should be grateful if further light could be thrown on my hypothesis by colleagues who have had ample material for psychiatric observation.

SOME SCHIZOID DEFENCES

It is generally agreed that schizoid patients are more difficult to analyse than manic-depressive types. Their withdrawn, unemotional attitude, the narcissistic elements in their object relations (to which I referred earlier), a kind of detached hostility which pervades the whole relation to the analyst create a very difficult type of resistance. I believe that it is largely the splitting processes which account for the patient's failure in contact with the analyst and for his lack of response to the analyst's interpretations. The patient himself feels estranged and far away, and this feeling corresponds to the analyst's impression that considerable parts of the patient's personality and of his emotions are not available. Patients with schizoid features may say: 'I hear what you are saying. You may be right, but it has no meaning for me.' Or again they say they feel they are not there. The expression 'no meaning' in such cases does not imply an active rejection of the interpretation but suggests that parts of the personality and of the emotions are split off. These patients can, therefore, not deal with the interpretation; they can neither accept it nor reject it.

I shall illustrate the processes underlying such states by a piece of material taken from the analysis of a man patient. The session I have in mind started with the patient's telling me that he felt anxiety and did not know why. He then made comparisons with people more successful and fortunate than himself. These remarks also had a reference to me. Very strong feelings of frustration, envy and grievance came to the fore. When I interpreted – to give here again only the gist of my interpretations – that these feelings were directed against the analyst and that he wanted to destroy me, his mood changed abruptly. The tone of his voice became flat, he spoke in a slow, expressionless way, and he said that he felt detached from the whole situation. He added that my interpretation seemed correct, but that it did not matter. In fact, he no longer had any wishes, and nothing was worth bothering about.

My next interpretations centred on the causes for this change of mood. I suggested that at the moment of my interpretation the danger of destroying me had become very real to him and the immediate consequence was the fear of losing me. Instead of feeling guilt and depression, which at certain stages of his analysis followed such interpretations, he now attempted to deal with these dangers by a particular method of splitting. As we know, under the pressure of ambivalence, conflict and guilt, the patient often splits the figure of the analyst; then the analyst may at certain moments be loved, at other moments hated. Or the relations to the analyst may be split in such a way that he remains the good (or bad) figure while somebody else becomes the opposite figure. But this was not the kind of splitting which occurred in this particular instance. The patient split off those parts of himself, i.e. of his ego, which he felt to be dangerous and hostile towards the analyst. He turned his destructive impulses from his object *towards his ego*, with the result that parts of his ego temporarily went out of existence. In unconscious phantasy this amounted to annihilation of part of his personality. The particular mechanism of turning the destructive impulse against one part of his personality, and the ensuing dispersal of emotions, kept his anxiety in a latent state.

My interpretation of these processes had the effect of again altering the patient's mood. He became emotional, said he felt like crying, was depressed, but felt more integrated; then he also expressed a feeling of hunger.[22]

The violent splitting off and destroying of one part of the personality under the pressure of anxiety and guilt is in my experience an important schizoid mechanism. To refer briefly to another instance: a woman patient had dreamed that she had to deal with a wicked girl child who was determined to murder somebody. The patient tried to influence or control the child and to extort a confession from her which would have been to the child's benefit; but she was unsuccessful. I also entered into the dream and the patient felt that I might help her in dealing with the child. Then the patient strung up the child on a tree in order to frighten her and also prevent her from doing harm. When the patient was about to pull the rope and kill the child, she woke. During this part of the dream the analyst was also present but again remained inactive.

I shall give here only the essence of the conclusions I arrived at from the analysis of this dream. In the dream the patient's personality was split into two parts: the wicked and uncontrollable child on the one hand, and on the other hand the person who tried to influence and control her. The child, of course, stood also for various figures in the past, but in this context she mainly represented one part of the patient's self. Another conclusion was that the analyst was the person whom the child was going to murder; and my role in the dream was partly to prevent this murder from taking place. Killing the child – to which the patient had to resort – represented the annihilation of one part of her personality.

The question arises how the schizoid mechanism of annihilating part of the self connects with repression which, as we know, is directed against dangerous impulses. This, however, is a problem with which I cannot deal here.

Changes of mood, of course, do not always appear as dramatically within a session as in the first instance I have given in this section. But I have repeatedly found that advances in synthesis are brought about by interpretations of the specific causes for splitting. Such interpretations must deal in detail with the transference situation at that moment, including of course the connection with the past, and must contain a reference to the details of the anxiety situations which drive the ego to regress to schizoid mechanisms. The synthesis resulting from interpretations on these lines goes along with depression and anxieties of various kinds. Gradually such waves of depression – followed by greater integration – lead to a lessening of schizoid phenomena and also to fundamental changes in object relations.

LATENT ANXIETY IN SCHIZOID PATIENTS

I have already referred to the lack of emotion which makes schizoid patients unresponsive. This is accompanied by an absence of anxiety. An important support for the analytic work is therefore lacking. For with other types of patients who have strong manifest and latent anxiety, the relief of anxiety derived from analytic interpretation becomes an experience which furthers their capacity to co-operate in the analysis.

This lack of anxiety in schizoid patients is only apparent. For the schizoid mechanisms imply a dispersal of emotions including anxiety, but these dispersed elements still exist in the patient. Such patients have a certain form of latent anxiety; it is kept latent by the particular method of dispersal. The feeling of being disintegrated, of being unable to experience emotions, of losing one's objects, is in fact the equivalent of anxiety. This becomes clearer when advances in synthesis have been made. The great relief which a patient then experiences derives from a feeling that his inner and outer worlds have not only come more together but back to life again. At such moments it appears in retrospect that when emotions were lacking, relations were vague and uncertain and parts of the personality were felt to be lost, everything seemed to be dead. All this is the equivalent of anxiety of a very serious nature. This anxiety, kept latent by dispersal, is to some extent experienced all along, but its form differs from the latent anxiety which we can recognize in other types of cases.

Interpretations which tend towards synthesizing the split in the self, including the dispersal of emotions, make it possible for the anxiety gradually to be experienced as such, though for long stretches we may in fact only be able to bring the ideational contents together but not to elicit the emotions of anxiety.

I have also found that interpretations of schizoid states make particular demands on our capacity to put the interpretations in an intellectually clear form in which the links between the conscious, preconscious and unconscious are established. This is, of course, always one of our aims, but it is of special importance at times when the patient's emotions are not available and we seem to address ourselves only to his intellect, however much broken up.

It is possible that the few hints I have given may to some extent apply as well to the technique of analysing schizophrenic patients.

SUMMARY OF CONCLUSIONS

I will now summarize some of the conclusions presented in this paper. One of my main points was the suggestion that in the first few months of life anxiety is predominantly experienced as fear of persecution and that this contributes to certain mechanisms and defences which are significant for the paranoid-schizoid position. Outstanding among these defences are the mechanisms of splitting internal and external objects, emotions and the ego. These mechanisms and defences are part of normal development and at the same time form the basis for later schizophrenic illness. I described the processes underlying identification by projection as a combination of splitting off parts of the self and projecting them on to another person, and some of the effects this identification has on normal and schizoid object relations. The onset of the depressive position is the juncture at which by regression schizoid mechanisms may be reinforced. I also suggested a close connection between the manic-depressive and schizoid disorders, based on the interaction between the infantile paranoid-schizoid and depressive positions.

APPENDIX

Freud's analysis of the Schreber case[23] contains a wealth of material which is very relevant to my topic but from which I shall here draw only a few conclusions.

Schreber described vividly the splitting of the soul of his physician Flechsig (his loved and persecuting figure). The 'Flechsig soul' at one time introduced the system of 'soul divisions', splitting into as many as forty to sixty sub-divisions. These souls having multiplied till they became a 'nuisance', God made a raid on them and as a result the Flechsig soul survived in 'only one or two shapes'. Another point which Schreber mentions is that the fragments of the Flechsig soul slowly lost both their intelligence and their power.

One of the conclusions Freud arrived at in his analysis of this case was that the persecutor was split into God and Flechsig, and also that God and Flechsig represented the patient's father and brother. In discussing the various forms of Schreber's delusion of the destruction of the world, Freud states: 'In any case the end of the world was the consequence of the conflict which had broken out between him, Schreber, and Flechsig, or, according to the aetiology adopted in the second phase of his delusion, of the indissoluble bond which had been formed between him and God . . .'

I would suggest, in keeping with the hypotheses outlined in the present chapter, that the division of the Flechsig soul into many souls was not only splitting of the object but also a projection of Schreber's feeling that his ego was split. I shall here only mention the connection of such splitting processes with processes of introjection. The conclusion suggests itself that God and Flechsig also represented parts of Schreber's self. The conflict between Schreber and Flechsig, to which Freud attributed a vital role in the world destruction delusion, found expression in the raid by God on the Flechsig souls. In my view this raid represents the annihilation by one part of the self of the other parts – which, as I contend, is a schizoid mechanism. The anxieties and phantasies about inner destruction and ego disintegration bound up with this mechanism are projected on to the external world and underlie the delusions of its destruction.

Regarding the processes which are at the bottom of the paranoiac 'world catastrophe', Freud arrived at the following conclusions: 'The patient has withdrawn from the people in his environment and from the external world generally the libidinal cathexis which he has hitherto directed on to them. Thus everything has become indifferent and irrelevant to him, and has to be explained by means of a secondary rationalization as being "miracled up, cursorily improvised". The end of the world is the projection of this internal catastrophe; for his subjective world has come to an end since he has withdrawn his love from it.' This explanation specifically concerns the disturbance in object libido and the ensuing breakdown in relation to people and the external world. But a little further on Freud considered another aspect of these disturbances. He said: 'We can no more dismiss the possibility that disturbances of the libido may react upon the egoistic cathexes than we can overlook the *converse possibility* – namely, that *a secondary or induced disturbance of the libidinal processes may result from abnormal changes in the ego. Indeed it is probable that processes of this kind constitute the distinctive characteristic of psychoses*' (my italics). It is particularly the possibility expressed in the last two sentences which provides the link between Freud's explanation of the 'world catastrophe' and my hypothesis. 'Abnormal changes in the ego' derive, as I have suggested in this chapter, from excessive splitting processes in the early ego. These processes are inextricably linked with instinctual development, and with the anxieties to which instinctual desires give rise. In the light of Freud's later theory of the life and death instincts, which replaced the concept of the egoistic and sexual instincts, disturbances in the distribution of the libido presuppose a defusion between the destructive impulse and the libido. The mechanism of one part of the ego annihilating other parts which, I suggest, underlies 'world catastrophe' phantasy (the raid by God on the Flechsig souls) implies a preponderance of the destructive impulse over the libido. Any disturbance in the distribution of the narcissistic libido is in turn bound up with the relation to introjected objects which (according to my work) from the beginning come to form part of the ego. The interaction between narcissistic libido and object libido corresponds thus to the interaction between the relation to introjected and external objects. If the ego and the internalized objects are felt to be in bits, an internal catastrophe is experienced by the infant which both extends to the external world and is projected on to it. Such anxiety states relating to an internal catastrophe arise, according to the hypothesis discussed in the present chapter, during the period of the infantile paranoid-schizoid position and form the basis for later schizophrenia. In Freud's view the dispositional fixation to dementia praecox is found in a very early stage of development. Referring to dementia praecox, which Freud distinguished from paranoia, he said: 'The dispositional point of fixation must therefore be situated further back than in paranoia, and must lie somewhere at the beginning of the course of development from auto-erotism to object-love.'

I wish to draw one more conclusion from Freud's analysis of the Schreber case. I suggest that the raid, which ended in the Flechsig souls being reduced to one or two, was part of the attempt towards recovery. For the raid was to undo, or, one may say, heal the split in the ego by annihilating the split-off parts of the ego. As a result only one or two of the souls were left which, as we may assume, were meant to regain their intelligence and their power. This attempt towards recovery, however, was effected by very destructive means used by the ego against itself and its projected objects.

Freud's approach to the problems of schizophrenia and paranoia has proved of fundamental importance. His Schreber paper (and here we also have to remember Abraham's paper[24] quoted by Freud) opened up the possibility of understanding psychosis and the processes underlying it.

CHAPTER NINE

Melanie Klein gave this brief, but important paper at the International Congress of Psychoanalysis held in Amsterdam in 1951. It was published the following year in Part 3 of the *International Journal*. Part 2 had been a special issue brought out in celebration of Klein's seventieth birthday. The articles ranged from detailed clinical observations of acute psychosis to the application of Klein's theories to literature and aesthetics. As Ernest Jones commented, Klein's work was now established by her followers.

Klein's ideas on transference reflect the general tendency of her work discussed in the Introduction to this selection. Her emphasis is not, as in Freud's work, on the reconstruction of a past relationship which is transferred on to the analyst, but rather on the development *within* the analytic setting of a relationship which displays all the mechanisms, anxieties, love, guilt and phantasies which characterize the analysand's way of dealing with life in the world outside. These ways can be *transferred* on to or into the analyst and the setting and worked through in the analysis so that their severity is mitigated, and negative aspects can become more acceptable and be allowed to coexist with the more positive qualities.

THE ORIGINS OF TRANSFERENCE (1952)

In his *Fragment of an Analysis of a Case of Hysteria*[1] Freud defines the transference situation in the following way:

> What are transferences? They are new editions or facsimiles of the tendencies and phantasies which are aroused and made conscious during the progress of the analysis; but they have this peculiarity, which is characteristic for their species, that they replace some earlier person by the person of the physician. To put it another way: a whole series of psychological experiences are revived, not as belonging to the past, but as applying to the physician at the present moment.

In some form or other transference operates throughout life and influences all human relations, but here I am only concerned with the manifestations of transference in psycho-analysis. It is characteristic of psycho-analytic procedure that, as it begins to open up roads into the patient's unconscious, his past (in its conscious and unconscious aspects) is gradually being revived. Thereby his urge to transfer his early experiences, object relations and emotions, is reinforced and they come to focus on the psycho-analyst; this implies that the patient deals with the conflicts and anxieties which have been reactivated, by making use of the same mechanisms and defences as in earlier situations.

It follows that the deeper we are able to penetrate into the unconscious and the further back we can take the analysis, the greater will be our understanding of the transference. Therefore a brief summary of my conclusions about the earliest stages of development is relevant to my topic.

The first form of anxiety is of a persecutory nature. The working of the death instinct within – which according to Freud is directed against the organism – gives rise to the fear of annihilation, and this is the primordial cause of persecutory anxiety. Furthermore, from the beginning of post-natal life (I am not concerned here with pre-natal processes) destructive impulses against the object stir up fear of retaliation. These persecutory feelings from inner sources are intensified by painful external experiences, for, from the earliest days onwards, frustration and discomfort arouse in the infant the feeling that he is being attacked by hostile forces. Therefore the sensations experienced by the infant at birth and the difficulties of adapting himself to entirely new conditions give rise to persecutory anxiety. The comfort and care given after birth, particularly the first feeding experiences, are felt to come from good forces. In speaking of 'forces' I am using a rather adult word for what the young infant dimly conceives of as objects, either good or bad. The infant directs his feelings of gratification and love towards the 'good' breast, and his destructive impulses and feelings of persecution towards what he feels to be frustrating, i.e. the 'bad' breast. At this stage splitting processes are at their height, and love and hatred as well as the good and bad aspects of the breast are largely kept apart from one another. The infant's relative security is based on turning the good object into an ideal one as a protection against the dangerous and persecuting object. These processes – that is to say splitting, denial, omnipotence and idealization – are prevalent during the first three or four months of life (which I termed the 'paranoid-schizoid position' (1946). In these ways at a very early stage persecutory anxiety and its corollary, idealization, fundamentally influence object relations.

The primal processes of projection and introjection, being inextricably linked with the infant's emotions and anxieties, initiate object relations; by projecting, i.e. deflecting libido and aggression on to the mother's breast, the basis for object relations is established; by introjecting the object, first of all the breast, relations to internal objects come into being. My use of the term 'object relations' is based on my contention that the infant has from the beginning of post-natal life a relation to the mother (although focusing primarily on her breast) which is imbued with the fundamental elements of an object relation, i.e. love, hatred, phantasies, anxieties and defences.[2]

In my view – as I have explained in detail on other occasions – the introjection of the breast is the beginning of super-ego formation which extends over years. We have grounds for assuming that from the first feeding experience onwards the infant introjects the breast in its various aspects. The core of the super-ego is thus the mother's breast, both good and bad. Owing to the simultaneous operation of introjection and projection, relations to external and internal objects interact. The father too, who soon plays a role in the child's life, early on becomes part of the infant's internal world. It is characteristic of the infant's emotional life that there are rapid fluctuations between love and hate; between external and internal situations; between perception of reality and the phantasies relating to it; and, accordingly, an interplay between persecutory anxiety and idealization – both referring to internal and external objects; the idealized object being a corollary of the persecutory, extremely bad one.

The ego's growing capacity for integration and synthesis leads more and more, even during these first few months, to states in which love and hatred, and correspondingly the good and bad aspects of objects, are being synthesized; and this gives rise to the second form of anxiety – depressive anxiety – for the infant's aggressive impulses and desires towards the bad breast (mother) are now felt to be a danger to the good breast (mother) as well. In the second quarter of the first year these emotions are reinforced, because at this stage the infant increasingly perceives and introjects the mother as a person. Depressive anxiety is intensified, for the infant feels he has destroyed or is destroying a whole object by his greed and uncontrollable aggression. Moreover, owing to the growing synthesis of his emotions, he now feels that these destructive impulses are directed against a *loved person*. Similar processes operate in relation to the father and other members of the family. These anxieties and corresponding defences constitute the 'depressive position', which comes to a head about the middle of the first year and whose essence is the anxiety and guilt relating to the destruction and loss of the loved internal and external objects.

It is at this stage, and bound up with the depressive position, that the Oedipus complex sets in. Anxiety and guilt add a powerful impetus towards the beginning of the Oedipus complex. For anxiety and guilt increase the need to externalize (project) bad figures and to internalize (introject) good ones; to attach desires, love, feelings of guilt and reparative tendencies to some objects, and hate and anxiety to others; to find representatives for internal figures in the external world. It is, however, not only the search for new objects which dominates the infant's needs, but also the drive towards new aims: away from the breast towards the penis, i.e. from oral desires towards genital ones. Many factors contribute to these developments: the forward drive of the libido, the growing integration of the ego, physical and mental skills and progressive adaptation to the external world. These trends are bound up with the process of symbol formation, which enables the infant to transfer not only interest, but also emotions and phantasies, anxiety and guilt, from one object to another.

The processes I have described are linked with another fundamental phenomenon governing mental life. I believe that the pressure exerted by the earliest anxiety situations is one of the factors which bring about the repetition compulsion. I shall return to this hypothesis at a later point.

Some of my conclusions about the earliest stages of infancy are a continuation of Freud's discoveries; on certain points, however, divergencies have arisen, one of which is very relevant to my present topic. I am referring to my contention that object relations are operative from the beginning of post-natal life.

For many years I have held the view that auto-erotism and narcissism are in the young infant contemporaneous with the first relation to objects – external and internalized. I shall briefly restate my hypothesis: auto-erotism and narcissism include the love for and relation with the internalized good object which in phantasy forms part of the loved body and self. It is to this internalized object that in auto-erotic gratification and narcissistic *states* a withdrawal takes place. Concurrently, from birth onwards, a relation to objects, primarily the mother (her breast) is present. This hypothesis contradicts Freud's concept of auto-erotic and narcissistic *stages* which preclude an object relation. However, the difference between Freud's view and my own is less wide than appears at first sight, since Freud's statements on this issue are not unequivocal. In various contexts he explicitly and implicitly expressed opinions which suggested a relation to an object, the mother's breast, *preceding* auto-erotism and narcissism. One reference must suffice; in the first of two encyclopaedia articles,[3] Freud said:

> In the first instance the oral component instinct finds satisfaction by attaching itself to the sating of the desire for nourishment; and its object is the mother's breast. It then detaches itself, becomes independent and at the same time *auto-erotic*, that is, it finds an object in the child's own body.

Freud's use of the term object is here somewhat different from my use of this term, for he is referring to the object of an instinctual aim, while I mean, in addition to this, an object relation involving the infant's emotions, phantasies, anxieties and defences. Nevertheless, in the sentence referred to, Freud clearly speaks of a libidinal attachment to an object, the mother's breast, which precedes auto-erotism and narcissism.

In this context I wish to remind you also of Freud's findings about early identifications. In *The Ego and the Id*,[4] speaking of abandoned object cathexes, he said: '. . . the effects of the first identification in earliest childhood will be profound and lasting. This leads us back to the origin of the ego-ideal . . .' Freud then defines the first and most important identifications which lie hidden behind the ego ideal as the identification with the father, or with the parents, and places them, as he expresses it, in the 'pre-history of every person'. These formulations come close to what I described as the first introjected objects, for by definition identifications are the result of introjection. From the statement I have just discussed and the passage quoted from the encyclopaedia article it can be deduced that Freud, although he did not pursue this line of thought further, did assume that in earliest infancy both an object and introjective processes play a part.

That is to say, as regards auto-erotism and narcissism we meet with an inconsistency in Freud's views. Such inconsistencies which exist on a number of points of theory clearly show, I think, that on these particular issues Freud had not yet arrived at a final decision. In respect of the theory of anxiety he stated this explicitly in *Inhibitions, Symptoms and Anxiety*.[5] His realization that much about the early stages of development was still unknown or obscure to him is also exemplified by his speaking of the first years of the girl's life as '. . . lost in a past so dim and shadowy . . .'[6]

I do not know Anna Freud's view about this aspect of Freud's work. But, as regards the question of auto-erotism and narcissism, she seems only to have taken into account Freud's conclusion that an auto-erotic and a narcissistic stage precede object relations, and not to have allowed for the other possibilities implied in some of Freud's statements such as the ones I referred to above. This is one of the reasons why the divergence between Anna Freud's conception and my conception of early infancy is far greater than that between Freud's views, taken as a whole, and my view. I am stating this because I believe it is essential to clarify the extent and nature of the differences between the two schools of psycho-analytic thought represented by Anna Freud and myself. Such clarification is required in the interests of psycho-analytic training and also because it could help to open up fruitful discussions between psycho-analysts and thereby contribute to a greater general understanding of the fundamental problems of early infancy.

The hypothesis that a stage extending over several months precedes object relations implies that – except for the libido attached to the infant's own body – impulses, phantasies, anxieties and defences either are not present in him, or are not related to an object, that is to say they would operate *in vacuo*. The analysis of very young children has taught me that there is no instinctual urge, no anxiety situation, no mental process which does not involve objects, external or internal; in other words, object relations are at the *centre* of emotional life. Furthermore, love and hatred, phantasies, anxieties and defences are also operative from the beginning and are *ab initio* indivisibly linked with object relations. This insight showed me many phenomena in a new light.

I shall now draw the conclusion on which the present paper rests: I hold that transference originates in the same processes which in the earliest stages determine object relations. Therefore we have to go back again and again in analysis to the fluctuations between objects, loved and hated, external and internal, which dominate early infancy.

We can fully appreciate the interconnection between positive and negative transferences only if we explore the early interplay between love and hate, and the vicious circle of aggression, anxieties, feelings of guilt and increased aggression, as well as the various aspects of objects towards whom these conflicting emotions and anxieties are directed. On the other hand, through exploring these early processes I became convinced that the analysis of the negative transference, which had received relatively little attention[7] in psycho-analytic technique, is a precondition for analysing the deeper layers of the mind. The analysis of the negative as well as of the positive transference and of their interconnection is, as I have held for many years, an indispensable principle for the treatment of all types of patients, children and adults alike. I have substantiated this view in most of my writings from 1927 onwards.

This approach, which in the past made possible the psycho-analysis of very young children, has in recent years proved extremely fruitful for the analysis of schizophrenic patients. Until about 1920 it was assumed that schizophrenic patients were incapable of forming a transference and therefore could not be psycho-analysed. Since then the psycho-analysis of schizophrenics has been attempted by various techniques. The most radical change of view in this respect, however, has occurred more recently and is closely connected with the greater knowledge of the mechanisms, anxieties and defences operative in earliest infancy. Since some of these defences, evolved in primal object relations against both love and hatred, have been discovered, the fact that schizophrenic patients are capable of developing both a positive and a negative transference has been fully understood; this finding is confirmed if we consistently apply in the treatment of schizophrenic patients[8] the principle that it is as necessary to analyse the negative as the positive transference – that in fact the one cannot be analysed without the other.

Retrospectively it can be seen that these considerable advances in technique are supported in psycho-analytic theory by Freud's discovery of the life and death instincts, which has fundamentally added to the understanding of the origin of ambivalence. Because the life and death instincts, and therefore love and hatred, are at bottom in the closest interaction, negative and positive transference are basically interlinked.

The understanding of earliest object relations and the processes they imply has essentially influenced technique from various angles. It has long been known that the psycho-analyst in the transference situation may stand for mother, father or other people, that he is also at times playing in the patient's mind the part of the super-ego, at other times that of the id or the ego. Our present knowledge enables us to penetrate to the specific details of the various roles allotted by the patient to the analyst. There are in fact very few people in the young infant's life, but he feels them to be a multitude of objects because they appear to him in different aspects. Accordingly, the analyst may at a given moment represent a part of the self, of the super-ego or any one of a wide range of internalized figures. Similarly it does not carry us far enough if we realize that the analyst stands for the actual father or mother, unless we understand which aspect of the parents has been revived. The picture of the parents in the patient's mind has in varying degrees undergone distortion through the infantile processes of projection and idealization, and has often retained much of its phantastic nature. Altogether, in the young infant's mind every external experience is interwoven with his phantasies and on the other hand every phantasy contains elements of actual experience, and it is only by analysing the transference situation to its depth that we are able to discover the past both in its realistic and phantastic aspects. It is also the origin of these fluctuations in earliest infancy which accounts for their strength in the transference, and for the swift changes – sometimes even within one session – between father and mother, between omnipotently kind objects and dangerous persecutors, between internal and external figures. Sometimes the analyst appears simultaneously to represent both parents – in that case often in a hostile alliance against the patient, whereby the negative transference acquires great intensity. What has then been revived or has become manifest in the transference is the mixture in the patient's phantasy of the parents as one figure, the 'combined parent figure' as I described it elsewhere.[9] This is one of the phantasy formations characteristic of the earliest stages of the Oedipus complex and which, if maintained in strength, is detrimental both to object relations and to sexual development. The phantasy of the combined parents draws its force from another element of early emotional life – i.e. from the powerful envy associated with frustrated oral desires. Through the analysis of such early situations we learn that in the baby's mind when he is frustrated (or dissatisfied from inner causes) his frustration is coupled with the feeling that another object (soon represented by the father) receives from the mother the coveted gratification and love denied to himself at that moment. Here is one root of the phantasy that the parents are combined in an everlasting mutual gratification of an oral, anal and genital nature. And this is in my view the prototype of situations of both envy and jealousy.

There is another aspect of the analysis of transference which needs mentioning. We are accustomed to speak of the transference *situation*. But do we always keep in mind the fundamental importance of this concept? It is my experience that in unravelling the details of the transference it is essential to think in terms of *total situations* transferred from the past into the present, as well as of emotions, defences and object relations.

For many years – and this is up to a point still true today – transference was understood in terms of direct references to the analyst in the patient's material. My conception of transference as rooted in the earliest stages of development and in deep layers of the unconscious is much wider and entails a technique by which from the whole material presented the *unconscious elements* of the transference are deduced. For instance, reports of patients about their everyday life, relations and activities not only give an insight into the functioning of the ego, but also reveal – if we explore their unconscious content – the defences against the anxieties stirred up in the transference situation. For the patient is bound to deal with conflicts and anxieties re-experienced towards the analyst by the same methods he used in the past. That is to say, he turns away from the analyst as he attempted to turn away from his primal objects; he tries to split the relation to him, keeping him either as a good or as a bad figure; he deflects some of the feelings and attitudes experienced towards the analyst on to other people in his current life, and this is part of 'acting out'.[10]

In keeping with my subject matter, I have predominantly discussed here the earliest experiences, situations and emotions from which transference springs. On these foundations, however, are built the later object relations and the emotional and intellectual developments which necessitate the analyst's attention no less than the earliest ones; that is to say, our field of investigation covers *all* that lies between the current situation and the earliest experiences. In fact it is not possible to find access to earliest emotions and object relations except by examining their vicissitudes in the light of later developments. It is only by linking again and again (and that means hard and patient work) later experiences with earlier ones and vice versa, it is only by consistently exploring their interplay, that present and past can come together in the patient's mind. This is one aspect of the process of integration which, as the analysis progresses, encompasses the whole of the patient's mental life. When anxiety and guilt diminish and love and hate can be better synthesized, splitting processes – a fundamental defence against anxiety – as well as repressions lessen while the ego gains in strength and coherence; the cleavage between idealized and persecutory objects diminishes; the phantastic aspects of objects lose in strength; all of which implies that unconscious phantasy life – less sharply divided off from the unconscious part of the mind – can be better utilized in ego activities, with a consequent general enrichment of the personality. I am touching here on the *differences* – as contrasted with the similarities – between transference and the first object relations. These differences are a measure of the curative effect of the analytic procedure.

I suggested above that one of the factors which bring about the repetition compulsion is the pressure exerted by the earliest anxiety situations. When persecutory and depressive anxiety and guilt diminish, there is less urge to repeat fundamental experiences over and over again, and therefore early patterns and modes of feelings are maintained with less tenacity. These fundamental changes come about through the consistent analysis of the transference; they are bound up with a deep-reaching revision of the earliest object relations and are reflected in the patient's current life as well as in the altered attitudes towards the analyst.

CHAPTER TEN

In the summer of 1955, Klein read a paper at the Nineteenth International Congress held in Geneva. In February 1956 she delivered an expanded version to the British Society of Psychoanalysis. It is this lecture, called 'A Study of Envy and Gratitude', that is published here for the first time. Klein expanded the lecture into a short book, *Envy and Gratitude: A Study of Unconscious Sources* (London, Tavistock), which was published the following year. Klein's new notion is that the infant's primary envy of all that its mother possesses and deprives it of is of fundamental importance for its psychic development. The idea received a great deal of support but also a great deal of opposition from fellow-analysts. In some ways, the negative response resembled the first hostility expressed towards Freud's concept of a death drive: the notion was found unpalatable rather than unobservable. Debate often centred more on what characterized envy, rather than on whether or not envy could be seen as a key element in psychic processes. The countervailing notion of gratitude, with which Klein balanced her idea of the prevalence of envy, was and is, often forgotten in a debate that still, to an extent, continues today.

Although Klein wrote a few more essays, this lecture introduces her last major theoretical innovation.

A STUDY OF ENVY AND GRATITUDE (1956)

From the beginning of life, the infant turns to the mother for all his needs but, in my view, which I have substantiated in other connections, this first bond already contains the fundamental elements of an object relation. Furthermore, this relation is based on an innate factor; for the breast, towards which all his desires are directed, is instinctively felt to be not only the source of nourishment but of life itself. The relation to the gratifying breast in some measure restores, if things go well, the lost prenatal unity with the mother. This largely depends on the infant's capacity to cathect sufficiently the breast or its symbolic representative, the bottle: for in this way the mother is turned into a loved object. It may well be that his having formed part of the mother in the prenatal state contributes to the innate feeling that there exists an object which will give him all he needs and desires.

An element of frustration by the breast is bound, however, to enter into the infant's earliest relation to it, because even a happy feeding situation cannot altogether replace the prenatal unity with the mother. Also, the infant's longing for an inexhaustible and always present breast – which would not only satisfy him but prevent destructive impulses and persecutory anxiety – cannot ever be fully satisfied. These unavoidable grievances, together with happy experiences, reinforce the innate conflict between love and hatred, at bottom between life and death instincts, and result in the feeling that a good and bad breast exists. As a consequence, early emotional life is characterized by a sense of losing and regaining the good object. In speaking of an innate conflict between love and hatred, I am implying that both destructive impulses and the capacity for love are, to some extent, constitutional, varying individually in strength. They are increased by external circumstances. For instance, a difficult birth and unsatisfactory feeding – and possibly even unpleasant experiences in the prenatal state – undoubtedly intensify destructive impulses, persecutory anxiety, greed and envy.

In this paper I wish to draw attention to a particular aspect of earliest object relations and internalization processes. I am referring to the effects of envy on the development of the capacity for gratitude and happiness. The contention I wish to put forward is that envy contributes to the infant's difficulties, in that he feels that the gratification he was deprived of has been kept for itself by the breast which frustrated him.

A distinction should be drawn between envy, jealousy and greed. Envy is the angry feeling that another person possesses and enjoys something desirable – the envious impulse being to take it away or to spoil it. Moreover, envy implies the subject's relation to one person only and goes back to the earliest exclusive relation with the mother. Jealousy is based on envy, but it involves the subject's relation to at least two people. Jealousy is mainly concerned with love which the subject feels is his due and which has been taken away, or is in danger of being taken away from him. In the everyday conception of jealousy, a man or a woman feels deprived of the person they love by somebody else.

Greed is an impetuous and insatiable craving, exceeding what the subject needs and what the object can and wishes to give. At the unconscious level, greed aims primarily at completely scooping out, sucking dry and devouring the breast, that is to say, its aim is destructive introjection; whereas envy not only aims at robbing in this way, but also at putting badness, primarily bad excrements and bad parts of the self, into the mother – first of all into her breast – in order to spoil and destroy her; in the deepest sense this means destroying her creativeness. This process I have defined elsewhere as a destructive aspect of projective identification which starts from the beginning of life. The difference between greed and envy, although no rigid dividing line can be drawn since they are so closely associated, would accordingly be that greed is mainly bound up with introjection and envy with projection.

My work has shown me that the first object to be envied is the feeding breast, for the infant feels that it possesses everything that he desires and that it has an unlimited flow of milk and love which it keeps for its own gratification. This feeling adds to his sense of grievance and hatred. If envy is excessive – which would indicate that paranoid and schizoid features are strong – the result is a disturbed relation to the mother.

We find this primitive envy revived in the transference situation. For instance: the analyst has just given an interpretation which brought the patient relief and produced a change of mood from despair to hope and trust. With some patients, or with the same patient at other times, this helpful interpretation may soon become the object of criticism. It is then no longer felt to be something good he has received and which he has experienced as an enrichment. The envious patient grudges the analyst the success of his work; and if his envious criticism has the effect of making him feel that the analyst and the help he is giving have become spoilt, the patient cannot introject the analyst sufficiently as a good object and cannot accept his interpretations with real conviction. He may also feel, because of guilt about devaluing the help given, that he is unworthy to benefit by analysis.

In these ways, envy plays an important part in the negative therapeutic reaction, in addition to the factors discovered by Freud and further developed by Joan Riviere. Needless to say, our patients criticize us for a variety of reasons, sometimes with justification. But a patient's need to devalue the very help he has experienced is the expression of envy. This applies particularly to paranoid patients, who indulge in the sadistic pleasure of disparaging the analyst's work even though it has given them relief. On the other hand, some of our patients try to avoid criticism and are, up to a point, very co-operative. And yet we find that their doubts and uncertainties about the value of the analysis persist. In my experience the slow progress we make in such cases has also to do with envy. The patient has split off the envious and hostile part of his self; nevertheless it is bound to influence fundamentally the course of the analysis. Other patients try to avoid criticism by becoming confused. This confusion is not only a defence but also expresses the uncertainty as to whether the analyst is still a good figure, or whether he and the help he is giving have become bad because he has been spoilt by criticism.

All these attitudes are part of the negative therapeutic reaction because they interfere with the gradual building up of a good object in the transference situation and therefore – just as in the earliest situation the good food and the primal good object could not be assimilated – in the transference situation the result of the analysis is impaired.

Thus in the context of the analytic material we can sometimes gather how the patient felt as a baby towards the mother's breast. For instance, the infant may have a grievance that the milk comes too quickly or too slowly; or that he was not given the breast when he most craved for it, and therefore when it is offered, he does not want it any more. He turns away from it and sucks his fingers instead. When he accepts the breast he may not drink enough, or the feed is disturbed. Some infants obviously have great difficulty in overcoming such grievances. With others these feelings, even though based on actual frustrations, are soon overcome: the breast is taken and the feed is fully enjoyed.

It is in the nature of envy that it spoils the primal good object and gives added impetus to sadistic attacks on the breast, which I have often described in other connections. Excessive envy increases the intensity of such attacks and their duration, and thus makes it more difficult for the infant to regain the lost good object; whereas sadistic attacks on the breast which are less determined by envy pass more quickly and therefore do not, in the infant's mind, so strongly and lastingly destroy the goodness of the object; the breast which returns is felt as an evidence that it is not injured and that it is still good.

When envy is excessive, the infant does not sufficiently build up a good object, and therefore cannot preserve it internally. Hence, somewhat later he is unable to establish firmly other good objects in his inner world.

The contrary situation holds in children with a strong capacity for love. The relation to the good object is deeply rooted and can, without being fundamentally damaged, withstand temporary states of envy, hatred and grievance – which arise even in children who are loved and well mothered. Thus, when these negative states are transient, the good object is regained time and again. This is an essential factor in establishing the good object and in laying the foundations for stability and a strong ego.

The emotions and attitudes I have referred to arise in the earliest stage of infancy when for the baby the mother is the one and only object. How far this exclusive relation remains undisturbed depends partly on external factors. But the feelings which underlie it – above all the capacity for love – appear to be innate. I have repeatedly put forward the hypothesis that the primal good object, the mother's breast, forms the core of the ego and vitally contributes to its growth and integration. We find in the analysis of our patients that the breast in its good aspects is the prototype of maternal goodness and generosity, as well as of creativeness. All this is felt by the infant in much more primitive ways than language can express it.

Strong envy of the feeding breast interferes with the capacity for complete gratification which is of vital importance for the infant's development. For if the *undisturbed* enjoyment in being fed is *frequently* experienced, the introjection of the mother's breast as a good object comes about with relative security. The capacity to fully enjoy gratification at the breast forms the foundation for all later happiness, as well as for pleasure from various sources. It is significant that Freud attributed so much importance to the pleasure–pain principle.

A full gratification at the breast means that the infant feels he has received from his loved object a unique gift, which he wants to keep. This is the basis of gratitude. Gratitude includes belief in good objects and trust in them. It includes also the ability to assimilate the loved object – not only as a source of food – and to love it without envy interfering. The more often this gift received is fully accepted, the more often the feeling of enjoyment and gratitude – implying the wish to return pleasure – is experienced. Gratitude is closely bound up with generosity. For inner wealth derives from having assimilated the good object, and this enables the individual to share its gifts with others.

To clarify my argument, a reference to my views on the early ego is necessary. I believe that it exists in a rudimentary form from the beginning of post-natal life, and performs a number of important functions. It might well be that this early ego is identical with the unconscious part of the ego which Freud postulated. Though he did not assume that an ego exists from the beginning, he attributed to the organism a function which, as I see it, can only be performed by the ego. The threat of annihilation by the death instinct within is, in my view – which differs from Freud's on this point – the primordial anxiety and it is the ego which, in the services of the life instinct, possibly even called into operation by the life instinct, deflects to some extent that threat outwards. This fundamental defence against the death instinct Freud attributed to the organism, whereas I regard this process as the primary activity of the ego.

There are other primary activities of the ego which in my view derive from the imperative need to deal with the struggle between life and death instincts. One of these functions is gradual integration. The opposite tendency of the ego to split itself and its object is partly due to the ego lacking cohesion at birth, and partly it is a defence against the primordial anxiety. I have, for many years, attributed great importance to one particular process of splitting, the division of the breast into a good and bad object. I took this to be an expression of the innate conflict between love and hate and the ensuing anxieties. However, coexisting with this division there appear to be various processes of splitting, such as fragmenting the ego and its objects, whereby a dispersal of the destructive impulses is achieved. This is one of the characteristic defences during the paranoid-schizoid position which I believe normally extends over the first three or four months of life.

This does not of course mean that during that period the infant is not capable of fully enjoying his feeds, the relation to his mother and frequent states of physical comfort and well-being. What it does mean is that when anxiety arises, it is mainly of a paranoid nature and the defences against it, as well as the mechanisms used, are predominantly schizoid. The same applies, *mutatis mutandis*, to the infant's emotional life during the period characterized by the depressive position.

To return to the splitting process which I take to be a precondition for the young infant's relative stability: during the first few months he predominantly keeps the good object apart from the bad one and thus, in a fundamental way, preserves it. This primal division only succeeds if there is adequate capacity for love. Excessive envy, a corollary of destructive impulses, interferes with the building up of a good object and the primal split between the good and bad breast cannot be sufficiently achieved. The result is that later the differentiation between good and bad is disturbed in various connections. On the other hand, if the split between the two aspects of the object is too deep, the all-important processes of ego integration and object synthesis, as well as of mitigation of hatred by love, are impaired and the depressive position cannot be worked through. A very deep and sharp division between loved and hated objects indicates that destructive impulses, envy and persecutory anxiety are very strong and serve as a defence against these emotions.

I am touching here on the problem of idealization. This is an early process which I take to be universal, but the motive power behind it varies individually. As I discovered many years ago in my work with young children, idealization is a corollary to persecutory anxiety – a defence against it – and the ideal breast is the counterpart of the devouring breast. But I also found that idealization derives from the innate feeling that an extremely good breast exists, a feeling which leads to the longing for a good object. Infants whose capacity for love is strong have less need for idealization than those in whom destructive impulses and persecutory anxiety are paramount. Excessive idealization denotes that persecution is the main driving force. It becomes also an important defence against envy, because if the object is exalted so much that comparison with it becomes impossible, envy is counteracted. The idealized object, which largely replaces the good one, is much less integrated in the ego since it stems predominantly from persecution.

While people who have been able to establish the primal good object with relative security are capable of retaining their love for it in spite of its shortcomings, with others idealization is a characteristic of their love relations and friendships. This tends to break down and then one loved object may have to be frequently exchanged for another; for no such person can fully come up to expectations. The former idealized person is then often felt as a persecutor (which shows the origin of idealization as a counterpart to persecution) and on to him is projected the subject's envious and critical attitude.

There is a direct link between the envy experienced towards the mother's breast and the development of jealousy. Jealousy is based on the suspicion of and rivalry with the father, who is accused of having taken away the mother's breast, and the mother. This rivalry marks the early stages of the positive and negative Oedipus complexes which arise concurrently with the depressive position in the second quarter of the first year. The importance of the combined parent figure, expressed in such phantasies as the mother or the mother's breast containing the penis of the father, or the father containing the mother, have been elaborated by me in earlier writings. The influence of this combined parent figure on the infant's ability to differentiate between the parents and to establish good relations with each of them, is affected by the strength of envy and the ensuing jealousy. For the feeling that the parents are always getting sexual gratification from one another reinforces the phantasy – derived from various sources – that they are always combined. The consequence may be a lasting disturbance in the relation to both parents.

During the period characterized by the depressive position, when the infant progressively integrates his feelings of love and hatred and synthesizes the good and bad aspects of the mother, he goes through states of mourning bound up with feelings of guilt. He also begins to understand more of the external world and realizes that he cannot keep his mother to himself as his exclusive possession. Jealousy is, as we know, inherent in the Oedipus situation and is accompanied by hate and death wishes. Normally, however, the gain of new objects who can be loved – the father and siblings – and other compensations which the developing ego derives from the external world, mitigate jealousy and grievance to some extent. If paranoid and schizoid mechanisms are strong, jealousy – and at bottom envy – remain unmitigated.

All this has an essential bearing on the development of the Oedipus complex. Freud has shown how vital the relation of the girl to the mother is in her subsequent relations to men. I believe that if her first oral gratifications have been disturbed, mainly by internal factors such as strong envy, greed and hatred, her turning away from the breast towards the penis is largely a flight mechanism. If this is so, the relation to the father, and later on to other men, may suffer in different ways.

Freud's discovery of penis envy in women, and its link with aggressive impulses, was a basic contribution to the understanding of envy. When penis envy and castration wishes are strong, the envied object, the penis, is to be destroyed, and the man who owns it deprived of it. There are a number of factors contributing to penis envy which are, however, not relevant to my thesis. In this context I wish to consider the woman's penis envy only in so far as it is of oral origin. As we know, under the dominance of oral desires, the penis is strongly equated with the breast (as Abraham has shown) and in my experience penis envy can be traced back to envy of the mother's breast.

Much in the girl's relation to the father depends on whether envy of the mother's possession of the father prevails, or whether she is mainly intent on gaining his love entirely for herself. If envy is the main factor, her desire to spoil the father for the mother makes him into a valueless or bad object, undermines her relation to men and may express itself in frigidity. If jealousy about the father's love predominates, she may combine some hatred against the mother with love for the father.

In men, the envy of the mother's breast is also a very important factor. If it is strong and oral gratification thereby impaired, hatred and anxieties are transferred to the female genital. Whereas normally the genital development enables the boy to retain his mother as a love-object, a deep disturbance in the oral relation opens the way for severe difficulties in the genital relation to women. Excessive envy of the breast is likely to extend to all feminine attributes, in particular to the woman's capacity to bear children.

At bottom, envy is directed against creativeness: what the envied breast has to offer is unconsciously felt as the prototype of creativeness, because the breast and the milk it gives is felt to be the source of life. In both men and women this envy plays a major part in the desires to take away the attributes of the other sex, as well as to possess or spoil those of the parent of the same sex. It follows that paranoid jealousy and rivalry in the direct and inverted Oedipus situations are in both the male and female, however divergent their development, based on excessive envy towards the primal object: the mother and her breast.

I shall now illustrate some of my conclusions by clinical material. My first instance is taken from the analysis of a woman patient. She had been breast-fed, but circumstances had otherwise not been favourable and she was convinced that her babyhood and feeding had been wholly unsatisfactory. Her grievance about the past linked with hopelessness about the present and future. Envy of the feeding breast, and the ensuing difficulties in object relations, had already been extensively analysed prior to the material to which I am going to refer.

The patient telephoned and said that she could not come for treatment because of a pain in her shoulder. On the next day she rang me to say that she was still not well but expected to see me on the following day. When, on the third day, she actually came, she was full of complaints. She had been looked after by her maid, but nobody else had taken an interest in her. She described to me that at one moment her pain had suddenly increased, together with a sense of extreme coldness. She had felt an impetuous need for somebody to come at once and cover up her shoulder so that it should get warm, and go away again as soon as that was done. It occurred to her at that moment that this must be how she had felt as a baby when she wanted to be looked after and nobody came.

It was characteristic of the patient's attitude to people and threw light on her earliest relation to the breast that she desired to be looked after but at the same time repelled the very object which was to gratify her. The suspicion of the gift received, together with her impetuous need to be cared for, which ultimately meant a desire to be fed, expressed her ambivalent attitude towards the breast. I have referred to infants whose response to frustration is to make insufficient use of the gratification which even the delayed feed could give them. I would assume that though they do not give up their desire for a gratifying breast, they cannot enjoy it and therefore repel it. The case under discussion illustrates some of the reasons for this attitude: suspicion of the gift she wished to receive because the object was already spoilt by envy and hatred, and therefore deep resentment about every frustration. We also have to remember – and this applies to other adults in whom envy is marked – that many disappointing experiences, no doubt partly due to her own attitude, had even beforehand made her feel that the desired care would not be satisfactory.

In the course of this session the patient reported a dream: she was in a restaurant, sat down at a table, but nobody came to serve her. She decided to join a queue and fetch herself something to eat. In front of her was a woman who took two or three little cakes and went away with them. The patient also took two or three little cakes. From her associations I am selecting the following: the woman seemed very determined, and her figure reminded her of mine. There was a sudden doubt about the name of the cakes (actually *petits fours*) which she first thought were *petit fru*, which reminded her of *petit frau* and thus of *Frau Klein*.[1] The gist of my interpretations was that her grievance about the missed analytic sessions related to the unsatisfactory feeds and unhappiness in babyhood. The two cakes out of the 'two or three' stood for the breast which she felt she had been twice deprived of by missing analytic sessions. The fact that the woman was 'determined' and that the patient followed her example in taking the cakes pointed both to her identification with the analyst and at her projection of her greed on to her. In the context of this paper, one aspect of the dream is most relevant. The woman who went away with the two or three *petits fours* stood not only for the breast which was withheld, but also for the breast which was going to feed itself. (Taken together with the other material, the 'determined' analyst did not only represent a breast but a person with whose qualities, good or bad, the patient identified herself.)

To frustration was thus added envy of the breast. This envy gave rise to bitter resentment, for the mother was felt to be selfish and mean, feeding and loving herself rather than her baby. In this analytic situation I was suspected of having enjoyed myself during the time when she was absent, or of having given the time to other patients whom I preferred. The queue which the patient had to join referred to other more favoured rivals.

The response to the analysis of the dream was a striking change in the emotional situation. The patient now experienced a feeling of happiness and gratitude more vividly than in previous analytic sessions. She had tears in her eyes, which was unusual, and said that she felt as if now she had had an entirely satisfactory feed.

It also occurred to her that her breast-feeding and her infancy might have been happier than it appeared to her in retrospect. Moreover, she felt more hopeful about the future and about the result of her analysis. The patient had more fully realized one part of herself which was by no means unknown to her in other connections. She was fully aware that she was envious and jealous of various people but had not been able to recognize it sufficiently in the relation to the analyst because it was too painful to acknowledge that she was grudging me the success of the analysis on which her hopes were centred. In this session, after the interpretation of it, her envy had lessened; the capacity for enjoyment and gratitude had come to the fore, and she was able to experience a happy feed. This emotional situation had to be worked through over and over again, both in the positive and negative transference, until a more stable result was achieved.

We find that some patients are even quite able to express their dislike and criticism of the analyst; but this differs fundamentally from the realization that at bottom it was they who by their envy spoilt the analyst and his work. The envious part of the self is split off, but exerts its power and contributes to the negative therapeutic reaction.

To come back to the patient under discussion, it was by enabling her gradually to bring the split-off parts of her self together in relation to the analyst, and by her recognizing how envious and therefore suspicious she was of me, and in the first place of her mother, that the experience of that happy feed came about. This was bound up with feelings of gratitude. In the course of the analysis envy was diminished and feelings of gratitude became much more frequent and lasting.

In passing I would say that it is not only in children but also in adults that a full revival of the emotions felt during the earliest feeding experiences can come about in the transference situation. For instance, a feeling of hunger or thirst comes up very strongly during the session and has gone after the interpretation which was felt to have satisfied it. One of my patients, overcome by such feelings, got up from the couch and put his arms round one section of the arch which separated one part of my consulting room from the other. I have repeatedly heard the expression at the end of such a session, 'I have been well nourished.' The good object, in its earliest primitive form as the mother who takes care of the baby and feeds him, had been regained.

My next example is of a woman patient whom I would describe as fairly normal. She had in the course of time become more and more aware of envy experienced both towards an older sister and towards her mother. The envy of the sister had been counteracted by a feeling of strong intellectual superiority which had a basis in fact, and by an unconscious feeling that the sister was extremely neurotic. The envy towards the mother was counteracted by very strong feelings of love towards her and appreciation of her goodness.

The patient reported a dream in which she was alone in a railway carriage with a woman of whom she could only see the back; she was leaning towards the door of the compartment and was in great danger of falling out. The patient held her strongly, grasping her by the belt with one hand; with the other hand she wrote a notice and put it up on the window, to the effect that a doctor was engaged with a patient in this compartment and should not be disturbed.

The associations to the dream were as follows: the patient felt that the figure on whom she kept a tight grip was a part of herself and a mad part. In the dream she had an urgent feeling that she should not let the woman fall out but should keep her in the compartment (standing for herself) and deal with her. The associations to the hair, which was only seen from behind, were to her older sister. Further associations led to recognition of rivalry and envy in relation to her, going back to the time when the patient was still a child while her sister was already being courted.

These associations also led to a special dress which her mother wore and which as a child the patient had both admired and coveted. This dress had very clearly shown the shape of the breasts, and it became more evident than ever before (though none of this was entirely new), that what she originally envied and spoiled in her feelings was the mother's breast.

I said that the patient felt that she had to keep a grip on a mad, split-off part of herself, though this mad part was also linked with the internalization of the neurotic sister. The result of this realization, following the dream, on the patient who had reason to regard herself as reasonably normal, was a feeling of strong surprise and shock. An increased feeling of guilt, both towards her sister and her mother, was aroused through this realization, and this led to a further revision of her earliest relations. She arrived at a much more compassionate understanding of the deficiencies of her sister and felt that she had not loved her sufficiently. She also discovered that in her early childhood she had loved her much more than she had realized.

The feeling that she had to keep a firm hold on that figure implied that she should also have helped her sister more, prevented her, as it were, from falling, and this feeling was now re-experienced in connection with an internalized sister. The revision of her earliest relations was bound up with changes in her internal situation, in particular with changes in feelings towards her introjected early objects. The fact that that sister also represented the mad part of herself turned out to be partly a projection of her own schizoid and paranoid feelings on to the sister, but it was together with this realization that both the split in her ego diminished and a fuller integration came about.

In both these cases – and this applies to others as well – the relation to the analyst as an internal object turned out to be of fundamental importance. Generally speaking, when anxiety about envy and its consequences reaches a climax, the patient, in varying degrees, feels persecuted by the analyst as a grudging and envious internal object, disturbing his life, work and activities. When this occurs, the good object is felt to be lost, and with it inner security. My observations have shown me that when at any stage in life the relation to the good object is seriously disturbed, not only is inner security lost but character deterioration sets in. The prevalence of internal persecutory objects reinforces destructive impulses; whereas if the good object is well established, the identification with it strengthens the capacity for love and constructive impulses. This is in keeping with the hypothesis, put forward in this paper, that if the good object is deeply rooted, temporary disturbances can be withstood and the foundation is laid for mental health, character formation and a successful ego development.

I suggested above that the internalized persecuting object, which is felt to be grudging and envious owing to the individual's envy being projected on to it, is experienced as particularly dangerous because it has the effect of hampering all attempts at reparation and creativeness. Envy interferes most of all with these constructive attempts because the object which is to be restored is at the same time attacked and devalued by envy. Since these feelings are transferred to the analyst, the incapacity to make reparation, which shows itself in the incapacity to co-operate in the analysis, forms part of the negative therapeutic reaction, in addition to the factors I have mentioned earlier. We have to be prepared for lengthy work if we want to achieve a better and more stable balance in the deep layers, in which envy and destructive impulses originate. I have always been convinced of the importance of Freud's finding that working through is one of the main tasks of the analysis. My experiences in analysing the processes by which a deeply hated and despised part of the personality is split off and my attempts to heal this split and bring about integration have deepened further this conviction.

I can only touch here on the fluctuation and difficulties we encounter when we analyse the splitting processes which are bound up with the analysis of envy. For instance, the patient has experienced gratitude for and appreciation of the analyst's skill, but this very skill becomes the cause of the transformation of admiration into envy. Envy may be counteracted by pride in having a good analyst. But if this pride stirs up possessiveness and greed, there is a return to the baby's greedy attitude which could be described in the following terms: I have everything I want, the good mother belongs only to me. Such a greedy and controlling attitude is liable to spoil the relation to the good object. Guilt about destructive greed might soon lead to another defence, such as: I do not want to injure the analyst (mother); I rather refrain from accepting her gifts. Such an attitude in turn may easily give rise to guilt about not accepting the analyst's help.

Each of the changes I have just enumerated has to be analysed as it comes up in the transference situation. It is by working through a multitude of defences and the emotions which underlie these defences that we can in time help the patient to achieve a better balance. With this end in view we have again and again to analyse the splitting processes, which I now think is the most difficult part of the analytic procedure. Since no anxiety can be experienced without the ego using whatever defences are available, these splitting processes play an important role as defences against persecutory and depressive anxieties. It appears to me that the realization of envy and the harm done by it to the loved object, and the deep anxieties to which this realization gives rise, contributes to the strong resistance we meet in attempting to undo the split and to bring about steps in integration. It is of the greatest importance to observe every detail in the transference situation which throws light on the earliest difficulties. In this way we sometimes discover that even a strong positive transference may be deceptive for it may be based on idealization and a covering up of the hatred and envy which are split off.

I have described how painful it is for the patient to realize his harmful and spoiling envy against the loved mother, and why there is such a strong resistance against such insight. When the patient nevertheless, through the analytic procedure, comes face to face with this split-off hated and despised part of his personality, this is often experienced as a shock and leads to depression. The feeling of guilt resulting from the realization of destructive envy may lead to the patient temporarily inhibiting his own capacities. We encounter a very different line when the undoing of the split is felt as unbearable and the consequence is an increase of omnipotent and even megalomaniac phantasies. This can be a critical stage because the patient may take refuge in increasing his hostile attitudes. Thus he feels justified in hating the analyst and in thinking that he, the patient, is superior to him and undervalued by him. He feels that everything so far achieved in the analysis was his own doing. To go back to the early situation, the patient as an infant sometimes felt superior to the parents; I have also met with the phantasies that he or she created, as it were, the mother or gave birth to her and possessed the mother's breasts. It was thus the mother who robbed the patient of the breast and not the patient who robbed her. Projection, omnipotence and persecution are then at their highest.

I am stressing the difficulties arising at certain points in the analysis in patients whose envy is constitutionally strong; but we should remember that people whose analysis has never been carried into such depths, or who have never been analysed at all, may experience similar difficulties, and even break down, because the underlying envy and anxieties are operative and may come up under certain circumstances. Without being over-optimistic, because I realize the difficulties and limitations of psycho-analytic therapy, I believe that the analysis of those deep and severe disturbances is in many cases a safeguard against potential danger resulting from excessively envious and omnipotent attitudes.

The insight gained in the process of integration leads step by step to the patient recognizing that there are dangerous parts in his self; he becomes able to accept this because with growing integration the capacity for love increases and envy and hatred are mitigated. The pain which the patient goes through during these processes is gradually diminished by improvements bound up with integration. For instance, patients become able to make decisions which they were previously unable to come to make, and in general to use their gifts more freely. This is linked up with a lessening inhibition of their capacity to make reparation. Their powers of enjoyment may increase in many ways and hope comes up again and again.

The enrichment of the personality by integrating split-off parts of the self is a vital process. Together with hatred, envy and destructiveness, other important parts of the personality had been lost and are regained in the course of the analysis.

Freud accepted a number of factors as constitutional. For instance, in his view anal-erotism in many people is a constitutional factor.

In this paper I have particularly emphasized envy, greed, hatred and feelings of persecution in relation to the primal object, the mother's breast, as largely innate. I have linked these constitutional factors with the preponderance of the one or other instinct in the fusion of the life and death instincts assumed by Freud. Abraham, too, believed in innate factors. In particular he discovered the constitutional element in the strength of oral impulses, which he connected with the aetiology of manic-depressive illness. He found that envy is an oral trait but – and this is where my views differ from his – he assumed that envy and hostility belong to a later, the oral-sadistic stage. Abraham mentioned envy as an anal trait which, however, originates in the oral phase. He did not speak of gratitude but he described generosity as an oral feature.[2] Eisler (1919) had emphasized the constitutional factor in oral erotism and had recognized envy as an oral trait.[3] My concept of envy also includes the anal-sadistic tendencies which express themselves in splitting, projecting and putting badness first into the breast and then into the mother's body. The fact that not only oral-sadistic but also urethral- and anal-sadistic trends are operative from the beginning of life has been suggested by me as far back as my 'Psycho-Analysis of Children'.

The existence of constitutional factors points to the limitations of psycho-analytic therapy. While I am quite aware of them, my experience has taught me that nevertheless we are able in a number of cases to produce fundamental and favourable changes.

I have found that whenever integration has come about more fully and the patient has been able up to a point to accept the hating and hated part of his personality, he has also in retrospect established the primal good object more securely than he had done in infancy. We can, therefore, look from another angle at the aspects of technique which I am trying to convey. From the beginning all emotions attach themselves to the first object. If destructive impulses, envy and paranoid anxiety are excessive, the infant grossly distorts and magnifies every frustration from external sources which he experiences, and the mother's breast turns externally and internally predominantly into a persecutory object. Then even actual gratifications cannot be sufficiently accepted and cannot sufficiently counteract persecutory anxiety. In taking the analysis back to earliest infancy, we enable the patient to revive fundamental situations – a revival which I have often spoken of as 'memories in feelings'. This implies that in retrospect the patient lives more successfully through early frustrations. The means by which this is achieved is the analysis of the negative and positive transference which takes us back to earliest object relations. If we succeed, the patient realizes his own destructive impulses and projections, revises therefore his first object relations and establishes, in retrospect, his good object more securely, in particular by establishing the analyst as a good object in the transference. This can only come about if splitting processes, which have been largely used as a defence against persecution and guilt, lose in strength as a result of analysis. Thus the more integrated ego becomes capable of experiencing guilt and feelings of responsibility which it was unable to face in infancy; object synthesis and therefore a mitigation of hatred by love becomes possible, and greed and envy, which are corollaries of destructive impulses, lose in power. It is on these lines that also the psycho-analysis of psychotics can succeed.

To put it differently: by the consistent analysis of the negative as well as the positive transference, persecutory anxiety and schizoid mechanisms are diminished and the patient can work through the depressive position. When his initial inability to establish a good object is to some extent overcome, his capacity for enjoyment, and the appreciation of the gifts received from the good object, increases step by step and envy is diminished and gratitude becomes possible. These changes extend to many aspects of the patient's personality and range from earliest emotional life to adult experiences and relations. In the analysis of the effects of early disturbances on the whole development lies, I believe, our greatest hope of helping our patients.

NOTES

CHAPTER I: *The Psycho-Analytic Play Technique: Its History and Significance*

1. A description of this early approach is given in Anna Freud's book *Einführung in die Technik der Kinderanalyse*, 1927 (*Introduction to the Technique of Child Analysis*, Nervous and Mental Disease Monograph series, No. 48, 1929).

2. 'The Development of a Child', 1923; 'The Rôle of the School in the Libidinal Development of the Child', 1924; and 'Early Analysis', 1926. [*Editor's note:* Klein was able to make psychoanalytic interpretations to 'Fritz' in Hungary and later in Berlin because he was in fact her youngest son, Erich. Internal evidence makes this clear; further details are given by J.-M. Petot and P. Grosskurth (see p. 242).]

3. See also *On the Bringing up of Children* (ed. Rickman), 1936, and 'The Oedipus Complex in the Light of Early Anxieties', *CW*, Vol. I.

4. They are mainly: little wooden men and women, usually in two sizes, cars, wheelbarrows, swings, trains, aeroplanes, animals, trees, bricks, houses, fences, paper, scissors, a knife, pencils, chalks or paints, glue, balls and marbles, plasticine and string.

5. It has a washable floor, running water, a table, a few chairs, a little sofa, some cushions and a chest of drawers.

6. Instances both of play with toys and of the games described above can be found in *The Psycho-Analysis of Children*, *CW*, Vol. II (particularly in Chapters 2, 3 and 4). See also 'Personification in the Play of Children', *CW*, Vol. I.

7. This child, whose analysis was begun in 1924, was another of the cases that helped to develop my play technique.

8. Cf. *The Psycho-Analysis of Children*, *CW*, Vol. II.

9. Rita had eighty-three sessions, Trude eighty-two sessions.

10. See 'The Oedipus Complex in the Light of Early Anxieties', *CW*, Vol. I. p. 404.

11. Cf. 'A Short History of the Development of the Libido, Viewed in the Light of Mental Disorders', 1924, *Selected Papers*, Hogarth, 1927.

12. Ruth had 190 sessions, Peter 278 sessions.

13. This growing conviction about the fundamental importance of Abraham's discoveries was also the result of my analysis with him, which began in 1924 and was cut short fourteen months later through his illness and death.

14. Described under the name 'Erna' in *The Psycho-Analysis of Children*, Chapter 3, *CW*, Vol. II.

15. Cf. 'Early Stages of the Oedipus Conflict' (see this volume, Chapter 3).

16. Cf. 'The Importance of Symbol-Formation in the Development of the Ego' (see this volume, Chapter 5).

17. These and other conclusions are contained in the two papers I have already mentioned, 'Early Stages of the Oedipus Conflict' (see this volume, Chapter 3) and 'The Importance of Symbol-Formation in the Development of the Ego' (see this volume, Chapter 5). See also 'Personification in the Play of Children', *CW*, Vol. I.

18. It is possible that the understanding of the contents of psychotic anxieties and of the urgency to interpret them was brought home to me in the analysis of a paranoiac-schizophrenic man who came to me for one month only. In 1922 a colleague who was going on holiday asked me to take over for a month a schizophrenic patient of his. I found from the first hour onwards that I must not allow the patient to remain

silent for any length of time. I felt that his silence implied danger, and in every such instance I interpreted his suspicions of me, e.g. that I was plotting with his uncle and would have him certified again (he had recently been de-certified) – material which on other occasions he verbally expressed. Once when I had interpreted his silence in this way, connecting it with former material, the patient, sitting up, asked me in a threatening tone: 'Are you going to send me back to the asylum?' But he soon became quieter and began to speak more freely. That showed me that I had been on the right lines and should continue to interpret his suspicions and feelings of persecution. To some extent a positive as well as a negative transference to me came about; but at one point, when his fear of women came up very strongly, he demanded from me the name of a male analyst to whom he could turn. I gave him a name, but he never approached this colleague. During that month I saw the patient every day. The analyst who had asked me to take over found some progress on his return and wished me to continue the analysis. I refused, having become fully aware of the danger of treating a paranoiac without any protection or other suitable management. During the time when I analysed him, he often stood for hours opposite my house, looking up at my window, though it was only on a few occasions that he rang the bell and asked to see me. I may mention that after a short time he was again certified. Although I did not at the time draw any theoretical conclusions from this experience, I believe that this fragment of an analysis may have contributed to my later insight into the psychotic nature of infantile anxieties and to the development of my technique.

19. As we know, Freud found that there is no structural difference between the normal and the neurotic, and this discovery has been of the greatest importance in the understanding of mental processes in general. My hypothesis that anxieties of a psychotic nature are ubiquitous in infancy, and underlie the infantile neurosis, is an extension of Freud's discovery.

20. The conclusions I have presented in the last paragraph can be found fully dealt with in *The Psycho-Analysis of Children*, *CW*, Vol. II.

21. In this connection, cf. Dr Ernest Jones's important paper 'The Theory of Symbolism', 1916.

22. 'The Importance of Symbol-Formation in the Development of the Ego' (see this volume, Chapter 5).

23. This conclusion has since influenced the understanding of the schizophrenic mode of communication and has found its place in the treatment of schizophrenia.

24. I cannot deal here with the fundamental differences which, besides common features, exist between the normal, the neurotic and the psychotic.

25. 'Personification in the Play of Children', *CW*, Vol. I.

26. 'A Contribution to the Psychogenesis of Manic-Depressive States' (see this volume, Chapter 6).

27. 'Notes on Some Schizoid Mechanisms' (see this volume, Chapter 8).

28. W. R. D. Fairbairn, 'A Revised Psychopathology of the Psychoses and Neuroses', 1941.

29. The play technique has also influenced work with children in other fields, as for example in child guidance work and in education. The development of educational methods in England has been given fresh impetus by Susan Isaacs' research at the Malting House School. Her books about that work have been widely read and have had a lasting effect on educational techniques in this country, especially where young children are concerned. Her approach was strongly influenced by her great appreciation of child analysis, in particular of play technique; and it is largely due to her that in

England the psycho-analytic understanding of children has contributed to developments in education.

CHAPTER 2: *The Psychological Principles of Infant Analysis*

1. With this conclusion is very closely connected a second, which I can only indicate here.

In a number of children's analyses I discovered that the little girl's choice of the father as love-object ensued on weaning. This deprivation, which is followed by the training in cleanliness (a process which presents itself to the child as a new and grievous withdrawal of love), loosens the bond to the mother and brings into operation the heterosexual attraction, reinforced by the father's caresses, which are now construed as a seduction. As a love-object the father, too, subserves in the first instance the purpose of oral gratification. In the paper which I read at the Salzburg Congress in April 1924, I gave examples to show that children at first conceive of, and desire, coitus as an oral act.

I think that the effect of these deprivations on the development of the Oedipus complex in *boys* is at once inhibitory and promotive. The *inhibitory* effect of these traumas is seen in the fact that it is to which the boy subsequently reverts whenever he tries to escape from his mother fixation and which reinforce his inverted Oedipus attitude. The circumstance that these traumas, which pave the way for the castration complex, proceed from the mother is also, as I have proved, the reason why in both sexes it is the mother who in the deepest strata of the unconscious is specially dreaded as castrator.

On the other hand, however, the oral and anal deprivation of love appears to *promote* the development of the Oedipus situation in boys, for it compels them to change their libido position and to desire the mother as a genital love-object.

2. The close connection of such elaborations with anxiety has already been demonstrated by me in my paper on *Infant Analysis* (*Int. J. Psycho-Anal.*, Vol. VII, 1926), where I discussed the relation between anxiety and inhibition.

3. *Popo* = buttocks. *Kacki* = faeces. *Kucks, Kuchen* = cakes. *Gucken* = look.

4. Rita's castration complex manifested itself in a number of neurotic symptoms as well as in the development of her character. Her games, too, showed very clearly her very strong father identification and her fear of failing in the male role – an anxiety which had its origin in the castration complex.

5. Children cannot change the circumstances of their lives, as adults often do at the end of an analysis. But a child has been very greatly helped if, as a result of analysis, we enable him to feel more at ease in the existing circumstances and to develop better. Moreover, the clearing up of neurosis in children often diminishes the difficulties of their milieu. For instance, I have repeatedly proved that the mother's reactions were much less neurotic when favourable changes took place in her children after analysis.

6. My analyses repeatedly demonstrate how many different things dolls, for example, can mean in play. Sometimes they stand for the penis, sometimes for the child stolen from the mother, sometimes for the little patient itself, etc. It is only by examining the minutest details of the game and their interpretation that the connections are revealed, without which our results must remain imperfect. The *material* that children produce during an analytic hour, as they pass from play with toys to dramatization in their own persons and, again, to playing with water, cutting out paper, or drawing; the *manner* in which they do this; the *reason* why they change from one to another; the *means* they choose for their representations – all this medley

of factors, which so often seems confused and meaningless, is seen to be in perfect conformity with a plan and the underlying sources and thoughts are revealed to us if we interpret them just like dreams. Moreover, in their play children often represent the same thing as has appeared in some dream which they have narrated before and they often produce associations to a dream by means of the play which follows it and which is their most important mode of expressing themselves.

7. *Collected Papers*, Vol. III, p. 475, and SE, Vol. XVII, pp. 8–9.

8. At the Eighth International Psycho-Analytical Congress, held in Salzburg in 1924, I showed that a fundamental mechanism in children's play and in all subsequent sublimations is the discharge of masturbation phantasies. This underlies all play activity and serves as a constant stimulus to play (compulsion to repetition). Inhibitions in play and in learning have their origin in an exaggerated repression of these phantasies and, with them, of all phantasy. Sexual experiences are associated with the masturbation phantasies and, with these, find representation and abreaction in play. Amongst the experiences dramatized, representations of the primal scene play a prominent part and they regularly appear in the foreground of the analyses of young children. It is only after a considerable amount of analysis, which has partially revealed the primal scene and the genital development, that we come on representations of pregenital experiences and phantasies.

9. This training, which Erna had felt as a most cruel act of coercion, was in reality accomplished without any sort of harshness and so easily that, at the age of one year, she was perfectly clean in her habits. A strong incentive was her unusually early developed ambition, which, however, caused her to face all the measures taken to train her from the very beginning as an outrage. This early ambition was the primary condition of her sensitiveness to blame and of the precocious and marked development of her sense of guilt. But it is a common thing to see these feelings of guilt already playing a very big part in the training in cleanliness, and we can recognize in them the first beginnings of the super-ego.

CHAPTER 3: *Early Stages of the Oedipus Conflict*

1. *Internationale Zeitschrift für Psychoanalyse*, Vol. XI, 1925.

2. Cf. here Reich: *Die Funktion des Orgasmus*, Internationaler Psycho-analytischer Verlag.

3. H. Deutsch: *Psychoanalyse der weiblichen Sexualfunktion*.

4. We regularly come across the unconscious reproach that the mother has seduced the child whilst tending it. The explanation is that at the period when she had to minister to its bodily needs the Oedipus tendencies were awaking.

5. Cf. Hárnik's paper at the Innsbruck Psycho-Analytical Congress: 'Die ökonomischen Beziehungen zwischen dem Schuldgefühl und dem weiblichen Narzissmus'.

6. Karl Abraham, *Selected Papers*, International Psycho-Analytical Library, No. 13.

CHAPTER 5: *The Importance of Symbol Formation in the Development of the Ego*

1. Cf. my 'Early Stages of the Oedipus Conflict' (this volume, Chapter 3).

2. *Hemmung, Symptom und Angst*, Vienna, *Gesammelte Schriften*, Vol. XI, 23, and *SE*, Vol. XX, p. 104.

3. 'Infant Analysis', *Int. J. Psycho-Anal.* Vol. VII, 1926.

4. By the end of his first year it struck her that the child was abnormal, and this had a still worse effect on her attitude towards him.

5. In Dick's analysis, moreover, this symptom has hitherto been the most difficult to overcome.

6. This applies only to the introductory phase of the analysis and to other limited portions of it. When once access to the Ucs has been gained and the degree of anxiety has been diminished, play activities, speech associations and all the other modes of representation begin to make their appearance, alongside of the ego development which is made possible by the analytic work.

7. Here I found the explanation of a peculiar apprehensiveness which Dick's mother had noticed in him when he was about five months old and again from time to time at later periods. When the child was defecating and urinating, his expression was one of great anxiety. Since the faeces were not hard, the fact that he suffered from *prolapsus ani* and haemorrhoids did not seem enough to account for his apprehensiveness, especially as it manifested itself in just the same way when he was passing urine. During the analytic hour this anxiety reached such a pitch that when Dick told me he wanted to urinate or defecate he did so – in either case – only after long hesitation, with every indication of deep anxiety and with tears in his eyes. After we had analysed this anxiety his attitude towards both these functions was very different and is now almost normal.

8. Cf. my paper on 'Personification in the Play of Children', *Int. J. Psycho-Anal.*, Vol. X, 1929.

9. The fact, however, that analysis made it possible to establish contact with Dick's mind and brought about some advance in so comparatively short a time suggests the possibility that there had already been some latent development as well as the slight development outwardly manifest. But, even if we suppose this, the total development was so abnormally meagre that the hypothesis of a regression from a stage already successfully reached will hardly meet the case.

10. I will cite elsewhere the material upon which I am basing this view and will give more detailed reasons in support of it. (See *The Psycho-Analysis of Children*, *CW*, Vol. II.)

CHAPTER 6: *A Contribution to the Psychogenesis of Manic-Depressive States*

1. *The Psycho-Analysis of Children*, Chapters 8 and 9, *CW*, Vol. II.

2. 'A Psycho-Analytic Approach to the Classification of Mental Disorders', *Journal of Mental Science*, October 1932.

3. I would refer the reader to my account of the phase in which the child makes onslaughts on the mother's body. This phase is initiated by the onset of oral sadism and in my view it is the basis of paranoia (cf. *The Psycho-Analysis of Children*, Chapter 8, *CW*, Vol. II).

4. Klein, 'Infantile Anxiety Situations Reflected in a Work of Art and in the Creative Impulse' (see this volume, Chapter 4); also *The Psycho-Analysis of Children*.

5. For many years now I have supported the view that the source of a child's fixation to its mother is not simply its dependence on her, but also its anxiety and sense of guilt, and that these feelings are connected with its early aggression against her.

6. I have explained that, gradually, by unifying and then splitting up the good and bad, the phantastic and the real, the external and the internal objects, the ego makes

its way towards a more realistic conception both of the external and of the internal objects and thus obtains a satisfactory relation to both.

7. In his *The Ego and the Id*, Freud has pointed out that in melancholia the destructive component has become concentrated in the super-ego and is directed against the ego.

8. It is well known that some children display an urgent need to be kept under strict discipline and thus to be stopped by external agency from doing wrong.

9. 'Notes upon a Case of Obsessional Neurosis' (1909), *Collected Papers*, Vol. III, and *SE*, Vol. X, p. 241.

10. As Melitta Schmideberg has pointed out, cf. 'The Role of Psychotic Mechanisms in Cultural Development', *Int. J. Psycho-Anal.* Vol. XII, 1931.

11. Melanie Klein, *The Psycho-Analysis of Children*, p. 206, *CW*, Vol. II.

12. Dr Clifford Scott mentioned in his course of lectures on psychoses, at the Institute of Psycho-Analysis, in the autumn of 1934, that in his experience in schizophrenia clinically the hypochondriacal symptoms are more manifold and bizarre and are linked to persecutions and part-object functions. This may be seen even after a short examination. In depressive reactions clinically the hypochondriacal symptoms are less varied and more related in their expression to ego functions.

13. This brings me to another question of terminology. In my former work I have described the psychotic anxieties and mechanisms of the child in terms of phases of development. The genetic connection between them, it is true, is given full justice by this description, and so is the fluctuation which goes on between them under the pressure of anxiety until more stability is reached; but since in normal development the psychotic anxieties and mechanisms never solely predominate (a fact which, of course, I have emphasized) the term psychotic phases is not really satisfactory. I am now using the term 'position' in relation to the child's early developmental psychotic anxieties and defences. It seems to me easier to associate with this term, than with the words 'mechanisms' or 'phases', the differences between the developmental psychotic anxieties of the child and the psychoses of the adult: e.g. the quick change-over that occurs from a persecution anxiety or depressed feeling to a normal attitude – a change-over that is so characteristic for the child.

14. These reasons are largely responsible for that state of mind in the melancholic in which he breaks off all relations with the external world.

15. 'Zur Psychologie der manisch depressiven Zustände', *Internationale Zeitschrift für Psychoanalyse*, Vol. XIX, 1933.

16. This 'reparation', in accordance with the phantastic character of the whole position, is nearly always of a quite unpractical and unrealizable nature. Cf. Helene Deutsch, loc. cit.

17. Bertram Lewin reported about an acute manic patient who identified herself with both parents in intercourse (*Psycho-Analytic Quarterly*, 1933).

18. In my experience the paranoiac conception of a dead object within is one of a secret and uncanny persecutor. He is felt as not being fully dead and may reappear at any time in cunning and plotting ways, and seems all the more dangerous and hostile because the subject tried to do away with him by killing him (the conception of a dangerous ghost).

19. Edward Glover makes the suggestion that the child in its development goes through phases which provide the foundation for the psychotic disorders of melancholia and mania ('A Psycho-Analytic Approach to the Classification of Mental Disorders', *Journal of Mental Science*, 1932).

20. Dr Susan Isaacs has suggested in her remarks on 'Anxiety in the First Year of Life' (to the British Psycho-Analytical Society, January 1934), that the child's earliest experiences of painful external and internal stimuli provide a basis for phantasies about hostile external and internal objects and that they largely contribute to the building up of such phantasies. It seems that in the very earliest stage every unpleasant stimulus is related to the 'bad', denying, persecuting breasts, every pleasant stimulus to the 'good', gratifying breasts.

21. M. Klein, 'Early Stages of the Oedipus Conflict' (see this volume, Chapter 3); and 'Personification in the Play of Children', *CW*, Vol. I, 1929.

22. M. Klein, *The Psycho-Analysis of Children*, Chapter 8, *CW*, Vol. II.

23. Sándor Radó, 'The Problem of Melancholia', *Int. J. Psycho-Anal.*, Vol. IX, 1928.

24. M. Schmideberg, 'Psychotic Mechanisms in Cultural Development', *Int. J. Psycho-Anal.*, Vol. XI, 1930.

CHAPTER 7: *Mourning and Its Relation to Manic-Depressive States*

1. *Collected Papers*, Vol. IV, p. 163, and *SE*, Vol. XIV, p. 242.

2. Ibid., p. 154, and *SE*, Vol. XIV, p. 245.

3. Ibid., p. 166, and *SE*, Vol. XIV, p. 255.

4. (See this volume, Chapter 6.) The present paper is a continuation of that paper, and much of what I have now to say will of necessity assume the conclusions I arrived at there.

5. Here I can only refer in passing to the great impetus which these anxieties afford to the development of interests and sublimations of all kinds. If these anxieties are over-strong, they may interfere with or even check intellectual development. (Cf. Klein, 'A Contribution to the Theory of Intellectual Inhibition', *CW*, Vol. I, 1931.)

6. *The Psycho-Analysis of Children*, 1932; in particular, Chapter 8.

7. In the same book (p. 149), referring to my view that every child passes through a neurosis differing only in degree from one individual to another, I added: 'This view, which I have maintained for a number of years now, has lately received valuable support. In his book *Die Frage der Laienanalyse* (1926) [*The Question of Lay Analysis* (*SE*, Vol. XX)], Freud writes: "Since we have learnt to see more clearly we are almost inclined to say that the occurrence of a neurosis in childhood is not the exception but the rule. It seems as though it is a thing that cannot be avoided in the course of development from the infantile disposition to the social life of the adult." (p. 215).'

8. At every juncture the child's feelings, fears and defences are linked up with his libidinal wishes and fixations, and the outcome of his sexual development in childhood is always interdependent with the processes I am describing in this paper. I think that new light will be thrown on the child's libidinal development if we consider it in connection with the depressive position and the defences used against that position. It is, however, a subject of such importance that it needs to be dealt with fully, and is therefore beyond the scope of this paper.

9. 'A Contribution to the Psychogenesis of Manic-Depressive States' (see this volume, Chapter 6).

10. I have pointed out in various connections (first of all in 'The Early Stages of the Oedipus Conflict', see this volume, Chapter 3) that the fear of phantastically 'bad' persecutors and the belief in phantastically 'good' objects are bound up with each other. Idealization is an essential process in the young child's mind, since he cannot

yet cope in any other way with his fears of persecution (a result of his own hatred). Not until early anxieties have been sufficiently relieved owing to experiences which increase love and trust, is it possible to establish the all-important process of bringing together more closely the various aspects of objects (external, internal, 'good' and 'bad', loved and hated), and thus for hatred to become actually mitigated by love – which means a decrease of ambivalence. While the separation of these contrasting *aspects* – felt in the unconscious as contrasting *objects* – operates strongly, feelings of hatred and love are also so much divorced from each other that love cannot mitigate hatred.

The flight to the internalized 'good' object, which Melitta Schmideberg (in 'Psychotic Mechanisms in Cultural Development', *Int. J. of Psycho-Anal.*, Vol. XI, 1930) has found to be a fundamental mechanism in schizophrenia, thus also enters into the process of idealization which the young child normally resorts to in his depressive anxieties. Melitta Schmideberg has also repeatedly drawn attention to the connections between idealization and distrust of the object.

11. 'A Contribution to the Psychogenesis of Manic-Depressive States' (see this volume, Chapter 6, pp. 143-4).

12. *The Psycho-Analysis of Children*, *CW*, Vol. II, pp. 116 and 202.

13. Ibid., Chapter 9.

14. These facts I think go some way towards answering Freud's question which I have quoted at the beginning of this paper: 'Why this process of carrying out the behest of reality bit by bit, which is in the nature of a compromise, should be so extraordinarily painful is not at all easy to explain in terms of mental economics. It is worth noting that this pain seems natural to us.'

15. 'Mourning and Melancholia', *Collected Papers*, Vol. IV, p. 166, and *SE*, Vol. XIV, p. 255.

16. Abraham (1924) writes of a situation of this kind: 'We have only to reverse [Freud's] statement that "the shadow of the lost love-object falls upon the ego" and say that in this case it was not the shadow but the bright radiance of his loved mother which was shed upon her son.' (*Selected Papers*, p. 442.)

17. *Collected Papers*, Vol. IV, p. 166, and *SE*, Vol. XIV, p. 255.

18. I have often found that processes which the patient unconsciously feels are going on inside him are represented as something happening on top of or closely round him. By means of the well-known principle of representation by the contrary, an external happening can stand for an internal one. Whether the emphasis lies on the internal or the external situation becomes clear from the whole context – from the details of associations and the nature and intensity of affects. For instance, certain manifestations of very acute anxiety and the specific defence mechanisms against this anxiety (particularly an increase in denial of psychic reality) indicate that an internal situation predominates at the time.

19. An attack on the outside of the body often stands for one which is felt to happen internally. I have already pointed out that something represented as being on top of or tightly round the body often covers the deeper meaning of being inside.

CHAPTER 8: *Notes on Some Schizoid Mechanisms*

1. [footnote to 1952 version:] This paper has been left unchanged and then published, apart from a few slight alterations (in particular the addition of one paragraph and some footnotes).

2. Before completing this paper I discussed its main aspects with Paula Heimann

and am much indebted to her for stimulating suggestions in working out and formulating a number of the concepts presented here.

3. Cf. my *Psycho-Analysis of Children*, *CW*, Vol. II, 1932, and 'A Contribution to the Psychogenesis of Manic-Depressive States', 1935 (see this volume, Chapter 6).

4. When this paper was first published in 1946, I was using my term 'paranoid position' synonymously with W. R. D. Fairbairn's 'schizoid position'. On further deliberation I decided to combine Fairbairn's term with mine and throughout the present book [*Developments in Psycho-Analysis*, 1952, in which this paper was first published] I am using the expression 'paranoid-schizoid position'.

5. Cf. 'A Revised Psychopathology of the Psychoses and Neuroses', 'Endopsychic Structure Considered in Terms of Object-Relationships' and 'Object-Relationships and Dynamic Structure'.

6. Cf. 'A Revised Psychopathology', 1941.

7. Cf. D. W. Winnicott, 'Primitive Emotional Development', 1945. In this paper Winnicott also described the pathological outcome of states of unintegration, for instance the case of a woman patient who could not distinguish between her twin sister and herself.

8. The greater or lesser cohesiveness of the ego at the beginning of postnatal life should be considered in connection with the greater or lesser capacity of the ego to tolerate anxiety which, as I have previously contended (*The Psycho-Analysis of Children*, *CW*, Vol. II, particularly p. 49), is a constitutional factor.

9. Ferenczi in 'Notes and Fragments', 1930, suggests that most likely every living organism reacts to unpleasant stimuli by fragmentation, which might be an expression of the death instinct. Possibly, complicated mechanisms (living organisms) are only kept as an entity through the impact of external conditions. When these conditions become unfavourable the organism falls to pieces.

10. D. W. Winnicott (loc. cit.) referred to the same process from another angle: he described how integration and adaptation to reality depend essentially on the infant's experience of the mother's love and care.

11. In the discussion following the reading of this paper, Dr W. C. M. Scott referred to another aspect of splitting. He stressed the importance of the breaks in continuity of experiences, which imply a splitting in time rather than in space. He referred as an instance to the alternation between states of being asleep and states of being awake. I fully agree with his point of view.

12. The description of such primitive processes suffers from a great handicap, for these phantasies arise at a time when the infant has not yet begun to think in words. In this context, for instance, I am using the expression 'to project *into* another person' because this seems to me the only way of conveying the unconscious process I am trying to describe.

13. M. G. Evans, in a short unpublished communication (read to the British Psycho-Analytical Society, January 1946) gave some instances of patients in whom the following phenomena were marked: lack of sense of reality, a feeling of being divided and parts of the personality having entered the mother's body in order to rob and control her; as a consequence the mother and other people similarly attacked came to represent the patient. M. G. Evans related these processes to a very primitive stage of development.

14. W. C. M. Scott in an unpublished paper, read to the British Psycho-Analytical Society a few years ago, described three interconnected features which he came upon in a schizophrenic patient: a strong disturbance of her sense of reality, her feeling that

the world round her was a cemetery, and the mechanism of putting all good parts of herself into another person – Greta Garbo – who came to stand for the patient.

15. Cf. 'A Contribution to the Problem of Sublimation and Its Relation to the Processes of Internalization', 1942, where Paula Heimann described a condition in which the internal objects act as foreign bodies embedded in the self. Whilst this is more obvious with regard to the bad objects, it is true even for the good ones, if the ego is compulsively subordinated to their preservation. When the ego serves its good internal objects excessively, they are felt as a source of danger to the self and come close to exerting a persecuting influence. Paula Heimann introduced the concept of the assimilation of the internal objects and applied it specifically to sublimation. As regards ego development, she pointed out that such assimilation is essential for the successful exercise of ego functions and for the achievement of independence.

16. Looked at in this light, the mother's love and understanding of the infant can be seen as the infant's greatest standby in overcoming states of disintegration and anxieties of a psychotic nature.

17. Herbert Rosenfeld, in 'Analysis of a Schizophrenic State with Depersonalization', 1947, has presented case material to illustrate how the splitting mechanisms which are bound up with projective identification were responsible both for a schizophrenic state and for depersonalization. In his paper 'A Note on the Psychopathology of Confusional States in Chronic Schizophrenias', 1950, he also pointed out that a confusional state comes about if the subject loses the capacity to differentiate between good and bad objects, between aggressive and libidinal impulses, and so on. He suggested that in such states of confusion splitting mechanisms are frequently reinforced for defensive purposes.

18. Herbert Rosenfeld, in 'Analysis of a Schizophrenic State with Depersonalization' and 'Remarks on the Relation of Male Homosexuality to Paranoia', 1949, discussed the clinical importance of those paranoid anxieties which are connected with projective identification in psychotic patients. In the two schizophrenic cases he described, it became evident that the patients were dominated by the fear that the analyst was trying to force himself into the patient. When these fears were analysed in the transference situation, improvement could take place. Rosenfeld has further connected projective identification (and the corresponding persecutory fears) with female sexual frigidity on the one hand and on the other with the frequent combination of homosexuality and paranoia in men.

19. *Psycho-Analysis of Children*, *CW*, Vol. II, Chapter 8, particularly p. 131, and Chapter 12, particularly p. 242.

20. Joan Riviere, in an unpublished paper 'Paranoid Attitudes Seen in Everyday Life and in Analysis' (read before the British Psycho-Analytical Society in 1948), reported a great deal of clinical material in which projective identification became apparent. Unconscious phantasies of forcing the whole self into the inside of the object (to obtain control and possession) led, through the fear of retaliation, to a variety of persecutory anxieties such as claustrophobia, or to such common phobias as of burglars, spiders, invasion in wartime. These fears are connected with the unconscious 'catastrophic' phantasies of being dismembered, disembowelled, torn to pieces and of total internal disruption of the body and personality and loss of identity – fears which are an elaboration of the fear of annihilation (death) and have the effect of reinforcing the mechanisms of splitting and the process of ego disintegration as found in psychotics.

21. I may mention that the analysis was resumed after a break.

22. The feeling of hunger indicated that the process of introjection had been set going again under the dominance of the libido. While to my first interpretation of his fear of destroying me by his aggression he had responded at once with the violent splitting off and annihilation of parts of his personality, he now experienced more fully the emotions of grief, guilt and fear of loss, as well as some relief of these depressive anxieties. The relief of anxiety resulted in the analyst again coming to stand for a good object which he could trust. Therefore the desire to introject me as a good object could come to the fore. If he could build up again the good breast inside himself, he would strengthen and integrate his ego, would be less afraid of his destructive impulses; in fact he could then preserve himself and the analyst.

23. 'Psycho-Analytic Notes upon an Autobiographical Account of a Case of Paranoia (Dementia Paranoides)', *S E*, Vol. XII.

24. 'The Psycho-Sexual Differences between Hysteria and Dementia Praecox', 1908.

CHAPTER 9: *The Origins of Transference*

1. 1905. Contained in *Collected Papers*, Vol. III, p. 139, and *S E*, Vol. VII, p. 116.

2. It is an essential feature of this earliest of all object relations that it is the prototype of a relation between *two* people into which no other object enters. This is of vital importance for later object relations, though in that exclusive form it possibly does not last longer than a very few months, for the phantasies relating to the father and his penis – phantasies which initiate the early stages of the Oedipus complex – introduce the relation to more than one object. In the analysis of adults and children the patient sometimes comes to experience feelings of blissful happiness through the revival of this early exclusive relation with the mother and her breast. Such experiences often follow the analysis of jealousy and rivalry situations in which a third object, ultimately the father, is involved.

3. 'Psycho-Analysis', 1922. In *Collected Papers*, Vol. V, p. 107, and as the first of 'Two Encyclopaedia Articles', *S E*, Vol. XVIII, p. 235.

4. p. 39. On the same page Freud suggests – still referring to these first identifications – that they are a direct and immediate identification which takes place earlier than any object cathexis. This suggestion seems to imply that introjection even precedes object relations.

5. 1926. Chapter 8.

6. 1931. 'Female Sexuality'; contained in *Collected Papers*, Vol. V, p. 254, and *S E*, Vol. XXI, p. 226.

7. This was largely due to the undervaluation of the importance of aggression.

8. This technique is illustrated by H. Segal's paper 'Some Aspects of the Analysis of a Schizophrenic', *Int. J. of Psycho-Anal.*, Vol. XXXI, 1950, and H. Rosenfeld's papers 'Notes on the Psycho-Analysis of the Super-ego Conflict of an Acute Schizophrenic Patient', 1952, and 'Transference Phenomena and Transference Analysis in an Acute Catatonic Schizophrenic Patient', 1952, in *Psychotic States*, 1965, London, Hogarth Press.

9. See *The Psycho-Analysis of Children*, *CW*, Vol. II, particularly Chapters 8 and 11.

10. The patient may at times try to escape from the present into the past rather than realize that his emotions, anxieties and phantasies are at the time operative in full strength and focused on the analyst. At other times, as we know, the defences are mainly directed against re-experiencing the past in relation to the original objects.

CHAPTER 10: *A Study of Envy and Gratitude*

1. *Klein* = little.

2. Karl Abraham, 'Contributions to the Theory of the Anal Character', 1921, in *Selected Papers on Psycho-Analysis*, 1973, pp. 382–3, London, Hogarth Press.

3. M. J. Eisler, 'Pleasure in Sleep and the Disturbed Capacity for Sleep. A Contribution to the Study of the Oral Phase of the Development of the Libido', *Int. J. Psycho-Anal.*, 1922, Vol. III.

SELECTED BIBLIOGRAPHY

ABRAHAM, Karl, 'A Short Study of the Development of the Libido, Viewed in the Light of Mental Disorders', 1924, in *Selected Papers of Karl Abraham*, 1927, London, Hogarth Press.

ANZIEU, A., ANZIEU, D., FORNARI, F., GIBEAULT, A., and PETOT, J.-M., 'Avec Melanie Klein', *L'Archaïque*, 26, Autumn 1982, Paris, Gallimard.

FERENCZI, Sándor, 'Stages in the Development of a Sense of Reality', *Internationale Zeitschrift für Psychanalyse*, 1913, Vol. I, pp. 124–38, and in *Sex and Psycho-Analysis*, 1956, pp. 181–203, London, Dover Publications.

FREUD, Anna, *The Psychoanalytical Treatment of Children*, 1946, London, Imago.

FREUD, Sigmund, *The Complete Psychological Works*, *SE*, Vols. I–XXIV, 1966, London, Hogarth Press.

GROSSKURTH, Phyllis, *Melanie Klein. A Biography*, forthcoming (1986), London, Hodder & Stoughton.

ISAACS, Susan, 'The Nature and Function of Phantasy', in *Developments in Psycho-Analysis* (ed. Klein et al.), 1958, London, Hogarth Press.

JONES, Ernest, 'The Theory of Symbolism' and 'Early Female Sexuality', in *Papers on Psycho-Analysis*, 1948, London, Bailliere, Tindall and Cox.

KLEIN, Melanie, et al., *Developments in Psycho-Analysis* (ed. Joan Riviere), London, Hogarth Press, and *New Directions in Psycho-Analysis: The Significance of Infant Conflict in the Pattern of Adult Behaviour* (eds. Melanie Klein, Paula Heimann and R. E. Money-Kyrle), 1955, London, Tavistock Publications.

LAPLANCHE, J., and PONTALIS, J.-B., *The Language of Psycho-Analysis*, p. 11, 1973, London, Hogarth Press.

MCCLINTOCK, Barbara, quoted in Evelyn Keller, *A Feeling for the Organism: The Life and Work of Barbara McClintock*, p. 117, 1983, New York, W. H. Freeman and Co.

PETOT, Jean-Michel, *Melanie Klein. Premières découvertes, premier système* (1919–1932), 1979, and *Melanie Klein, le moi & le bon objet* (1932–1960), 1982, Paris, Dunod.

SEGAL, Hanna, *An Introduction to the Work of Melanie Klein*, 1964, London, Heinemann, and *Klein*, 1979, p. 73, London, Fontana/Collins.

STEINER, Riccardo, 'Some Thoughts about Tradition and Change Arising from an Examination of the British Psychoanalytical Society's Controversial Discussions (1943–1944)', *International Journal of Psycho-Analysis*, Vol. XII, No. 1, 1985, pp. 27–71.

THE WRITINGS OF MELANIE KLEIN

1920 'Der Familienroman in Statu Nascendi', *Internationale Zeitschrift für Psychanalyse*, 1920

1921 'Eine Kinderentwicklung', *Imago*, p. 270, and as 'The Development of a Child', *International Journal of Psycho-Analysis*, 1923, Vol. IV, pp. 419-74.

1922 'Inhibitions and Difficulties in Puberty', *Die neue Erziehung*, Vol. IV.

1923 'Die Rolle der Schule in der libidinösen Entwicklung des Kindes', *Internationale Zeitschrift für Psychoanalyse*, Vol. IX, p. 340, and as 'The Role of the School in the Libidinal Development of the Child', *International Journal of Psycho-Analysis*, 1924, Vol. V, pp. 312-31.

1925 'A Contribution to the Psychogenesis of Tics', *Internationale Zeitschrift für die Psychoanalyse*, Vol. XI.

1926 'Infant Analysis', *International Journal of Psycho-Analysis*, Vol. VII, pp. 31-63, and as 'Early Analysis', *CW*, Vol. I.

1926 'Die psychologischen Grundlagen der Frühanalyse', *Imago*, Vol. XII, pp. 371-3, and as 'The Psychological Principles of Infant Analysis', *International Journal of Psycho-Analysis*, Vol. VIII, pp. 25-37, and 'The Psychological Principles of Early Analysis', *CW*, Vol. I.

1927 'Symposium on Child Analysis', *International Journal of Psycho-Analysis*, Vol. VIII, pp. 339-70.

1927 'Criminal Tendencies in Normal Children', *British Journal of Medical Psychology*, Vol. VII, pp. 177-92.

1928 'Early Stages of the Oedipus Conflict', *International Journal of Psycho-Analysis*, Vol. IX, pp. 167-80.

1929 'Personification in the play of children', ibid., Vol. X, pp. 193-204.

1929 'Infantile Anxiety Situations Reflected in a Work of Art and in the Creative Impulse', ibid., Vol. X, pp. 436-43.

1930 'The Importance of Symbol Formation in the Development of the Ego', ibid., Vol. 11, pp. 24-39.

1930 'The Psychotherapy of the Psychoses', *British Journal of Medical Psychology*, Vol. X, pp. 242-4.

1931 'A Contribution to the Theory of Intellectual Inhibition', *International Journal of Psycho-Analysis*, Vol. XII, pp. 206-18.

1932 '*The Psycho-Analysis of Children*', London, Hogarth Press.

1934 'On criminality', *British Journal of Medical Psychology*, Vol. XIV, pp. 312-15.

1935 'A Contribution to the Psychogenesis of Manic-Depressive States', *International Journal of Psycho-Analysis*, Vol. XVI, pp. 145-74.

1936 'Weaning', in *On the Bringing Up of Children* (ed. J. Rickman), London, Kegan Paul.

1937 'Love, Guilt and Reparation', in *Love, Hate and Reparation* (eds. M. Klein and J. Riviere), London, Hogarth Press.

1940 'Mourning and Its Relation to Manic-Depressive States', *International Journal of Psycho-Analysis*, Vol. XXI, pp. 125–53.

1944 'The Early Development of Conscience in the Child', in *Psychoanalysis Today* (ed. S. Lornand), pp. 64–74, New York, International Universities Press.

1945 'The Oedipus Complex in the Light of Early Anxieties', *International Journal of Psycho-Analysis*, Vol. XXVI, pp. 11–33.

1946 'Notes on Some Schizoid Mechanisms', ibid., Vol. XXVII, pp. 99–110.

1948 *Contributions to Psycho-Analysis, 1921–1945*, London, Hogarth Press.

1948 'A Contribution to the Theory of Anxiety and Guilt', *International Journal of Psycho-Analysis*, Vol. XXIX, 114–23.

1950 Contribution to the First World Congress of Psychiatry, Paris.

1950 'On the Criteria for the Termination of a Psycho-Analysis', *International Journal of Psycho-Analysis*, Vol. XXXI, pp. 78–80.

1952 'The Origins of Transference', *International Journal of Psycho-Analysis*, Vol. XXXIII, pp. 433–8.

1952 'The Mutual Influences in the Development of Ego and Id' (a discussion by Melanie Klein et al.), *Psychoanalytic Study of the Child*, Vol. VII, pp. 51–68.

1952 'Some Theoretical Conclusions Regarding the Emotional Life of the Infant', in *Developments in Psycho-Analysis* (eds. M. Klein and J. Riviere), London, Hogarth Press.

1952 'On Observing the Behaviour of Young Infants', ibid.

1955 'The Psycho-Analytic Play Technique: Its History and Significance', *New Directions in Psycho-Analysis: The Significance of Infant Conflict in the Pattern of Adult Behaviour* (eds. M. Klein, P. Heimann and R. E. Money-Kyrle), London, Tavistock Publications.

1955 'On Identification', ibid.

1957 *Envy and Gratitude: A Study of Unconscious Sources*, London, Tavistock Publications.

1958 'The Development of Mental Functioning', *International Journal of Psycho-Analysis*, Vol. XXXIX, pp. 84–90.

1959 *The Psycho-Analysis of Children*, London, Hogarth Press.

1959 'Our Adult World and Its Roots in Infancy', *Human Relations*, Vol. XII, No. 4, pp. 291–303.

1960 'A Note on Depression in the Schizophrenic', *International Journal of Psycho-Analysis*, Vol. XLI, pp. 509–11.

1960 'On Mental Health', *British Journal of Medical Psychology*, Vol. XXXIII, pp. 237–41.

1960 *The Psycho-Analysis of Children*, New York, Grove Press.

1961 *Narrative of a Child Analysis: The Conduct of the Psycho-Analysis of Children as Seen in the Treatment of a Ten-Year-Old Boy*, London, Hogarth Press.

1963 'Some Reflections on the *Oresteia*', in *Our Adult World and Other Essays* (ed. M. Klein), London, Heinemann Medical.

1963 'On the Sense of Loneliness', ibid.

1975 *Collected Works of Melanie Klein*: Vol. I, *Love, Guilt and Reparation, and Other Works*; Vol. II, *The Psycho-Analysis of Children*; Vol. III, *Envy and Gratitude, and Other Works*; Vol. IV, *Narrative of a Child Analysis*; London, Hogarth Press and Institute of Psychoanalysis.

Index